Organizational Knowledge in the Making

Organizational Knowledge in the Making

*How Firms Create, Use, and
Institutionalize Knowledge*

GERARDO PATRIOTTA

OXFORD
UNIVERSITY PRESS

OXFORD

UNIVERSITY PRESS

Great Clarendon Street, Oxford OX2 6DP

Oxford University Press is a department of the University of Oxford.
It furthers the University's objective of excellence in research, scholarship,
and education by publishing worldwide in

Oxford New York

Auckland Bangkok Buenos Aires Cape Town Chennai
Dar es Salaam Delhi Hong Kong Istanbul Karachi Kolkata
Kuala Lumpur Madrid Melbourne Mexico City Mumbai Nairobi
São Paulo Shanghai Taipei Tokyo Toronto

Oxford is a registered trade mark of Oxford University Press
in the UK and in certain other countries

Published in the United States
by Oxford University Press Inc., New York

British Library Cataloguing in Publication Data
Data available

Library of Congress Cataloging in Publication Data
Data available

ISBN 0–19–925678–0
ISBN 0–19–927524–6 (Pbk.)

1 3 5 7 9 10 8 6 4 2

Typeset by Newgen Imaging Systems (P) Ltd., Chennai, India
Printed in Great Britain
on acid-free paper by
Biddles Ltd., King's Lynn, Norfolk

Contents

Foreword

This is an eloquent, timely, and scholarly study of knowing in the context of organizing. The book's critical edge is of the essence. This is not yet another static and inert treatment of organizational knowledge where knowledge is portrayed as a simple commodity that can be parceled up into tidy bundles and through unstated mechanisms deliver competitive performance. Rather we have here a processual treatment of knowing in its organizational context, where the core questions are about how knowledge is created, utilized, legitimated, and institutionalized in the manufacturing setting of Fiat Auto in Italy. Throughout the manuscript knowing is seen as a highly situational, relational, interactive, and contestable process.

Organizational Knowledge in the Making also makes a significant contribution to the empirical study of knowing in organizational settings. Knowing is approached through the three complementary lenses of time, breakdowns, and narratives. Through these lenses both manifest and tacit knowledge are made transparent and real. In achieving this, Gerardo Patriotta has found a practical bridge between the abstract language of knowledge and knowing and the experience of knowledge and knowing. This is a signal contribution which others can build on for years to come.

The knowledge movement is sweeping through the management and social sciences. Interest in knowledge and its exploitation is also very much at home in the salons of the global consultancy industry and in senior executive corridors. Lord Browne, regularly voted the most successful Chief Executive Officer (CEO) in Britain, is happy to go public on the significance of knowledge and learning to BP's corporate development and enhanced performance (Prokesch 1997). However, it is still fair to say that no scholar has yet done the impossible and isolated the impact of knowledge resources from other competing and complementary determinants of organizational performance.

Anecdotal experience suggests that at the beginning of the twenty-first century large numbers of doctoral theses in Europe have knowledge and/or learning in their titles, or core vocabulary. Should we be excited, worried, or indifferent to this apparent closure around the theme of organizational knowledge? Whenever I witness this kind of over-focusing on a single topic, I always ask the sociology of knowledge question—why? What are the features of contemporary context and action driving knowledge and learning so vigorously on to the front stage? I am reminded of an equivalent closure around the theme of organizational culture in the 1980s. Explanations to the same sociology of knowledge question about culture picked up the problems of control then so evident in many Western economies (and certainly in the United Kingdom). In the early 1980s the managerial and scholarly interest in culture at work was part of a search to find alternative methods and mechanisms of controlling and motivating employees, as the traditional hierarchical methods of control were being found more and more wanting.

The easy explanation for the rise and rise of knowledge as a topic for research and management action lies in the rhetoric about the emergence of the post-industrial society, knowledge economy, and firm. But are there deeper and/or more instrumental explanations? Time will no doubt expose these phenomena. I foresee another cycle of Ph. D.s on the sociology of knowledge about knowledge.

Meanwhile, where are we in the treatment of knowledge and knowing in the management literatures, and does Gerardo's book provide us with some firmer stepping-stones into the future? Gerardo's book is wise, humane, evocative, critical, and timely. He characterizes the knowledge literature in the fields of management and organization as adolescent. This is fair. With the rapid rise of interest in the topic has come a welter of inconsistent and often incoherent language, an over emphasis on the simple dichotomy of manifest and tacit knowledge, and an over-elaboration of theoretical frameworks which have not yet been subject to the disciplines of empirical analysis. But alongside this conceptual and linguistic ground clearing, we also need some challenging of the hype about the easy association between knowledge assets and resources and the competitive performance of the firm.

There is now a vast literature on the measurement of corporate performance and of performance management. The literature on the determinants of performance is much less extensive. However, the field of strategic management is full of studies, nearly all using cross-sectional data, which purport to show a relationship between a limited set of independent variables and the dependent variable of performance. In an extended review and critique of these literatures on the determinants of organizational performance (Pettigrew et al. 1999; Pettigrew 2000), two essential points can be made. Firstly, the tendency to link one determinant on its own to performance (whether it be human resource management, IT, knowledge, or strategy) is a less than fruitful exercise. Secondly, we need to know not just about the likely interactive set of factors, which determine performance, but also the processes which deliver those performance outcomes. These difficulties suggest that we put into brackets the causal link between knowledge assets and performance, at least until we have found out more about the more basic questions about what knowledge and knowing are, how knowledge is made, and how it might link theoretically and empirically with other complementary determinants of performance improvement. Part of that build up, Gerardo suggests, is to empirically examine knowledge making, use, and institutionalization as situational and relational processes. His mechanism to do this lies through the triple and complementary lenses of time, breakdowns, and narratives.

The setting for this analysis of knowing and organizing (the two Fiat plants in Italy) is itself counterintuitive and rich in its possibilities. Thus far research on knowledge has tended to theorize and study the phenomenon in the supposedly richer knowledge settings of, for example, high technology firms or global professional service firms. This is a legitimate enough strategy, but tends to ignore the real possibilities in more established settings. The empirical virtue of the more traditional manufacturing context is here complemented by a research design which exposes real contextual variation in the settings for knowing and organizing. So Gerardo is able to compare the old established Fiat car-pressing plant of Mirafiori (the brownfield site), with the new assembly plant at Melfi (the greenfield site). Comparing the Melfi plant at two points in time then enriches this temporal and situational variation by revealing two points in the process of creating, utilizing, and institutionalizing knowledge. The two points in time are as the plant is being designed and constructed, and as it reaches its full operating state. So unusually for an empirical study in the social and management sciences, there is a good match between the theoretical questions being asked and the contextual variation in the research design. The resultant empirical variation does therefore have some chance of exposing the phenomena that might provide answers to the theoretical questions.

But what of the possibilities of revealing knowing and organizing through the triple lenses of time, breakdowns, and narratives? These three lenses are the operational devices to disentangle knowing and organizing from the tacit background against which knowledge is used in a day-to-day situational basis. We know (to paraphrase Gerardo) that knowledge recedes to the background in the sedimentation of history, so time becomes important as a lens to uncover it. We also know that knowledge has a habitual basis and we use it almost automatically. So breakdowns or disruptures in a system become revelatory. And finally, we also appreciate that knowledge is experience related and so knowledge can be exposed through our narratives. In this book all these lenses are used with effect to reveal how knowledge is made and put to use.

The books which are noticed and last in the social and management sciences seem to me to have a number of scholarly characteristics. They pursue big, enduring themes which are deeply embedded in the social and management sciences. They are critical and reflective and draw upon a wide, but integrated body of knowledge. They also help other scholars to see links between features of study they may not have recognized. They are also clear in the questions they ask. If they are empirical, they provide a study design which directly exposes the phenomena under investigation and the phenomena is operationalized clearly and simply. And they are written in a scholarly but accessible manner. *Organizational Knowledge in the Making* achieves all these requirements. It deserves to be noticed and in my view should have a big impact on future research on knowing and organizing in organizational settings.

Samoreau, France   Andrew Pettigrew
May 2002

Acknowledgements

This book is the tangible outcome of an intense intellectual journey—almost a rite of passage—that has carried me through different literatures, countries, institutions, people, and learning experiences. Throughout this long journey I was comforted and supported by a good number of friends, academics, and practitioners. I am grateful to my colleagues at Erasmus University in Rotterdam for their openness to discussion and knowledge exchange. The ongoing professional relationship with Andrew Pettigrew, Harry Scarbrough, and Giovan Francesco Lanzara has considerably influenced my research style and my intellectual thinking. Andrew has been the initiator of this book project. I have greatly benefited from his proverbial methodological rigour and professional touch. Harry is an original thinker. He is able to direct one's attention towards apparently peripheral details and turn them into major sources of scholarly production. Giovan Francesco has taught me the importance of self-reflection and systematic questioning. His ongoing support, collaboration, and valuable friendship have helped me to see beyond the mere intellectual exercise of writing a book. I would like to thank Luciano Massone, Personnel Director of Fiat Auto and Lancia, Luisella Erlicher of ISVOR-Fiat, and the workers in Melfi and Mirafiori for their availability and collaborative attitude throughout the duration of the project. My last word of gratitude goes to Anna, for having supported this endeavour with love, creativity, and patience, and having joined me in a common life project.

List of Figures

List of Tables

Abbreviations

ANT	Actor-network theory
D/A	disassemble/reassemble
CEO	chief executive officer
GM	General Motors
HRM	human resource management
ICT	Information and Communication Technology
IR	industrial relations
IT	information technology
JIT	just-in-time
KBT	knowledge-based theories
MAC	automated measuring devices
PC	personal computer
OU	operating units
RBT	resource-based theories
TPM	total productive maintenance
TQM	total quality management
TV	television
UTE	elementary technical units
VCR	video casette recorder
WBS	work breakdown structures

What really *exists* is not things made but things in the making. Once made, they are dead, and an infinite number of alternative conceptual decompositions can be used in defining them. But put yourself *in the making* by a stroke of intuitive sympathy with the thing and, the whole range of possible decompositions coming at once into your possession, you are no longer troubled by the question of which of them is the more absolutely true.

William James (1977:117)

Part One

Epistemological Foundations

1

Introduction

1.1 The nature of knowledge in organizations

In a recent essay the Czech writer Milan Kundera (1997) examines a novel written at the beginning of the century by his fellow-countryman Jaromir John. A forest ranger under the old monarchy, having spent most of his life in the Bohemian countryside, moves back to his native Prague where he plans to spend his retirement. Here he is confronted with a world that is profoundly different from the one he left. The new-born Czech republic has replaced the old monarchy, while Prague has become an emblem of the modern city. Interestingly, however, the feature that strikes him most is not the presence of democracy or the changed political climate; rather, the hallmark of modernity—what will become a nightmare for the main character of the book—seems to be an increased level of noise. It is a new noise, that of the cars and machinery, what he calls the 'monster engines'. As the forest ranger arrives in the city he moves to a mansion located in a residential area. Here, because of the 'monster engines', he witnesses for the first time the presence of the evil sound that will deeply affect his existence and turn his life into an endless escape. He moves across different parts of the city until he resolves to spend his nights in the trains. These, with their pleasant and archaic sound, can finally give him relatively calm sleep.

In Kundera's view, what is interesting in the above account is the method of inquiry followed by the novelist in the construction of his story. In fact, rather than taking for granted the distinctive traits of the world we dwell in, the author has chosen to proceed in an inductive way by detailing the existence of a real person. The findings of the inquiry are astonishing. The noise of the cars has managed to radically change the life of the main character more than the independence achieved by his country. Freedom, national independence, and capitalism are shorn of their sacredness, relegated to the background, while human conduct is explained by recourse to such a mundane category as noise. Ultimately, the most salient feature of the novel is precisely the apparent inversion of foreground and background, here instantiated by a reversed relationship between noise and silence.

Kundera observes that at the time John wrote his novel there probably was one car for every hundred inhabitants in Prague, or maybe even one for every thousand. At a time when environmental sonority was still minor, the irruption of noise turned out to be a sort of 'cosmology episode' for the forest ranger, an event that abruptly displaced him from his established habits of thinking and acting and seriously impaired his sense-making capabilities (Weick 1993; Lanzara and Patriotta 2001). It was precisely then that the phenomenon of noise could manifest itself in such powerful fashion and astonishing novelty. From this, Kundera tentatively elicits a general rule of method: a social phenomenon is more conspicuous not at the moment of its greatest expansion but in its incipient phase, when it is still innocent, hesitant, comparatively weaker than it will become in the future. The forest ranger could still feel a sense of wonder at the presence of noise. For him noise was a noticeable phenomenon, one that carried an existential meaning and dramatically affected his lifestyle. In contrast, the next generation was born in a world of noise, one in which noise had receded in the background and had become an established feature of everyday life. As a result, the pervasiveness of noise was not astonishing any more. The essence of man had been changed and man had been turned into a different type of man: the man of noise.

What does the frustration of the character depicted in the above story have to do with a book on organizational knowledge? Let me tackle the above question in two steps. The first requires explaining the link between pre-interpretation and the specificity of human knowing. The second involves relating the nature of human knowing to organizational knowledge.

With reference to human knowing the predicament contained in the story of the man of noise can be reframed as follows: how do we make sense of experiences that are deeply entrenched in routine contexts and therefore not amenable to observation? How can we understand phenomena of which we ourselves are part and which we often contribute to creating? In sum, how do we break into the ontological blindness of pre-interpretation?[1]

The argument depicted in the novel by John is essentially a phenomenological one, since it has to do with the ways in which individuals construct reality on a day-to-day basis. The world before the transition to modernity, as portrayed in the novel, was a simple one. Just like darkness follows daylight, so the ordinary, everyday nature of the forest

---

[1] As well known, ontology is that branch of philosophy concerned with establishing the nature of the fundamental kinds of things that must exist in the world. As such, ontology constitutes a theory of being aimed at determining the foundations of what it means to exist.

ranger was punctuated by the regular succession of periods of work and rest. Within such a world, the city provided a reference system for the forest ranger, a practical background for thinking and acting. Indeed, the intricate nexus of equipment, communication infrastructures, machinery, and conventions defining the modern city constituted a pre-interpreted, self-contained, and self-organized world. The sudden loss of this reference system, occasioned by a reversed relationship between silence and noise, made manifest in a dramatic way what was hidden in the ordinary, everyday experience of the forest ranger. From this we can infer that human knowing is a relational phenomenon; it is essentially about world making (Goodman 1978). As such it can only be understood in the presence of an organized world that defines and gives meaning to a particular mode of existence.

The story of the man of noise points out that we live in a pre-interpreted world which we ourselves have contributed to create and which serves as a backdrop for our everyday dealings. In a sense, the world we dwell in is self-explanatory and self-referential; it possesses an aura of naturalness. Pre-interpreted worlds can be seen as cosmologies; they point to a universe thought of as an ordered and integrated whole (Weick 1993). A cosmological order is one in which background and foreground stand in a stable relationship. For example, the cosmological order of the forest ranger was defined by a particular (and stable) configuration of silence and noise. In its turn, the dichotomy of silence and noise embodied a number of further oppositions between ontological states: blindness and conspicuousness, background and foreground, absence and presence, order and disorder, and so on. The ontological significance of the above opposites lies in the fact that any alteration in their configuration produces a disruption in the established order of things and thereby requires a redefinition of what it means to be in the world.

Pre-interpretation, organized worlds, and the relational nature of knowing seem to provide valuable points of entry for exploring the link between human and organizational knowledge. To be sure, organizations contain a collective dimension as well as a material one. They can be seen as assemblies (both in a material and social sense) of human and non-human 'actants' (Latour 1993) operating around a specific activity system.[2] Organizations are to such assemblies what the city was

---

[2] In semiotics the term 'actant' designates any entity (either human or non-human) endowed with the ability to act. More specifically, an actant can be thought of as that which accomplishes or undergoes an act, independently of all other determinations (Greimas and Courtés 1982). Unlike actors, actants are described in terms not of what they are, but of what they do and by their participation in a network of social actions and relations.

to the forest ranger. Just like cities, they constitute a background for the accomplishment of complex tasks. Such background consists of routines, standard operating procedures, technological implements, and organizational artefacts—the stuff of which organizations are made. Under these circumstances, the specificity of organizational knowing, and hence its *raison d'être*, lies in the structure of the work organization, in the nature of the task, and in the pattern of collective activity, that is, in the specific way in which knowledge is organized. Exploring the link between knowing and organizing implies looking at how knowledge is inscribed, internalized, encoded, distributed, and diffused in organizational structures of signification.

In this book I argue that studying knowledge in organizations is like seeing silence in a world of noise. It essentially amounts to understanding the subtle interaction between background and foreground, absence and presence, order and disorder within an organized setting. Understanding such relationships implies acknowledging the fact that the more something is obvious, the more it is hidden to observation; the more we get closer to the picture, the less we notice; the more we know, the less we see. Like silence, knowledge is seductive and elusive at the same time. Indeed, a common reference in the current literature on organizational knowledge is Polanyi's maxim that 'we know more than we can tell'. From the same literature we have also learned that organizational knowledge can be intangible, tacit, path dependent, and idiosyncratic. All these features make knowledge a valuable asset and a source of competitive advantage. The same features explain why knowledge-oriented phenomena are so difficult to grasp. Unfortunately, most organizational scholars have interpreted Polanyi's maxim as a problem of reconciliation between tacit and explicit knowledge. This has resulted in a prescriptive effort aimed at bridging the gap between what organizations know and what they can tell. Typically, the recipe put forward by mainstream knowledge-based theories of the firm suggests the development of management practices and conversion mechanisms able to render knowledge available throughout the organization. However, this approach does not take into full account the complexity of the phenomenon under study. Indeed, Polanyi's maxim reminds us that since we cannot express most of what we know, much of what we know remains silent. The presence of knowledge is 'silenced' by the practical background against which such knowledge is used and acquires meaning. But there is more than this. Proper functioning of our everyday life heuristics requires that part of our knowledge remain in the silent background of the things we take for granted.

In fact, not articulating the premises of our conduct is a precondition for efficient behavioural performance.

The strategy of inquiry followed in the book is similar to the one adopted in the story of the man of noise. It takes into account the fact that we live in a pre-interpreted world—where organizations provide ready-made backgrounds to human knowing—whose obviousness and familiarity are often deceiving. Following the tenets of the phenomenological method, the book seeks to dig into the 'life world' of organizations in order to capture the taken-for-granted stream of everyday routines, interaction, and events that constitute both individual and social practices. Such strategy requires a sort of 'skilled naivety'. This oxymoron designates the ability to see things as if for the first time, while exploiting the research skills accumulated by the observer through experience. Naivety evokes a form of intellectual curiosity based on the absence of preconceptions about what constitutes knowledge. At the same time, such naivety is skilled. It attempts to frame reality by crafting *ad hoc* tools for observation.

1.2 Purpose and scope of the book

This book is an inquiry into the inner workings of organizational knowing. It deals with the processes by which organizations create, use, and retain knowledge on a day-to-day basis. Knowledge has become increasingly relevant in organizations following a major shift in the dominant modes of industrial development and wealth creation in contemporary society. Peter Drucker (1993) has coined the term 'knowledge society' to stress the importance of knowledge as the defining feature of the post-capitalist world. In particular, the recombination of resources underlying present day modes of production has led to the emergence of a 'new economy' where physical assets and traditional factors of production have been gradually superseded by the power of data, information and knowledge. As a consequence of the above transformations, the post-industrial era will be increasingly populated by knowledge-intensive firms and knowledge workers while knowledge will displace capital as the engine of competitive performance.

Following the wider debate on the emergence of the information age and the knowledge society, recent years have seen an explosion of writings about organizational knowledge. To be sure, knowledge has been in the preserve of organization science ever since the appearance of Simon's notion of bounded rationality and the development of organizational theories of learning and cognition throughout the 1970s and the 1980s. Today, the widespread outgrowth of knowledge-based theories has resulted in the progressive consolidation of a managerial epistemology—significantly reflected in the sudden emergence of the knowledge-management movement—which has arguably established itself as the dominant discourse on organizational knowledge (e.g. Hedlund 1994; Sanchez and Heene 1997; Davenport and Prusak 1998; Boisot 1999; Scarbrough Swan and Preston 1999). Proponents of such a perspective have been paying increasing attention to the idea of the firm as a body of knowledge, stressing in turn the ability of firms to create, manage and transfer knowledge as a determinant of competitive performance.

Beyond the hype, however, there is a sense of incompleteness pervading today's conceptualizations of knowledge in organizations. While the theorizing on knowledge from different disciplinary perspectives and intellectual foci has produced a vast and diversified body of literature on the subject, the proliferation of organizational knowledge theories has not been accompanied by a parallel development of empirical studies. As a result of this absence of empirical focus, current literatures on knowledge seem to be marked by a widening gap between theory and practice.

In paradigmatic terms the managerial approach seems to be characterized by a functionalist understanding of knowledge-oriented phenomena in organizations. This functionalist view can be articulated in two main epistemological assumptions. First, knowledge is seen as a factor of production or resource that can be placed at the service of the organization. In its turn, the commodification of knowledge is instrumental in suggesting a causal relationship between organizational knowledge and competitive performance, and prescriptions to improve the way organizations manage their patrimony of knowledge. Knowledge is linked to such terms as best practices and world-class performance. The performativity of knowledge thus constitutes the second core assumption of the functionalist perspective.

Admittedly, the managerial approach has provided useful insights into the linkages between the capacity of a firm to generate new knowledge and its competitive performance. On the other hand, the analysis of everyday practices in organizations seems to pose a challenge to the epistemological foundations informing current mainstream theories of knowledge.

First, the presupposition that organizational knowledge can be managed implies that the main problem organizations have to face is how to render knowledge available (e.g. by converting tacit into explicit knowledge). In this regard, knowledge management emphasizes the need for devising systems and procedures able to create, encode, diffuse, and retain the knowledge that organizations produce in their day-to-day activities. On the other hand, the commodification of knowledge linked to the assumption of performativity has resulted in a sort of epistemological reification. Knowledge is mostly thought of as coming and circulating in canned packages. The facticity of knowledge—its 'matter-of-factness'—is taken for granted, while little attention is paid to the highly interactive, provisional, and contentious nature of knowledge making (Lanzara and Patriotta 2001).

Second, the empirical connection between knowledge and performance is somehow problematic. Knowledge is difficult to frame, let alone measure, while performance as an outcome variable is affected by several factors that are difficult to isolate. The difficulty suggests that we put into brackets the causal link between knowledge and performance and look at knowledge making as a relational phenomenon. From such perspective, the unfolding of knowledge processes is crucially affected by the activity system and the organizational context in which such processes take place.

Third, a purely managerial perspective tends to forget that what is accounted for as organizational knowledge might be invalidated or subverted in the near or distant future, or else revised and perfected, as a result of interaction, dispute, power play, agreement, and collective search and decision. Even the best established chunks of knowledge are subject to future revisions. As a result, interest in the instrumental and performative value of knowledge has displaced interest in generative, configurative, and evolutionary processes of knowledge making, which happen to be crucial for innovation and change in organizations.

Fourth, the quasi-exclusive focus on static epistemological categories has divorced knowledge-oriented phenomena from human action and the intricacies of everyday practice. Typically, organizational knowledge processes are reconnected to the dialectic between steady states (e.g. tacit/explicit), while little attention is paid to the ongoing transformations, translations and reconfigurations occurring along the knowledge chain. More generally, the over-reliance on the distinction between tacit and explicit as alternative types of knowledge points to an attributional conceptualization of knowledge based on formistic models and content theories. This 'alienation' of theory from practice underscores the need to engage with the study of processes, streams, flows, and flux (Weick 1979, 1995; Cooper and Law 1995; Pettigrew 1997), conceived as the cornerstones of a theory of knowing and organizing.

Fifth, current theories of knowledge seem to privilege knowledge creation over institutionalization dynamics. To be sure, as the managerial literature has pointed out, the ability of a firm to create and diffuse new knowledge can be a source of competitive advantage. However, a precondition for effective organizational performance is the ability of a firm to incorporate knowledge into stable organizational mechanisms such as structures, routines, procedures, artefacts, technological implements, and cognitive maps. In fact, the creation of knowledge generates controversies which, in turn, trigger a demand for closure. Hence, a new emphasis should be placed on the dynamics of institutionalization of knowledge, that is, the processes through which significant components of human knowledge and agency are inscribed and delegated to stable structures of signification.

A methodological problem seems to emerge from the above discussion. The gap between knowledge theory and practice suggests that a central issue for any inquiry into organizational knowledge is the possibility of studying knowledge as a dynamic empirical phenomenon. In other words, how do we empirically observe the processes whereby organizations create, use, and sustain knowledge? How can we understand the mechanics of knowledge creation? What are the micro-level foundations of knowledge in organizations? Secondly, if organization provides the backdrop for knowledge-making processes, any knowledge-based theory of the firm should be able to explain the co-evolution of knowing and organizing within and across a given social setting. This consideration leads to a further critical question, how can we capture the making of knowledge in the context of organizing?

This book aims to fill the gap between theory, method and practice by developing a phenomenological approach to the study of *knowing* in the context of *organizing*. The book contributes to the fields of strategy and organization in three ways. First it provides a critical review of the concepts, debates, and epistemological assumptions underpinning existing theories of organizational knowledge. Second, it develops a methodological framework for studying knowledge processes as an empirical phenomenon that is based on three methodological lenses: time, breakdowns, and narratives. Third, drawing on the three-lens framework the book presents a phenomenological inquiry into *knowing* and *organizing* processes within two large car-manufacturing plants at Fiat Auto, Italy. The book highlights the need to re-think organizational knowledge from an action-based perspective and suggests a new vocabulary for understanding knowledge-oriented phenomena in organizations.

The intellectual perspective developed in this book draws on a phenomenological tradition that goes back to the work of Martin Heidegger, Alfred Schutz, and Paul Ricoeur. Rather than stressing the performative, ready-made, and commodity-like character of organizational knowledge, the present book looks at the actual unfolding of knowledge-based phenomena in the work setting. Emphasis is placed on the provisional, transient, experimental, contested, and controversial nature of such phenomena. A linking theme of the book is that knowledge-making dynamics occur at the boundary between organization and disorganization. More specifically, knowledge making is seen as a process by which organizations appropriate order out of disorder and achieve closure. From this epistemological stance, organizations have to be understood as devices designed to counteract social entropy in a regulated fashion. The focus of analysis is on discontinuities, controversies, irregularities, breakdowns, and departures from standards.

Studying the interplay between knowing and organizing poses a dual challenge for the researcher. On the one hand, it entails spelling out how processes of knowledge creation and institutionalization may lead to the emergence of novel organizational arrangements. On the other hand, it involves understanding how specific features of organizational and institutional settings may facilitate or hinder the actors' capacity for sense making and collective inquiry. The making of knowledge is a way of enacting reality, giving existence to things and events, and organizing the world (Goodman 1978). Under these circumstances, knowledge making has less to do with performance, control or competition and more with sense making, existence, and ontology.

1.3 Organizational context: the choice of the automotive sector

The argument of the book draws on rich empirical evidence provided by three in-depth case studies, which were conducted at Fiat Auto, Italy. The choice of the auto industry may seem at odds with the project of a book on knowledge. Today, a typical study on knowledge would probably be conducted in the context of a consultancy firm, an Internet business, or a pharmaceutical company. These would be seen as knowledge-intensive settings characterized by a widespread deployment of knowledge as an input, throughput, and output. Indeed, when viewed as a commodity, knowledge is certainly more conspicuous in certain sectors or organizations. Accordingly, knowledge intensiveness may be defined as a function of the role that knowledge plays in the creation of value (e.g. the role of Research and Development (R&D) activities). However, the above argument mistakes the issue of knowledge intensiveness for the problem of the empirical relevance of knowledge within a given business domain. The argument fails on at least two grounds. First, the relevance of knowledge-oriented processes is to a great extent related to the new emphasis on knowledge which characterizes contemporary debates on organizations. What makes knowledge important in a firm is not the intrinsic nature of the business activities performed, but the interpretive apparatus with which we look at such activities. Second, and perhaps more important, as an experiential phenomenon knowledge pervades any type of activity both human and organizational. From a phenomenological perspective the importance of knowledge in organizations is inextricably linked to how organizations make sense of their world on an everyday basis.

More than fifty years ago, Peter Drucker (1946) defined car manufacturing as 'the industry of industries'. Today, the auto industry represents an archetype. It relies on traditional technologies like assembly lines, while the presence of avant-garde IT (Information Technology) systems is not so conspicuous as in other sectors. As a consequence, knowledge is not so much a by-product of IT, but rather stems from the complex nexus of equipment, conventions and institutions underlying organizational practices. Furthermore, car manufacturing embodies a mature sector characterized by consolidated industry recipes (Spender 1989) and where competition is most fierce. In the past decade, the industry of industries has undergone a major transition from Fordist mass production systems to new organizational models derived from the Toyota Production System (Womack, Jones, and Ross 1990). As a result of this critical transition, avant-garde organizational concepts such as lean production, total quality management, just in time, teamwork, along with the adoption of cutting edge technologies, have been pioneered in car manufacturing in response to competitive market forces. The above characteristics of the sector bear critical consequences for knowledge creation, change and innovation. The case studies contained in the book focus on knowledge creation, utilization, and institutionalization processes occurring on the shop floor of two of Fiat's most renowned factories: the Fiat SATA assembly plant in Melfi and the Mirafiori Pressing plant in Turin. Beyond their specific business operations, the selected plants can be seen as productive units characterized by distinctive combinations of product, production process, and work organization

(Abernathy 1978; Whipp and Clark 1986). In this respect they are characterized as knowledge systems in their own right.

The two plants stand in stark contrast as far as the institutional setting is concerned. Melfi is an avant-garde assembly plant, located in the South of Italy, built as a greenfield site in 1993 and opened officially in 1994. The plant is characterized by a novice workforce and holds one of the best productivity records in the world. Mirafiori is a brownfield set up in the 1950s and characterized by an experienced workforce. The two plants share the same organizational model, known as the 'integrated factory', introduced by Fiat at the beginning of the 1990s as a result of a major re-engineering process accompanying a radical shift from mass production systems to a Post-Fordist paradigm. However, while Melfi has been designed as an integrated factory, in Mirafiori the model has been superimposed on the existing organization. The two factories also differ in terms of technology since Melfi is a final assembly plant relying on an assembly line, whilst Mirafiori produces car parts and accordingly is organized as a batch production system. The distinct settings of two plants characterized by different stages of maturity constitute critical context variations in the study. These variations offer alternative perspectives for the observation of organizational knowledge processes.

1.4   Structure and content of the book

The book is organized according to a three-fold structure. Part One (Chapters 1–3) lays out the epistemological foundations of the study. In particular, Chapter 2 presents a systematic review of the existing perspectives on knowledge in organizations and identifies the main gaps in the literature. Chapter 3 develops a methodological framework for studying organizational knowledge processes as empirical phenomena. The framework is based on three methodological lenses: time, breakdowns, and narratives. Each lens provides a distinctive technique for accessing the tacit features of organization. At the same time the three lenses are part of a coherent framework and therefore can be deployed in a complementary fashion. Part Two (Chapters 4–7) contains the empirical core of the study. Specifically, the three-lens framework is applied in the setting of two large car-manufacturing plants at Fiat Auto Italy. Chapter 4 provides a brief profile of Fiat. Drawing on business history and labour history methods, the chapter outlines the main phases punctuating processes of organizational change and innovation at Fiat. In particular, the chapter analyses the evolution of production systems and organizational models within the company. Chapters 5–7 depict the Fiat case through three in-depth empirical studies. Chapter 5 contains a longitudinal analysis of the dynamics surrounding the coming into existence of an avant-garde auto assembly plant from the greenfield. The construction work, involving future workforce, is seen as a metaphor of knowledge creation and institutionalization. Chapter 6 considers the same plant once it has reached full production capacity. The focus of observation is on the variety of breakdowns punctuating the smooth functioning of the assembly line on the shop floor. The case study shows how breakdowns provide access to tacit knowledge, and in particular how they reveal the cognitive structures underlying the functioning of assembly lines. Chapter 7 focuses on narratives and storytelling as ways to disclose the distinctive sense-making processes through which operators frame the complexity of the shop floor. A main finding of the case study is that stories act as noticing devices or attention directors affecting the dynamics of knowledge creation and collective remembering. In this regard, stories possess a strong metaphorical character resulting in a double edge: they are prompts and reminders, collectors and transmitters of knowledge. Finally, stories in the form of notable experiences are part of a cultural system reflected in the conventional wisdom of the team members. Here, the value-driven character of knowledge as 'justified true belief' is emphasized. Part Three attempts to develop a systematic conceptualization of knowledge-oriented phenomena in organizations which is empirically grounded and methodologically sound. In Chapter 8, the empirical findings of the study provide the backbone for constructing a theoretical model of knowledge in organizations. The model highlights a standard knowledge cycle based on recursive processes of creation, utilization, and institutionalization and leading to the production of generic knowledge outcomes. When referred to the case studies the model reveals the linkages among process, content, and type of knowledge in different organizational settings and under different historical contingencies. In particular, the map of transformations that organizational knowledge undergoes over time defines a hypothetical knowledge trajectory. This trajectory identifies three main types of knowledge: foundational knowledge is connected to the design of organization; procedural knowledge refers to the routinization of organizational action in consolidated settings; experiential knowledge points to more mature stages in the co-evolutionary paths of knowing and organizing. Finally, Chapter 9 summarizes the main theoretical, methodological, and empirical contributions achieved by the book. It also outlines some possible directions for future research.

2

Knowing and Organizing

2.1 Introduction

Despite the long-established tradition of knowledge studies, the field of organization science seems to be characterized by a constellation of multiple and often fragmented perspectives. Echoing Scott (1987), it is appropriate to say that knowledge theories have just entered the adolescent phase with some perspectives still in an early stage of development. Historically, the evolution of organizational knowledge theories has been informed by a wide spectrum of theoretical traditions. Knowledge is a multifaceted phenomenon which has been debated in a variety of disciplinary contexts: from philosophy and sociology, to social psychology and cognitive science; from economics to management and organizational analysis. The breadth and depth of the subject under study makes it difficult to trace a genealogy of existing knowledge theories.

For Spender and Grant (1996) the beginning of the knowledge-based paradigm can be connected to Simon's (1947) notion of bounded rationality. Interestingly, the work of Simon epitomizes the encounter of two epistemological traditions: one derived from economics and emphasizing issues of individual self interest and rational decision-making, the other related to psychology and focusing on the link between cognition and action and its behavioural consequences. Likewise, Pentland (1992) identifies a divide between cognitive and structural theories of knowledge. For him the dual derivation of knowledge theories is neatly captured by what Ryle (1949) called 'the dogma of the Ghost in the Machine'. The cognitive approach directs our attention to the ghost: perception, belief and sense making. The structural approach focuses on the machine: structures, objects and routines.

Broadly speaking, existing theories of organizational knowledge can be connected to the dialectic between the above epistemological traditions. The 'cognitive turn' in organization studies was conceived as a way to bring the concepts of mind, intentionality, and sense making into the realm of organizational behaviour (Boland and Tenkasi 1993). Cognitive theories have looked at knowledge as a representational phenomenon associated with the image of organizations as brains (Morgan 1997). From this perspective, organizational knowledge is seen to reside in mental structures (Shank and Abelson 1977) such as frames, scripts, cognitive maps, and interpretative schemes which account for how organizations make sense of their activity and perform in the face of environmental changes.

The alternative approach has focused on the material and structural features of organization such as resources and routines within a ubiquitous conceptualization of knowledge as an 'intangible' asset or commodity. Knowledge is seen as a factor of production and causally linked to organizational performance. The increasing success of the theories generated within this strand has resulted in the progressive consolidation of a knowledge-based view of the firm (e.g. Nonaka and Takeuchi 1995; Grant 1996; Spender 1996; Boisot 1999; Eisenhardt and Santos 2001) which has been mainly developed within the realms of organizational economics and strategic management.

The theories of knowledge analysed above account for the vast majority of the literature that has been produced on the subject. The third strand analysed in the present chapter is referred to as the situated perspective and is characterized by a distinctive focus on organizational practices. It directs our attention to the body of organizational literature that has stressed the importance of the 'details of practice' (Brown and Duguid 1991), situated action (Lave and Wenger 1991; Suchman 1987) formative contexts (Unger 1987; Blackler 1992; Ciborra and Lanzara 1994), and activity systems (Engestrom 1987; Blackler 1995).

Finally, the fourth strand considered in this chapter can be labelled the 'techno-science' approach (Latour and Woolgar 1979; Knorr-Cetina 1981; Latour 1987; Bijker, Hughes, and Pinch 1989). Its roots are in the sociology of science and sociological studies of technology. The body of literature belonging to this strand emerges from the rejection of the traditional mind–body opposition and the recognition of the socially constructed nature of knowledge. The techno-science approach is primarily empirical in its focus. The laboratory serves as a metaphor underlying most of the empirical work in this strand, emphasizing the processes of knowledge production and transformation.

In the following sections I review the four main perspectives on organizational knowledge presented above in order to identify the gaps in the literature and derive a research agenda for this study.

2.2 Knowledge as representation: the cognitive approach

In its most paradigmatic formulation the cognitive approach to the study of knowledge has been variously characterized as rational cognitivism (Blackler 1993), planning model (Suchman 1987) or symbolic cognition (Norman 1993) and described according to the metaphor of the computer model of the mind (Boland and Tenkasi 1993). Following that metaphor, knowing is seen as a computational activity which involves the manipulation of symbols after the fashion of digital computers (Newell and Simon 1972). As Norman (1993) has pointed out, the caricature of the traditional symbolic approach to human cognition is that it focuses entirely upon the processing structures of the brain and the symbolic representations of the mind. All action is inside the head, yielding a natural distinction between the reality 'out there' and the processes taking place 'inside here'. Under these circumstances, the main problem confronting the knowing subject is the possibility of establishing some reasonably sure connection with the outside world through information gathering and processing activities. As Winograd and Flores (1986: 73) have pointed out:

At its simplest, the rationalistic view accepts the existence of an objective reality, made up of things bearing properties and entering into relations. A cognitive being 'gathers information' about those things and builds up a 'mental model' which will be in some respects correct (a faithful representation of reality) and in other respects incorrect. Knowledge is a *storehouse of representations*, which can be called upon for use in reasoning and which can be translated into language. Thinking is a process of manipulating representations—(Winograd and Flores 1986: 73, emphasis added).

In exploring the cognition–action linkages a fundamental hypothesis is that action always possesses a cognitive basis which is reflected in the representational activities of the mind. Cognitivism posits the existence of an isolated mind (a mind-in-a-vat) able to create inner representations that partly or fully correspond to the outer world, be it objects, events or states (Latour 1999*a*; Von Krogh, Roos and Klein 1998). The mind is depicted as a glassware mirroring an objective reality. The image of the glassware highlights a sense of disconnection, separation, filtering, mediation, transparency, gazing, and contemplation. It is a visual metaphor stressing the fact that knowing is seeing, or rather, 'seeing through'. A world that is totally outside, 'out there' and yet accessible through a tenuous connection with a mind 'in here'. Under these circumstances, the knowing subject appears as a bodiless observer, excised from the rest, and contemplating the outside world.

The duality of cognition and action underlies the conceptualization of knowing as a computational activity. Planning and intentionality are central to symbolic theories since human behaviour is always oriented towards a goal. The planning model in cognitive science treats a plan as a sequence of actions designed to accomplish some preconceived end. The model posits that action is a form of problem-solving, where the actor's problem is to find a path from some initial state to a desired goal state, given certain conditions along the way (Newell and Simon 1972 cited in Suchman 1987: 28). Under these circumstances, internal representations act as filters mediating between goal and situation. Representation is information about a situation which is stored in human memory as a result of previous experience and learning. As in a computer program, such representations contain a set of instructions on how to respond to a given situation. Accordingly, effective behavioural performance depends on the degree of accuracy in the representation of a problem. The essence of individual knowing resides in the possibility of establishing a correspondence between reality and language, the world and the word, things and names, events and representations, maps and territories (Weick 1990; Van Maanen 1995). Truth is a matter of accuracy, knowing is a problem of reference.

Cognitive theories are elaborated from the standpoint of the individual and then extended to organizations. Within cognitive theory, organizations are seen as having a mind of their own. Historically, they have been defined as information processing devices (Galbraith 1977), interpretation systems (Daft and Weick 1984), and thinking systems (Sims and Gioia 1986). In the classical Simonian view, organizations are considered as devices for accomplishing complex tasks that may exceed the bounded rationality of individuals. In this respect, human limitations are institutionalized in the structure and modes of functioning of our organizations (Morgan 1997). Hierarchy, for example, provides a powerful mechanism for simplification, capable of breaking a complex task down to its smallest components. Likewise, organizational routines and standard operating procedures act as programmes for action. More generally, organizations are viewed as decision-making mechanisms (March and Simon 1958) conveying a simplified image of reality and thereby helping individuals to make rational decisions.

In sum, cognitive theories lead us to understand organizations as kinds of institutionalized brains that fragment, routinize and bind the decision-making process to make it manageable (Morgan 1997). Furthermore, the conceptualization of knowledge as symbolic representation, related to problem-solving, bears important implications for organizational learning. According to Simon et al. (1992) a primary task for researchers on organizational learning is to understand how people acquire new problem representations for dealing with new problems. New problems need new problem representations because existing problem-solving procedures are based on selective searches through a problem space defined by a particular problem representation. Changes in problem representations imply fundamental change in organizational knowledge and individual skills.

2.2.1 *Organizational learning and cognition*

Organizational learning was brought to the forefront of management by Argyris and Schön (1978). Their aim was to explore the relationship between action and cognition in organizations in order to develop an action-oriented theory of organizational learning. In line with the brain metaphor they saw organizations as cognitive artefacts. Central to their framework was the notion of theories of action, conceived as cognitive structures underlying all deliberate human behaviour. A theory of action is a set of norms, strategies and assumptions informing human conduct. It contains hypotheses about the world aimed at realizing a correspondence among situations, intentions and behavioural outcomes. Typically, a theory of action consists of a set of interconnected propositions having an 'if . . . then' form. Theories of action are inferential structures characterized by an instrumental quality: in situation S, if you want to achieve consequence C, under assumptions a, . . . , n, do A . . . (Argyris and Schön 1978: 11).

For Argyris and Schön a crucial problem in effective action was that theories of action which people actually use may differ from theories of action they espouse. This potential split has important organizational consequences since it can lead to learning inefficiencies. There are various reasons why the two theories may not collide, which can be connected to the tacit nature of theory in use. Theory in use may remain tacit because its incongruity with espoused theory is undiscussable. In fact, theory in use reflects a set of assumptions, strategies, and norms which have sedimented over time and have come to be taken for granted: we act without being aware of the premises that govern our behaviour. Or it may remain tacit because people know more than they can tell (Polanyi 1966), since the theory in use is inaccessible to them. In this case, tacitness is related to the opacity of human behaviour and to the bounded rationality of individuals. A theory of action contains a huge number of instructions which it is impossible to codify or to describe. A further source of incongruence between espoused theory and theory in use is that people may deliberately hide the theories underlying their behaviour for opportunistic reasons.

Just as individual theories of action may be inferred from individual behaviour, so organizational theories of action may be inferred from patterns of organizational action. More specifically, a firm's theory of action is a set of shared norms, strategies, and assumptions informing organizational practice and directed to the achievement of corporate objectives. Furthermore, as individuals have espoused theories which may be incongruent with their theories in use, so have organizations. At the organizational level, espoused theory is reflected in formal corporate documents such as organizational charts, policy statements, and job descriptions while the organization's theory in use needs to be inferred from the observation of actual behaviour. According to Argyris and Schön, the largely tacit theory in use accounts for organizational identity and continuity. Organizational knowledge resides in the organization's theory in use. Consequently, theory in use constitutes the focus of any inquiry into organizational learning dynamics.

Organizational theory in use is encoded in private images and public maps of the organization. The latter are defined as shared descriptions which individuals jointly construct to guide their behaviour. Maps offer a simplified picture of reality, thus allowing for cognitive economies and providing guides to future action. In this regard, maps are both descriptive and prescriptive. Having introduced the notion of theory of action as a guide to individual behaviour in organizations, Argyris and Schön analyse how these theories are formed, how they come to change, and in what senses they may be considered adequate or inadequate. This analysis leads to a theory of organizational learning. Human action and human learning are placed in the larger context of knowing and defined as the construction, testing and restructuring of a certain kind of knowledge. Likewise, organizational learning can be defined as a stable modification of behaviour. It occurs as a result of modifications to individual's maps and images of the organization, which, in turn, may produce changes in organizational theory in use. Argyris and Schön distinguish between two types of learning. Single loop learning is based on a simple feedback mechanism that links expected outcomes of action to the theory informing them in order to keep organizational performance within the range set by organizational norms (keep the organization 'on course'). The norms themselves remain unchanged. In this situation, organizational members respond to changes in the internal and external environments of the organizations by detecting errors and correcting them within the existing theory in use. Single loop learning is effective for most of the day-to-day problems that organizations have to face. A typical example would be the modification of an organizational routine in response to a certain type of systematic disruption. The modification occurs within a constant framework of norms for performance. Double loop learning refers to situations of organizational change where complex issues cannot be tackled by means of existing cognitive and institutional resources. It implies changing existing norms and premises in order to solve the problem at hand. The authors also highlight the difficulties in succeeding in double loop learning. These difficulties are related to the tendency of organizations to resist change by enacting defensive routines (Argyris 1990). Hence, a crucial dilemma for organizations is the balance between control and innovation, between static and dynamic efficiency. In both cases, organizational learning implies testing and restructuring the existing theory in use. Put another way, learning does not take place if the modifications in strategies, norms, and assumptions are not embedded in organizational memory by means of their encoding in organizational maps. Organizational learning is the result of a collective inquiry into the strategies, norms, and assumptions underlying organizational practice.

2.2.2 *Knowledge and sense making*

Thus far, we have addressed only marginally the issue of meaning and interpretation of action, which is crucial for the construction of organizational knowledge. Consequently, our analysis needs to descend to a further level of detail in order to understand how organizations make sense of the flows and processes which characterize their activity. Karl Weick has been the scholar who has introduced the sense-making perspective into organizational study and made this concept the analytical cornerstone of his phenomenology of organizing (Weick 1979). Sense making literally means the making of sense (Weick 1995: 4). It deals with how social agents construct meaning out of a flow of action and events and how this meaning is crystallized into sensible structures. As Thomas, Clark, and Gioia (1993) have pointed out, the concept of sense making keeps action and cognition together. Like knowledge, of which it represents the 'processual' aspect, sense making is closely related to action, contexts, and time. Sense making is an ongoing activity related to how people cope with equivocal flows of action.

Although the concept of sense making seems to deal mostly with cognitive phenomena, when applied to organizations it proves to be extremely insightful. The ongoing character of sense-making activity is reflected in organizational routines conceived as carriers of tacit knowledge (Nelson and Winter, 1982). Also, in organizations we find a fundamental analogy between the workflow and the flow of meanings surrounding the execution of tasks and routines. If sense making keeps action and cognition together, the cognitive content of action emerges only in specific occasions, namely when action and cognition are set apart. This stresses the importance of breakdowns and triggers as entry points to tacit knowledge. Louis and Sutton's (1991) discussion of conditions for conscious cognitive processing, when people shift from automatic to active thinking, provides a valuable overview of occasions for sense making. The authors identify three kinds of situation in which actors are likely to become consciously engaged. First, switching to a conscious mode is provoked when one experiences a situation as unusual or novel—when something 'stands out of the ordinary', 'is unique', or when the 'unfamiliar' or 'previously unknown' is experienced. Second, switching is provoked by discrepancy—when 'acts are in some way frustrated', when there is 'an unexpected failure', 'a disruption', 'a troublesome . . . situation', when there is a significant difference between expectations and reality. A third condition exists of deliberate initiative, usually in response to an internal or external request for an increased level of conscious attention—as when people are 'asked to think' or 'explicitly questioned' or when they choose to 'try something new' (Louis and Sutton 1991: 60, also cited in Weick 1995).

Interruption is a common antecedent of sense-making occasions. However, the mere presence of discontinuities in action is not sufficient. The sense maker is an active agent, and realities and environments are 'enacted' by the actors who face them through processes of selection, punctuation, and retention (Weick 1977). In a similar vein, Louis and Sutton contend that 'the situation alone does not determine whether the previously unknown or discrepant event will be experienced as such, whether it will 'stand out'. Instead, the predispositions and experiences of the individual in the situation contribute to the actor's sensitivity and openness to environmental conditions' (Louis and Sutton 1991: 60–1). In other words, occasions for sense making are themselves constructed, after which they become a platform for further construction (Weick, 1995: 85). The last observation highlights the importance of contexts for sense making and the act of interpretation. An action can become an object of attention only after it has occurred, and the choice of what the action means is heavily influenced by the situational context (Weick 1995: 26). Hence a context affects both the process of noticing (Starbuck and Milliken 1988) and the interpretation of what is noticed. It defines the scope and meaning of action.

The above considerations have important empirical consequences because the presence of a major crisis or disruption makes sense-making activities particularly conspicuous. A good example of the above is Weick's classical study of a group of fire fighters facing a major disaster in Mann Gulch (Weick 1993). Drawing on secondary data provided by Norman Maclean's (1992) book, *Young Men and Fire*, Weick describes in detail how a group of 'smoke jumpers' performed in the face of a major fire. Failure of co-ordination between the group of fire fighters and their leader is connected to discrepancies in the group's 'cosmology'; that is, the cognitive structure governing the sense-making processes of the group. Specifically, the cosmology operating in Mann Gulch enabled certain types of action while disallowing others (e.g. following certain types of orders). A major finding of the study is that serious dysfunctions in minimal organizations' performance may derive from the concurrent failure of sense-making capacities (e.g. the ability to improvize) and organizational structures (e.g. the role system). The notion of cosmology points to the rigidities inherent in the institutionalization of a knowledge system; that is, what the members of a community have come to take for granted over the years. The Mann Gulch disaster underscores the consequences of such rigidities in a dramatic fashion and this, aside from the author's elegant prose, is probably one of the narrative devices that make Weick's account so compelling.

2.2.3   *Critical remarks*

While the cognitive focus has added to our understanding of organizations in many ways, the predominant vision that has guided a major portion of cognitive studies has been symbolic cognition and the computer model of the mind. Boland and Tenkasi (1993) contend that this metaphor confuses information processing with meaning making. In fact, while a digital computer operates on the physical form of the symbols it computes without any concern for their meaning (syntax), the human mind is not indifferent with respect to meaning. Put another way, the computer model of the mind neglects the semantic dimension of knowledge-making processes.

More generally, the two chief assumptions underlying the cognitive approach—all types of action have a cognitive basis, and organizational cognition is an extension of individual cognition—raise major criticisms. A first point of controversy is that the view of knowledge propounded by the cognitive approach is informed by an exclusive preoccupation with the mind. In contrast with the planning model, the situated cognition perspective (e.g. Suchman 1987; Winograd and Flores 1986) has pointed out that knowledge does not necessarily need to be explicitly represented (more on this later). Argyris and Schön have made clear that theories in use do not need to be explicit. Advocates of the 'thinking organization' (Sims and Gioia 1986) recognize that mental structures often operate unconsciously. Even Simon (Vera and Simon 1993), in an article written in response to the criticism levelled by the situated cognition approach, has made a clear distinction between cognitive processing and conscious awareness. Secondly, organizational cognition is derived from individual cognition without a clear explanation of how individual knowledge is organizationally amplified. For example, Argyris and Schön recognize that organizational knowledge creation stems from the interplay between private images and public maps of the organizations, but they do not explain the process that leads to sharing those images. Since the socially constructed nature of organizational knowledge is neglected, the cognitive perspective is not able to explain the genesis and evolution of a certain belief system. Furthermore, the emphasis on cognition overlooks the institutional dimension of knowledge and the role of contextual factors. As a consequence, the taken-for-granted aspects of knowledge underlying organizational behaviour are underestimated. The separation between cognition and action, and between individual and organization represents a major obstacle for understanding how organizations think. Indeed, the term 'thinking organizations', coined by Sims and Gioia, provides a way to capture a paradox: organizations are the products of the thought and action of their members; they do not behave independently of the people who construct and manage them. At the same time, organizations also seem to take on a life of their own, thus offering a view of a 'corporate mind'.

In sum, the cognitive approach—based on a pervasive analogy with the computer model of the mind—seems to suggest an abstracted, disembodied view of knowing and thinking. According to this view, invisible, ordered patterns are assumed to lie beneath the conscious activity of the human subject (Boland and Tenkasi 1993). In so doing, paradigmatic cognitive theories overlook and reify the fluid, shifting, and often contradictory nature of human understanding, and relegate the complexity of knowledge-making dynamics to a fixed and static image. This position, which reflects the traditional Cartesian split between the mind and the body, has been nicely captured by Gilbert Ryle (1949) as the 'dogma of the ghost in the machine'. The ghost is represented by the invisible knowledge structures animating the human body and producing human behaviour. Given the 'ghostly' nature of knowledge, it is always problematic to empirically derive specific actions and decisions from internal (invisible) representations of organizational actors. As a consequence, the problem of studying knowledge empirically remains unresolved. On the other hand, the sense-making perspective seems to close the gap between organizational theory and practice, and therefore provides the conceptual basis for an empirical study of knowledge. In this respect, it makes a distinctive contribution towards the construction of a theory of knowledge in organizations that recognizes the cognitive dimension while taking into account the importance of meaning and context.

2.3 Knowledge as commodity: the knowledge-based view of the firm

A great deal of the current literature has looked at knowledge as an intangible asset or commodity which can be made readily available throughout the organization in order to enhance competitive performance. The increasing importance ascribed to knowledge as a strategic factor of production has resulted in the progressive consolidation of a knowledge-based view of the firm (e.g. Nonaka and Takeuchi 1995; Grant 1996; Spender 1996; Boisot 1999; Eisenhardt and Santos 2001), which has arguably established itself as the mainstream literature informing the discourse on knowledge in organizations. The most distinctive trait of such a theory is the conceptualization of the firm itself as a body of knowledge. In particular, the knowledge-based approach emphasizes firm-specific, difficult to imitate assets as a source of sustainable competitive advantage. The idiosyncratic knowledge base underlying a firm's performance includes resources (Penrose 1959; Wernerfelt 1984; Barney 1991; Grant 1991; Peteraf 1993; Collis and Montgomery 1995); routines (Nelson and Winter 1982); competencies (Prahalad and Hamel 1990); capabilities (Leonard-Barton 1992*a*; Kogut and Zander 1992; Amit and Schoemaker 1993; Teece, Pisano, and Schuen 1997; Eisenhardt and Martin 2000); and intellectual capital (Quinn 1992; Nahapiet and Goshal 1998).

The knowledge-based view of the firm can be seen as an outgrowth of the resource-based theory (RBT) within the field of strategic management. The resource-based perspective attempts to develop a theory of strategy formulation which is an alternative to the traditional competitive forces approach developed by Porter (1980) and regarded as the dominant paradigm in the field during the 1980s. According to Porter, competitive advantage results from the strategic positioning of a firm with respect to its environment, the latter being defined by the industry sector in which a firm operates. In particular, industry structure strongly influences competitive rules of the game and thereby the repertoire of strategic choices potentially available to firms. This perspective emphasizes the actions a firm can take to create a defensible position against competitive forces (Teece, Pisano, and Schuen 1997).

In contrast to the competitive forces approach, the RBT underscores the role of endogenous factors as the fundamental determinants of firm performance. Although the influence of the business environment is not denied, resource-based theorists argue that firms are heterogeneous in nature (Rumelt 1991). Accordingly, the capacity of a firm to achieve superior performance should be understood from an inward looking perspective. At the heart of the firm's competitive strength is a set of unique assets, capabilities, and organizational processes that differentiate a company strategically and deliver competitive advantage. More specifically, firm resources can become the source of sustainable competitive advantage if they are valuable, rare, and difficult to imitate or substitute (Barney 1991).

The rejection of market determinism by resource-based theorists makes organizational knowledge a central theoretical concern. In particular, the knowledge base of a firm—as instanced by its configuration of resources, competencies and capabilities—is seen as a source of distinction; that is, what makes the firm what it is. As a consequence, difference and uniqueness are the ultimate causes of competitive advantage. A case in point is Prahalad and Hamel's (1990) conceptualization of core competence. Drawing on anecdotal evidence about American and Japanese firms operating in the same business, the authors argue that the superior competitive performance of the latter can be clearly connected to distinctive core competencies. Core competencies are defined as the collective learning in the organization, especially how to coordinate diverse production skills and streams of technologies. Examples of core competencies include Sony's capacity for miniaturization, Honda's distinctive competence in engines and power trains, NEC's digital technology and system integration skills, JVC's technology in video recording, and Casio's competence in display systems. And among non-Japanese innovative firms, Philips' optical-media expertise (laser disc), and 3M's competence with sticky tape.

To be sure, the RBT has provided a significant contribution to understanding the conditions under which firms achieve and sustain competitive advantage. On the other hand, the conceptualization of the firm as a static bundle of idiosyncratic resources fails to explain how and why certain firms have competitive advantage in regimes of rapid and unpredictable change. The need to account for the dynamic aspects of organizational knowledge is the main focus of the dynamic capabilities framework. As elaborated by Teece, Pisano, and Schuen (1997), dynamic capabilities refer to the firm's processes and routines that use resources in order to address rapidly changing environments. In this regard, dynamic capabilities reflect a firm's ability to achieve new and innovative forms of competitive advantage by changing its resource base.

More recently, Eisenhardt and Martin (2000) have proposed a reconceptualization of dynamic capabilities in order to understand how those capabilities are influenced by market dynamism and their evolution over time. Echoing Teece, Pisano, and Schuen, dynamic capabilities are defined as 'the organizational and strategic routines by which firms achieve new resource configurations as markets emerge, collide, split, evolve and die' (Teece, Pisano, and Schuen 1997: 1107). Examples of dynamic capabilities include such organizational and strategic processes as product innovation, decision-making, and alliancing. Although dynamic capabilities are idiosyncratic in their details and path dependent in their emergence, they have significant commonalities across firms. In this respect, dynamic capabilities can be equated to best practices, subject to imitation and diffusion within a certain sector. Accordingly, the fundamental assumptions of heterogeneity and resource immobility underlying the resource based view of the firm are called into question. In particular, RBT framework breaks down in high velocity environments where the duration of competitive advantage is inherently unpredictable. Therefore, the strategic challenge of firms operating in such environments is to build new resource configurations in the pursuit of temporary (rather than long-term) advantage.

Finally, the focus on endogenous, firm-specific resources as competitive forces raises important implications for the interaction between knowledge-based factors and organizational learning. The relevance of organizational learning processes is at least two-fold. Firstly, firm-level resources are based on tacit know-how and therefore highly idiosyncratic. These idiosyncratic resources result from the firm's specific learning trajectories which have been developed over time. Secondly, the set of existing competencies and capabilities may enable or constrain the learning potentials of a firm through path-dependency. As Teece, Pisano, and Schuen (1997: 514) have pointed out: 'resource endowments are "sticky": at least in the short run, firms are to some degree stuck with what they have and may have to live with what they lack'. This point is consistent with Leonard Barton's (1992a) notion of 'core rigidities'.[1] She sees capabilities as institutionalized assets (literally infused with value), which organizational actors have come to take for granted. Building upon illustrative cases of new product development in five American companies, the author finds that firm-specific capabilities are characterized by a fundamental duality: they can promote competitive advantage, or, conversely, provide a source of incumbent inertia. A major managerial challenge, therefore, derives from the firm's ability to handle the paradox of core capabilities and core rigidities. More generally, the notion of path dependency points to the institutional features of organizational knowledge and highlights important learning dilemmas.

2.3.1   *Tacit and explicit knowledge*

Most dynamic knowledge theories can be connected to the path breaking studies of Nonaka and Takeuchi (1995) and Nelson and Winter (1982). Both works assume Polanyi's distinction of tacit and explicit knowledge as their point of departure. However, the two conceptualizations reach different conclusions about the entities involved in knowledge creation dynamics and, ultimately, the evolution of the firm.

Nonaka and Takeuchi's (1995: 3) theory of knowledge creation attempts to explain the systematic capacity of Japanese firms to outperform their Western competitors.[2] By organizational knowledge creation the authors mean 'the capability of a company as a whole to create new knowledge, disseminate it throughout the organization, and embody it in products, services and systems'. At the heart of Nonaka

---

[1] The presence of core rigidities relates to Hedberg's (1981) work on 'unlearning'. As Pettigrew and Whipp (1991: 277) have pointed out, the jettisoning or refashioning of entrenched knowledge and beliefs may play a critical role in the dynamics of competition and strategic change.

[2] Most of the management literature on knowledge builds upon the increasing success of Japanese firms throughout the 1980s and the relative competitive decline of Western companies. Indeed, the opposition Western/Eastern is a leitmotiv of most influential knowledge-based theories. Interestingly, however, this point contrasts with the difficulties of Japanese firms during the 1990s. In other words, the early debate on knowledge and competitive performance seems to be grounded in historical as well as contextual contingencies that do not hold true any more.

and Takeuchi's framework is Polanyi's (1966) distinction between tacit and explicit knowledge. Tacit knowledge is related to experience and is idiosyncratic. It can be defined as the stock of background knowledge that individuals take for granted in their everyday coping with the world. Explicit knowledge refers to knowledge that can be codified and articulated and therefore transmitted in a formal way. The two alternative types of knowledge are often referred to as know-how and know-that (Ryle 1949). While the former is created 'here and now' in a specific, practical context and conveyed through analogies and metaphors, the latter is contained in manuals and procedures and oriented towards a context-free theory.

According to Nonaka and Takeuchi (1995), knowledge is created and expanded through a continuous and dynamic interaction between tacit and explicit knowledge. Specifically, knowledge creation occurs through four modes of conversion of tacit and explicit knowledge—which they call socialization, externalization, internalization, and combination—each characterized by a particular content. This theory of knowledge creation encompasses both an epistemological dimension (types of knowledge at hand), and an ontological one (knowledge creating entities). As far as the latter is concerned, Nonaka and Takeuchi contend that knowledge is created only by individuals, although the conversion process is a social process between individuals and not confined within the individual. Subsequently, knowledge is 'organizationally' expanded and amplified through the four modes of knowledge conversion and crystallized at higher ontological levels (group, organization, and inter-organization). To exemplify this process the authors use the metaphor of the knowledge spiral, in which the interaction between tacit and explicit knowledge becomes larger in scale as it moves up the ontological levels.

Nonaka and Takeuchi (1995: 56) hint at the primacy of tacit knowledge over the explicit when they affirm that 'the key to knowledge creation lies in the mobilization and conversion of tacit knowledge' and accordingly emphasize the role of individuals as carriers of knowledge and organizational innovation. In fact, unlike information, knowledge is about beliefs and commitment and therefore essentially relates to human action (Kolb 1979). Accordingly, knowledge creation is linked with dynamics of interpretation and sense making. However, the authors do not develop this important aspect of their theory and leave the problem of agency unresolved (Spender 1996).

The conceptualization of knowledge as a commodity and the above-mentioned distinction between tacit and explicit knowledge also inform

Nelson and Winter's (1982) knowledge-based theory of the firm. They see organizations as knowledge repositories. The knowledge of a firm resides essentially in its memory, and is stored in organizational routines. The authors suggest that the routinization of activity constitutes the most important form of storage of organizational knowledge and that organizations essentially 'remember by doing'. Accordingly, they identify the routinization of activity as the 'locus' of operational knowledge in an organization.

Following Polanyi (1966), Nelson and Winter argue that much operational knowledge in organizations exists at a tacit level and that routines are the carriers of such knowledge. First of all, routines are ways of doing things that have consolidated over time. They constitute quasi-automatic responses that have been deeply internalized by organizational actors and therefore are executed without conscious volition. Routines are characterized by opacity and rigidity. Secondly, routines are to organizations what skills represent for human behaviour. Like humans, organizations are characterized by bounded rationality. Accordingly, they find it difficult or impossible to articulate a full account of the details of their performance and, most of all, to be aware of the relationships that link those details.

The authors recognize to some extent the role of the individual as a knowledge agent. Information is actually stored primarily in the memories of the members of the organization, in which resides all the knowledge, articulable and tacit, that constitutes their individual skills (Polani 1996: 104). Accordingly a firm's performance depends on the ability of its members to 'continue to know their jobs' and on their capacity to interpret correctly and respond to the messages they receive from the working environment. However, the knowledge stored in human memories is meaningful and effective only in a certain context. In this respect, organizations provide the context that underlies the acts of interpretation performed by its members and consequently the background knowledge that informs the execution of skilled performance. The context typically includes, firstly, various forms of external memory—files, message boards, manuals, computer memories, magnetic tapes—maintained in large part as a routine organizational function. Secondly, the context includes the physical state of equipment and of the work environment generally. Performance of an organizational memory function is in part implicit in the simple fact that equipment and structures are relatively durable. Finally, the context of the information possessed by an individual member is established by the information possessed by all other members. Individual memories are linked by shared experiences of the past—experiences that have established the extremely detailed and specific communication system that underlies routine performance (Nelson and Winter 1982: 105).

In sum, Nelson and Winter's conceptualization of knowledge implies that organizations are able to 'know' independently of their members. Routines constitute the 'genetic' material of organizations and evolve by genetic mutations, that is, through the adaptation of the knowledge shared by organizational members to the environmental conditions. Accordingly, the evolution of a firm seems to be governed more by stochastic processes than by deliberate choice.

2.3.2   *Critical remarks*

The development of an inside-out approach to the study of firms' competitive strategies has produced a paradigm shift with respect to the dominant positioning approach developed by Porter in the 1980s. More importantly, the focus on endogenous factors to explain how firms achieve superior performance has led strategy theorists to develop a theory of the firm based on a knowledge perspective. The most innovative aspect of the knowledge-based approach is the re-conceptualization of the firm as a knowledge architecture. For example, Prahalad and Hamel (1990) compare the firm to a large (knowledge) tree articulated according to a series of planes—end products, business units, core products, and core competencies—each reflecting in a more or less in-depth way the distinctive body of knowledge of a firm. Rumelt (1984: 561) notes that the strategic firm 'is characterized by a bundle of linked and idiosyncratic resources and resource conversion activities'. Sanchez and Mahoney's (1996) modular perspective of the firm highlights the isomorphism between knowledge structures and the firm's core products. Finally, Nonaka and Takeuchi's (1995) hypertext organization is made up of interconnected layers or contexts providing a structural base for knowledge creation. A major consequence of the above re-conceptualization of the firm is that the traditional functional structure, based on the division of labour and the employment relationship, is replaced by a more subtle division of knowledge. Within the firm context, knowledge acts as a generative principle reflected in the structure of core products, and core businesses.

The knowledge-based view of the firm developed in the field of strategy constitutes the epitome of the managerialist epistemology mentioned in the introductory chapter. As explained earlier, most existing knowledge-based theories of the firm seem to be governed by what can be called a 'functional' view of knowledge. This view is characterized by a conceptualization of knowledge as an objective, transferable commodity which can be made readily available throughout the organization. Secondly, the knowledge-based perspective posits a functional/causal link between knowledge and competitive performance. The examples of core competencies cited in Prahalad and Hamel (1990: 85) provide an exemplification of the pervasive analogy between visible inputs/outputs (resources and products) and the stock of knowledge underlying their production (core competencies and capabilities). Competence seems to result from a mix of technology and production skills: 'core products are the tangible link between identified core competencies and end products—the physical embodiments of one or more core competencies'. As a consequence of this 'commodification' of knowledge, a firm's core product is implicitly related to the way knowledge is utilized.

The above statements characterize the knowledge-based view of the firm and explain the success of such theoretical streams. Indeed, the fact that knowledge management has established itself as one of the 'buzzwords' of the late 1990s does not come as a surprise. In fact, the way knowledge is conceptualized by the knowledge-based approach constitutes a sort of wishful thinking for the firm: the durability of knowledge (commodity) enables the firm to use it instrumentally. This perspective is therefore consistent with the image of organization as a machine, and knowledge is connected to the production process. On the other hand, the above assumptions underlying knowledge-based theories of the firm highlight major methodological difficulties. Competencies, resources and capabilities may well provide a sound terminology for a theory of knowledge, but at the same time they seem to be problematic as far as empirical validation is concerned. In fact, the difficulty implicit in the search for a conceptual definition of knowledge-based factors seems to conceal a deeper methodological problem. The assumption of the performativity of knowledge underlying the resource-based approach implies treating knowledge as an independent variable. However, as Scarbrough (1998) has noted, knowledge-based concepts such as those mentioned above defy measurement. As a consequence, it is difficult to appreciate to what extent organizational performance is really affected by its knowledge base.

Furthermore, the equation of knowledge and commodities bears dangerous empirical consequences, since the fundamental conversion process that transforms inputs into outputs is only implied rather than scrutinized. The theories analysed above display a tendency to abstract knowledge from practice and accordingly overlook the importance of action. In different versions, they all imply some kind of transformation process that leads to knowledge production as its outcome. The resource-based approach, for example, highlights the way resources are transformed into core capabilities within a structuralist, static view of the firm; Nonaka and Takeuchi see knowledge as being generated through a dynamic interaction (conversion) between tacit and explicit knowledge; and finally, for Nelson and Winter the evolution of the firm results from a process whereby knowledge is stored and memorized in organizational routines. How these transformation processes occur is not explained since emphasis is placed on outcomes, rather than on the processes that lead to such outcomes. Nonaka and Takeuchi's framework probably provides the best exemplification of this critical omission. The interaction between tacit and explicit knowledge is explained by drawing on the metaphor of the spiral. But this image of a seemingly evolving process is itself a kind of black box—a tacit and unexplained bridge between organizational resources and knowledge outcomes. As a consequence, the spiral glosses over the sense-making dynamics and interpretation processes which lead to knowledge creation. A direct consequence of the above gap between theory and practice, outcomes and processes, and so on, is a drift of these dynamic theories of knowledge towards stasis. As Spender (1996) and Tsoukas (1996) have pointed out the models proposed by the above authors appear to be formistic and based on Weberian ideal types as they implicitly assume that knowledge can be harnessed into static categories. Accordingly, the knowledge-based perspective tends to produce a content theory (Scarbrough 1998; Spender 1996), and gloss over the processual aspects of knowledge creation. More importantly, the commodification of knowledge makes it unproblematic and purely instrumental with respect to organizational performance. Organizational knowledge is not allowed to be controversial; it is not about hypotheses, let alone about disputes. Instead, making knowledge is about codifying experience and rendering it transparent.

To recap: in attempting to explain the causes of the firm's competitive advantage, knowledge-based theories of the firm posit a functional link between knowledge-oriented factors and competitive performance. This causal correlation raises important theoretical and methodological issues. Indeed the very notion of 'intangible asset' seems to be permeated by an intrinsic tension. This makes the definition of knowledge-oriented factors somewhat problematic, at times tautological (skill, capability, etc.), or based on analogy ('glue that binds existing businesses', 'roots of competitive advantage', 'knowledge spiral'), or deduced from visible outputs (knowledge is equated to products). Put another way, knowledge seems to refer to a commodity that transcends commodities, and ultimately to a commodity which is not a commodity. As a result, the endeavour to build a knowledge-based theory of the firm seems to end up in a kind of reification of knowledge in the attempt to bring to the surface something that by definition is not visible or empirically observable. As Scarbrough (1998) has pointed out, a major risk related to the above conceptualizations is that of opening the black box of organization only to find another black box.

2.4   The situated approach

The situated approach (Lave and Wenger 1991; Brown and Duguid 1991; Pentland 1992) has offered a pragmatic definition of knowledge which is oriented towards the interpretation of organizational perform- ance through the observation of everyday practices in the workplace. The roots of this perspective are to be found in sociological theories of practice (Bourdieu 1977) and in philosophical pragmatism (Dewey 1938; Rorty 1979), which hold that knowledge is embodied in praxis (Pentland 1992). From a situated perspective, knowledge is neither a disembodied cognitive structure nor an objectified commodity (nei- ther ghost nor machine). It does not exist outside the nexus of equip- ment, practices, institutions, and conventions in which it is generated and utilized, but it is somehow 'immanent' to them. The hypothesis of immanence underlies the notions of distributed knowledge systems (Hutchins 1993; Tsoukas 1996), activity systems theories (Blackler 1995; Engestrom 1987), and formative contexts (Unger 1987; Blackler 1992; Ciborra and Lanzara 1994). Central to the situated approach is the problem of the context in which human action and interaction takes place. The context is described as a fabric of interrelated meanings rather than as a mere container of activity divorced from everyday practice. Most of the contributions within this perspective have in com- mon a view of learning and knowing as predominantly social activities which take place through participation within a 'community of prac- tice' (Lave and Wenger 1991; Brown and Duguid 1991; Wenger 1998). From such an epistemological stance, knowledge is not the property of the individual but is distributed across a social system.

Two important elements can be highlighted within the situated approach. The first is the attempt to move away from the disembodied view of knowledge suggested by symbolic cognition in order to stress the social, situated nature of representations. In particular, situated cognition (Suchman 1987) goes beyond the traditional dichotomies between thought–action and individual–organization by reconceptualizing the 'world of social activity' in relational terms (Chaicklin and Lave 1993). Likewise, Blackler (1995) underscores the distinctive features of the situated approach by counterposing a static view of knowledge, with its connotations of abstraction, progress, permanency, and mentalism, against action-based knowing, which is situated, distributed and material.

A second distinctive element within this perspective is its primary focus on knowledge-producing practices in the workplace. According to Turner (1994), the meaning of practice is difficult to grasp, since it refers to and overlaps with a broader family of terms such as paradigm, tacit knowledge, *Weltanschauung*, tradition, ideology, and framework. From an analytical point of view it is useful to distinguish between practices and practice. The former refers to habits, customs, beliefs, and principles, pointing to the fact that practices are shared. Conversely, the meaning of the term 'practice' can be grasped as opposed to theory. What is emphasized here is the telic connotation of practice as activity seeking a goal. The two meanings are closely interconnected in that practices provide a shared background of readiness to hand for the execution of goal-oriented activities (practice). In this respect, practices provide the causes for practical activities. The above distinction raises a crucial question for understanding the production and transfer of organizational knowledge. Turner asks: 'to what extent does a practice in the telic sense require "practices" in the sense of ingrained habits or bits of tacit knowledge?' (Turner 1994: 8). When applied to organizations, the question emphasizes the relationship between purposeful actions and the tacit premises governing their execution. Practices work as an institution as they connect organizational activities (doing) with a particular perspective on the world (seeing). They involve issues of identity, trust, and commitment. In the following sections I review the main contribution to knowledge theories provided by the situated cognition approach and practice theories.

2.4.1 *The situated cognition perspective*

The situated cognition approach was conceived as a reaction to the paradigmatic model of cognition proposed by rational cognitivism. Proponents of this perspective reject the ontological distinction between a reality 'out there' and the internal representations of a knowing subject. In fact, a common theme uniting many situated approaches to cognition is a shift in the way the person/environment relationship is conceived. Rather than a person 'being' in an environment, the activities of person and environment are parts of a mutually constructed whole. The inside/outside relationship between person and environment is replaced by a part/whole relationship (Bredo 1994). This shift in view is made more plausible by viewing person and environment in terms of their contributions to an activity rather than as separately described things. Viewed actively, the adaptation of person and environment involves dynamic mutual modification rather than static matching. Such an 'interactivist' (Bickard 1992) 'relational' (Lave and Wenger 1991; Scarbrough 1998) or 'dialectical' (Clancey 1991) view is central to work on situated cognition.

Most of the contributions within this perspective derive from psychology and cognitive anthropology and are characterized by a distinctive empirical focus on the activity of knowing. Hutchins' (1993, 1996) ethnographic study of the work practices of a navigation team represents one of the best empirical inquiries into situated cognition. The study considers navigation as an activity system providing a distinctive context for thinking and learning. The routine activity on a naval vessel is centred around the task of making fixes at regular intervals in order to establish the position of the ship. This task setting requires complex computations that exceed the capabilities of any individual and therefore need to be divided across a navigation team. Finally, the co-operative nature of the task requires substantial sharing of information, while the presence of overlapping regions in the role system underlying navigational computations qualifies the team as a socially distributed knowledge system. Following the cognitive tradition, Hutchins' study emphasizes the role of information processing and representation. However, it does so by taking a situated and relational perspective. A major strength of Hutchins' study lies precisely in its ability to subtly conceptualize the navigation activity as a knowledge system. Under these circumstances, the context of navigation identifies a minimal form of organization, relating the task, the role system, the representational artefacts, and the equipment (e.g. nautical charts and measuring instruments) supporting the team's activities. The notion of a distributed knowledge system emphasizes the fact that knowledge does not reside in the heads of the team members, but rather is situated in a variety of organizational structures and sense-making devices connecting the team's activities in a coherent whole.

The problem of the context also informs those related theories of learning and cognition that have explored the implications of thinking in action. According to Scribner (1987), learning is centred around problem-solving and is intricately related to the context; understanding by 'context' here (a) the problem's conceptual structure as well as (b) the purpose of the activity and (c) the social milieu in which it is embedded. Doing and knowing, or what she calls 'practical thinking', are seen as open-ended processes of improvisation with the social, material, and experiential resources at hand. In the workplace setting, learners acquire knowledge, competencies and skills through engaging in activities, continuously trying out new strategies, routines and interventions, and drawing on all available resources in the solution of practical problems. Practical problem-solving is thus an open system that includes components lying outside the formal problem itself— objects and information in the environment, goals, and interests of the problem-solver, and social relations between workers.

2.4.2 *Situated knowledge and the role of praxis*

The situated perspective is informed by a conceptualization of work as practice as opposed to the traditional employment relationship. Canonical descriptions of work organization rely on the analysis of procedures, data flows, activities, 'objects', transactions and processes, assuming that 'work' can be ultimately decomposed into such constituent elements. However, the study of situated work practices has pointed out, in a variety of office and manufacturing settings, that work is more than a random collection of analytical abstractions and models to be rationalized (Wynn 1979; Suchman 1987; Zuboff 1988; Brown and Duguid 1991; Ciborra, Patriotta, and Erlicher 1996). Rather, it is a complex bundle of situated actions and interpretations aimed at making sense of resources and structures, and maintaining the identity of the members and the working community confronted by both routine and breakdown events. Within the situated perspective, the canonical, formalized organization contained in organizational maps and prescriptive documentation is counterposed against non-canonical, emerging communities of practice engaged in everyday coping with the world.

The situated approach has produced a rich body of empirical studies. Orr's ethnography of photocopy repair technicians (reps) probably provides one of the most classical applications of this perspective. By following in detail the technician's 'talk about machines', Orr discovers that the practices enacted by the reps in their everyday dealing with

troubled machines is much richer and more complex than the prescriptive documentation provided by the company manuals would suggest.
For example, narratives and storytelling constitute a fundamental
aspect of the technicians' job.[3] Narratives have at least three functions.
Firstly, they act as diagnostic tools and provide sense-making devices;
diagnoses and repair interventions are based on the successful solutions of problematic situations of the past; and learning occurs through
success stories. Secondly, they foster knowledge transfer; knowledge is
created day-by-day and maintained through the circulation of success
stories. Finally, the circulation of success stories contributes to building
the technician's identity as a competent worker:

> Narratives form a primary element of this practice. The actual process of dia-
> gnosis involves the creation of a coherent account of the troubled state of the
> machine from available pieces of integrated information, and in this respect,
> diagnosis happens through a narrative process. A coherent diagnostic narrat-
> ive constitutes a technician's mastery of the problematic situation. Narratives
> preserve such diagnosis as they are told to colleagues; the accounts constructed
> in diagnosis become the basis for technicians' discourse about their experience
> and thereby the means for the social distribution of experiential knowledge
> through community interaction. The circulation of stories among the commun-
> ity of technicians is the principal means by which the technicians stay
> informed of the developing subtleties of machine behaviour in the field. The
> telling of these narratives demonstrates and shares the technicians' mastery
> and so both celebrates and creates the technicians' identities as masters of the
> black arts of dealing with machines and of the only somewhat less difficult arts
> of dealing with customers . . . (Orr 1996: 2).

The empirical implications of the situational approach are very important. Firstly, if knowledge is embodied in practice it has to be retrieved by
following organizational actors in their everyday dealings. Secondly, situations and not individuals become the most appropriate level for organizational analysis. The actions of organizational members are always
shaped, to some degree, by the situation in which they find themselves.
The situation provides the point of contact between the individual and
the organization (Pentland 1992: 529). In operational terms, Pentland
introduces the concept of the 'move' (Goffmann 1981) as a unit of analysis in the study of organizational knowledge. The move is the elementary
unit of organizational performance, be it a problem-solving procedure

---

[3] As I will show in Chapter 6, Orr's emphasis on the narrative dimension of knowledge
strongly accords with the findings of one of the case studies presented in this work.

or a different kind of routine. Drawing on empirical evidence of technical service interaction in software support hot lines, Pentland identifies
a set of organizing moves with which technical support operators
respond to customer calls. The analysis of such moves leads him to
conclude that the moves that specific actors use in certain situations
both enact and reflect the structure of the organization. Knowledge is
situated in the sense that it is highly contingent upon the interaction
among people, resources, and routines present in a given situation.
Accordingly, each time we study knowledge in organization we must
start from the question: 'where is knowledge situated?' and look for
those features of a situation which constrain or induce intentional performances or at least fall within the scope of attention of the actors in
the situation (Ciborra, Patriotta, and Erlicher 1996).

2.4.3 *Formative contexts: the two-fold structure of practical knowledge*

A further insight into the concept of practical knowledge is offered by
the notion of formative context (Unger 1987; Blackler 1992; Ciborra and
Lanzara 1994). According to this perspective, practical knowledge that
informs human action is structured into two distinct levels: it has a
visible aspect which refers to the level of practices and routines. The
execution of work routines is, however, governed by a stock of background knowledge that people usually take for granted and apply in
situated actions. This second level, which is labelled formative context,
relates to the tacit, unstated dimension of knowledge within which
routines are 'formed' and from which they receive their scope and
meaning. The formative context directs our attention to the cognitive,
social and material foundations of the context that inform actions.
Ciborra and Lanzara (1994: 70), in extending Unger's (1987) ideas
about formative context and applying it to organizational analysis,
have defined the term as 'the set of pre-existing institutional arrangements, cognitive frames and imageries that actors bring and routinely
enact in a situation of action. A formative context thus comprises both
an organizational and a cognitive dimension and has far-reaching,
subtle influences: it constitutes a background condition for action,
enforcing constraints, giving direction and meaning, and setting the
range of opportunities for undertaking action'.

The distinctive feature of the formative context, as elaborated by
Ciborra and Lanzara, is its dual emphasis on the cognitive and the

institutional. When enacted in a situation of action, formative contexts are expressions of a social cognition that transcends the individual. 'Such cognition may well be embodied in material or symbolic artefacts, organizational structures and procedures, institutional settings, and, most crucially, in the relationships or "couplings" binding actors and their work tools in a sort of micro-ecology of stable uses and shared meanings' (Unger 1987: 72).

The context is 'formative' in that it shapes the ways people perceive, understand, perform and get organized in a situation bounded in space and time. It is 'formative' because it may help people to see and do things in new ways, or on the contrary, make them stick stubbornly to old ways. Accordingly, the formative context sets a path for learning. For example, in their analysis of the process of innovation in a large European computer manufacturer, Ciborra and Lanzara (1994) connected phenomena of resistance to change and emerging work practices of the users to the interaction between the pre-existing hierarchical formative context and the emergent network-based one. Their findings point to the conventional distinction between a conceptualization of work as employment relationship and work as practice, contrasting the official, formalized organization with emergent communities of practice enacted by the daily acts of re-invention and improvisation performed by the users.

The outcome of a formative context is a texture of routines, roles and tasks, a division of labour, and a set of co-ordination mechanisms that come to possess 'an aura of naturalness' for those who execute routines within that context. Given its tacit nature, a formative context is empirically unveiled when organizational actors experience a situation of displacement, when new objects and routines are introduced in a pre-existing context or, conversely, when familiar objects and routines are withdrawn from that context. As we shall see later on in greater depth, one of these conditions is represented by the situations of breakdown when the obviousness of daily routine becomes problematic.

2.4.4 *Critical remarks*

Situated theories attempt to reconcile the split between cognitive and normative elements of knowledge-making processes within a relational perspective on knowledge. The contribution of the situated perspective to the study of knowledge becomes apparent if compared to the other approaches encountered earlier. First of all, the situated perspective rejects the idea—suggested by symbolic cognition—that knowledge emerges from manipulating representations of an objective reality (Scarbrough 1998). Secondly, the situated approach differs from the current knowledge-based theories (KBT) of the firm developed in the field of strategy. Within the knowledge-based view the firm is characterized as a stable configuration of resources, competencies, and capabilities which can be made readily available throughout the organization. Knowledge is treated as a strategic asset or commodity and causally linked to competitive performance. Learning is seen as an incremental process based on changes in organizational routines and path-dependency. In contrast, theorists of the situated approach see the firm as an activity system characterized by a distinctive task and an idiosyncratic set of practices. Their focus is on the processes of social construction and the role of organizational contexts in shaping the dynamics of learning and knowledge acquisition. A final point of divergence concerns the view on management. As it was said earlier, KBT are characterized by a managerial focus, emphasizing the role of the manager as a decision-maker. From a situated perspective, instead, the focus of analysis is on the interdependencies among the task, the role system, the representational artefacts and equipment supporting the activity of a particular community of practice.

Despite the wealth of empirical studies produced within the situated approach, this body of literature has failed, at least so far, to develop a consistent theory of knowledge. On the other hand, the focus on communities of practice, suggested by the situated approach, can provide the backbone for the development of an organizational perspective on knowledge. In particular, the emphasis on the tacit features of organizations opens up the possibility of integrating the insights of the situated approach with the theoretical apparatus offered by institutional theories of organization (Powell and Di Maggio 1991). According to Zucker, institutionalization is a 'phenomenological process by which certain social relationships and actions come to be taken for granted' (Zucker 1983: 2). In other words, institutionalization refers to the degree of tacitness of knowledge and, in that sense, it can be seen both as a process and a variable. The taken-for-granted quality of certain practices and their reproduction in existing institutional arrangements is seen as a source of persistence (Zucker 1977), which accounts for the accumulation and maintenance of knowledge in organizations. The presence of reproduction mechanisms also highlights the ritual and ceremonial aspect of knowledge creation (Meyer and Rowan 1977). Finally, the institutional approach takes into account the political dimension of knowledge making, that is, the conditions whereby a community reaches consensus about what is valid knowledge. The latter emphasizes the socially constructed nature of knowledge and the role of power and legitimization.

2.5   Knowledge and the laboratory: the techno-science approach

In the previous sections, we have come across a number of oppositions that represent the tension between alternative modes of thinking about knowledge in organizations. But knowledge itself is subject to this tension. In analytical terms we have to distinguish between knowledge, the physical product, the outcome on the one hand, and knowing, the process that leads to the social construction of commodified knowledge on the other. In order to resolve this dialectic tension, we now need to address the way the two terms of the opposition are translated into each other. That implies 'opening' organizational black boxes and exploring their content.

The techno-science approach takes a 'constructionist' stance on knowledge-related phenomena and refers to that branch of the sociology of knowledge which is interested in the process of social construction of reality (Berger and Luckmann 1967). As the label indicates, this perspective derives from the sociology of science and technology and focuses mainly on the work of scientists, inventors, and engineers, and the organizations of which they are part. The laboratory, conceived as the locus where knowledge is produced and transformed, is the pervasive metaphor underlying this body of literature. With some notable exceptions (e.g. see, Tsoukas 1996), the techno-science perspective has not been extensively or explicitly applied to the fields of strategy and organization theory. However, some of the principles informing it can be complementary in understanding the process of organizational knowledge making and offer an additional insight into the tacit features of organizations.

The techno-science approach offers a contested view of knowledge. As for science in general, knowledge is about the 'making of facts' and is thus linked to discourse. Scientific discourse undergoes a process of validation whereby knowledge is initially provisional and contested before being turned into agreed facts. For science, making knowledge is about resolving controversies. It is about reality and sense making. However, once controversies are turned into facts, knowledge is closed off and becomes a 'black box'. Here again, emphasis is placed on the durability of knowledge, but this durability is the outcome of an epistemological closure of controversies rather than an instrumental resource.

The techno-science approach rejects the traditional separation of science and technology based on the conventional wisdom whereby 'science discovers, technology applies'. Instead, scientific facts and technological artefacts are connected to the same dynamics of knowledge production and institutionalization. More generally, the techno-science approach denies conventional dichotomies deriving from the subject–object distinction, such as those between mind and body, nature and science, technology and society, and internal and external. In contrast to traditional dualistic epistemologies, the authors within this perspective take a holistic, systemic approach to knowing, and favour a more comprehensive definition of the entities involved in knowledge-making dynamics.

The rejection of dichotomies in favour of systems and networks is informed by the assumption that knowledge creation in science and technology eludes any categorization. 'System builders are no respecters of disciplinary and knowledge boundaries.' Rather, their work encompasses a seamless web of interactions, associations and translations. In the work of scientists, inventors, engineers, and managers—and the organizations of which they are part—technical, scientific, social, economic, and political matters tend to overlap. Accordingly, the observation of professionals at work must equally blur the above categories in order to account for the messy interactions occurring within knowledge-producing networks.

In line with the above assumptions, the chemical transformations occurring in laboratories and the electrical networks underlying the functioning of technological systems become an analogy of the knowledge-creation process. This view seeks to counter the determinism of hard sciences which sees the development of scientific and technological innovations as a set of linear and mechanical interconnections. Furthermore, knowledge making is not defined as an exclusively endogenous process. The systemic approach and the notion of a seamless web, highlight the role of the wider socio-institutional context in shaping knowledge-making dynamics through mechanisms of legitimization and epistemological closure.

2.5.1 *Actor-network theory*

Actor-network theory (ANT) is oriented towards the development of an epistemology of action. Knowledge making is seen as an action-based process that unfolds in a controversial manner. Fundamental to ANT is the problem of epistemological closure; that is, the processes by which knowledge is socially legitimized and made durable. In the pursuit of knowledge, ANT addresses a number of related questions: how controversies are settled, how processes and flows are turned into 'things', how artefacts are translated into facts.

In order to tackle the above issues, actor-network moves away from a static, abstract definition of knowledge. Within this perspective, knowledge making has to do with controversy, displacement, movement, and tension. As Law and Hassard (1999) have pointed out, 'actor-network' is an intentionally oxymoronic term that combines—and elides the distinction between—structure and agency. Important to the actor-network approach is the notion of translation, which captures the tension between a number of epistemological divides: subject and object, structure and agency, actor and system, difference and identity, order and disorder, and so on.

An early sketch of the actor-network approach is provided by Michel Callon (1980) in his study of electrical vehicle development in France. The term 'actor-network' designates a relational entity, a web of references consisting of both human and non-human actants, a nexus of *ad hoc* performances unfolding in the form of translations. For example in the case of the electrical vehicle, Callon's actors include electrons, catalysts, accumulators, users, researchers, manufacturers, and ministerial departments enforcing regulations affecting technology. These and many other actors interact through networks to create a coherent actor world. Callon's actor-network posits the 'indeterminacy' of the actor, opening the actor world to non-human entities and allowing them to speak.

ANT offers a semiotic approach to the study of knowledge making. The semiotic approach suggests that knowledge is produced in relations among heterogeneous materials. Knowledge agents are caught up in a network of relations, in a flow of intermediaries, which circulate, connect, link and reconstitute identities (Callon 1999: 187). As a consequence, knowledge is continuously subject to drifts and controversies. It is never given in the order of things.

Given the provisional, contested and controversial character of knowledge making, a main challenge for the researcher is to understand how durability is achieved. How it is that things are performed (and perform themselves) into relations that are relatively stable and stay in place (Law 1999). The solution provided by ANT is particularly original and insightful. Durability is the result of a temporary hooking up with circulating entities, the outcome of a technical black boxing of controversies (Latour 1999b). In this respect, what we regard as 'knowledge', as a coherent unity, is an assemblage of heterogeneous materials and multiple relations that have reached a stable yet provisional configuration. To have transformed knowledge from what was a commodity, into a circulation—a dynamic phenomenon—is probably the most useful contribution of ANT. Under these circumstances, ANT calls into question the performativity of knowledge. But it is a different kind of performativity. It does not refer to the instrumental character of knowledge with respect to socio-organizational performance; rather it has to do with actantiality and the relational nature of networks.

At the methodological level, ANT deals with two types of equally powerful dissatisfactions (Latour 1999*b*). On the one hand, studying knowledge-making dynamics requires following the actors while they are 'busy at work', that is, zooming into local practices, face-to-face interactions, and controversies. On the other hand, what gives shape to micro-interactions is not always directly visible in the local situation. In order to understand knowledge-making dynamics a broader level of analysis needs to be invoked, involving such notions as society, norms, values, cultures, structure, and social context.

ANT provides a useful apparatus for dealing with the above dissatisfactions. However, as Latour (1999*b*) has pointed out, ANT does not aim to overcome the divide between micro and macro by reconciling the opposites. Rather, it offers a bypassing strategy which deliberately glosses over the divide between local and global and concentrates attention on the 'whereabouts' of knowledge: 'in the social domain there is no change of scale . . . it is always flat and folded' (Latour 1999*b*: 18). Translation provides a connecting term for studying the back and forth movement between micro and macro, the tension between opposites, the shifting trajectory through which knowledge-making processes unfold.

In sum, ANT is not a theory of the social. It is more a method for mapping processes of knowledge creation and institutionalization (the whereabouts of knowledge). It is a strategy for framing the actors and their relations in the process of knowledge making. The method consists in following the actants—both humans and non-humans—while they are busy at work. It implies following movements and trajectories by which knowledge is temporarily hooked up to circulating entities and thereby is made durable. It is a method and not a theory, a way to travel from one spot to the next, from one field site to the next, not an interpretation of what actors do simply glossed in a different and more universalist language (Latour 1999*b*).

2.5.2   *The social construction of technological systems*

As stated in the introduction, the techno-science approach is primarily empirical in its focus. The empirical literature produced in this field is quite rich, encompassing social constructionist approaches to science and technology, social shaping of technology, history and sociology of technology, laboratory studies, actor-networks, and so on. A first strand of literature analysed in this section focuses on the social construction of technological systems.

Drawing on history and sociology of technology, Pinch and Bijker (1989) attempt to sketch a theory for studying the social construction of scientific facts and technological systems. From the early history of the bicycle, the authors provide examples of closure and stabilization, social shaping, interpretative flexibility, and the influence of social groups. Their focus is on the controversies surrounding the development of this technological artefact. More specifically, what interests them are the conflicting perceptions of different social groups engaged in the definition of problems and the invention of solutions through processes of negotiation and collective interpretation. The interplay among relevant social actors, problems, and solutions leads to a temporary closure and stabilization of the technology, which is nonetheless subject to the emergence of further controversies. The case history of the bicycle presents technological development as a non-determined, multidirectional flux that involves constant negotiation and renegotiation among and between groups shaping the technology. Their model is far from the rigid, categorized, linear one sometimes presented for technological development. Furthermore, the findings of the case suggest a three-stage framework to analyse the processes whereby knowledge, in the form of scientific facts or technological artefacts, is created and institutionalized within a given social context.

In the first stage, the interpretative flexibility of scientific findings is displayed; in other words, it is shown that scientific findings are open to more than one interpretation. This shifts the focus for the explanation of scientific developments from the natural world to the social world. Interpretative flexibility highlights the contentious nature of knowledge and the equivocality of action by focusing on technological controversies. Also, by stressing the equivocality of action, it directs our attention towards processes of collective sense making. Although this interpretative flexibility can be recovered in certain circumstances, it remains the case that such flexibility soon disappears in science; that is, a scientific consensus as to what the 'truth' is in any particular instance usually emerges.

Social mechanisms that limit interpretative flexibility and thus allow scientific controversies to be terminated are described in the second stage. This level of analysis focuses on closure and stabilization, that is, on those mechanisms whereby knowledge is stabilized, made durable and turned into a black box. 'Closure occurs in science when a consensus emerges that the "truth" has been winnowed from the various interpretations; it occurs in technology when a consensus emerges that a problem arising during the development of technology has been solved. When the social groups involved in designing and using the technology decide that the problem is solved, they stabilize the technology' (Pinch and Bijker 1989: 12). Closure mechanisms highlight issues of consensus, legitimization, institutionalization, and articulation.

A third stage, which according to the authors has not yet been carried through in any study of contemporary science, involves relating such 'closure mechanisms' to the wider socio-cultural milieu. Basically, this third stage challenges the assumption that knowledge creation is an endogenous process. In this respect, knowledge making can be likened to the creation of a public good: it is a matter of consensus, legitimization, and institutionalization within the wider social context.

2.5.3 *Opening organizational black boxes*

A second rich strand of empirical literature produced within the techno-science approach concerns the study of laboratory life (Latour and Woolgar 1979; Latour 1987) and the manufacture of scientific knowledge (Knorr-Cetina 1981).

In *Science and Action*, Latour (1987) offers a brilliant theory of method for studying the 'fabrication' of scientific facts and technical artefacts.[4] The latter are conceived as black boxes that have undergone a controversial process of social construction. The term 'black box', borrowed from cybernetics, is used metaphorically by Latour to indicate a final product, be it a fact or a piece of equipment, that has become taken for granted by the community of users. The task that a researcher has to face in order to deconstruct a fact is precisely that of re-opening the black box. But how is this mission to be accomplished? Again, we are looking for a way to access a particular system of knowledge, be it a scientific fact or an organizational system.

---

[4] It is interesting to note how facts and machines are both conceptualized as black boxes, as durable outcomes of a social construction process.

In the introduction of *Science and Action*, Latour asks: 'where can we start a study of science and technology?' (Latour 1987: 2). The proposed strategy, or 'rule of method' to enter facts and machines is a tricky one. He invites us to forget about end products and to look at science 'in the making' as opposed to 'ready-made' science: 'We go from final products to production, from "cold" stable objects to "warm" and unstable ones. Instead of black boxing the technical aspects of science and then looking for social influences and biases, we realized how much simpler it was to be there before the box closes and becomes black' (Latour 1987: 21). This temporal inversion in the choice of a point of departure is the key for studying knowledge making as a process of social construction. Controversies and not finished products provide a way in. The analyst will then follow the characters involved in the construction of a fact 'while they are busy at work', and attempt to reconstruct the network of events, decisions, physical artefacts, and institutions, surrounding the 'making' of things.

The technique adopted by Latour is that of the flashback, of the journey in space and time, since any process of social construction always has a historical dimension. The flashback takes us back to a moment when knowledge has not been institutionalized, when the black box has not yet been closed. During the flashback, the black box gets re-opened, allowing the analyst to trace back retrospectively the processes that have led to a certain outcome. Although the technique is fascinating, the task is not an easy one. The 'actor-network' is characterized by a variety of heterogeneous processes occurring alongside and intersecting with each other. Latour seems to be aware of the complexity of the interactionist field and of the risk of drifting endlessly: 'How are we going to account for the closing of the black boxes? It is all very well to choose the controversies as a way in, but we need to follow the closure of these controversies.' In other words, we also need a way out.

The complexity of the knowledge-in-the-making arena is captured by the notion of the actor-network (Callon 1980). The concept emphasizes the equivocal nature of action and processes and the social construction of categories under which we synthesize processes belonging to different domains. The actor-network is a 'quasi-object' (Latour 1993), a hybrid made of people, institutions, physical artefacts, and social practices. The actor-network contains a story that gives some unity to the heterogeneous material of which it consists. However, it is a shifting story, or rather a shifting trajectory, that acquires different meanings as we shift our focus of attention. In other words, the boundaries of the actor-network are brittle and the plot that it is made out of it crucially depends on the judgements of the external observer. The narrator's account, as the phenomena observed, is itself socially constructed. It depends on contingent factors, such as the narrator's past experience, the institutional and cultural setting in which he/she conducts the research, or even, as Pettigrew (1990) pointed out, the moment in which he/she decides to put pen to paper. The observer him/herself is part of an actor-network.

Like Latour, Knorr-Cetina (1981) is interested in the problem of 'facticity' of knowledge. Facts are seen as laboratory fabrications (from the Latin *facere* = to make) as opposed to given entities. More specifically, by focusing on the practices of knowledge production and reproduction in the laboratory setting, Knorr-Cetina seeks to build an ethnography of knowledge that eventually leads to a theory of such practices (see Bourdieu 1977). The above conceptualization of scientific facts has crucial implications for the study of knowledge as an empirical phenomenon: Once we see scientific products as the first and foremost result of a process of construction, we can begin to substitute philosophical theories of knowledge with an empirical theory of knowledge (Knorr-Cetina 1981: 3).

More generally, the laboratory challenges the epistemological concept of 'truth', stressing a pragmatic definition of knowledge related to 'making things work'. The laboratory, conceived as a workshop where knowledge is instrumentally manufactured, is described in phenomenological terms as a 'local accumulation of instruments and devices within a working space composed of chairs and tables' (Knorr-Cetina 1981: 3). The main argument derived from the study of laboratories is that 'products of science are contextually specific constructions which bear the mark of the situational contingency and interest structure of the process by which they are generated, and which cannot be adequately understood without an analysis of their construction. This means that what happens in the process of construction is not irrelevant to the product we obtain. It also means that the products of science have to be seen as highly internally structured through the process of production, independent of the question of their external structuring through some match or mismatch with reality' (Knorr-Cetina 1981: 5).

Processes of fabrication of facts highlight the controversial nature of knowledge. They involve chains of decisions and negotiations through which their outcomes are selected and derived. The process of social construction refers precisely to a decision-laden fabrication of scientific products. In turn, decisions and interpretations within the laboratory are contingent upon the historical context (context of selection) in which they are situated. (Knorr-Cetina 1981: 9). In sum, the approach followed by Knorr-Cetina in the study of laboratory practices attempts to establish the symbolic, contextually contingent character of the scientific manufacture of knowledge. In this respect, her approach bears important similarities with the situated perspective encountered before.

2.5.4 *Critical remarks*

The techno-science approach highlights the pivotal role of social relations between producers and users in shaping scientific facts and technological artefacts. Empirical evidence is presented to illustrate how social forces such as politics, culture, and gender, influence the changes in underlying knowledge structures and processes. A main contribution of the techno-science approach lies in the recognition of the contested and provisional nature of knowledge making. As in science, knowledge is treated as an empirical phenomenon, which is subject to conflicts of interpretation and controversies. This perspective contrasts with the commodified view of knowledge propounded by mainstream knowledge management theories. Like phenomenology, the techno-science approach deals with problems of epistemological closure. The focus is on how controversies are turned into 'things' and how society is made durable through processes of inscription and delegation. However the two perspectives present important differences as far as the vocabulary and units of analysis are concerned. Phenomenology inquires into knowledge-making processes as a result of the interplay between action and cognition, event and meaning. Social constructionism, on the other hand, investigates the relationship between things and society, and therefore deals with problems of legitimization and social acceptance. A second important contribution relates to the role of non-humans in knowledge-making processes. Indeed, the techno-science approach deals simultaneously with human and non-human agencies. Within such perspective any form of dualism and essentialist division is blurred in favour of an action-based view of knowing. Everything is action and knowledge is produced in a seamless web of relations between human and non-human entities.

On the other hand, the above approach is not immune from criticism. The techno-science assumes the radical indeterminacy of the actor. The actor's size, its psychological make up, and the motivations behind its actions—none of these are pre-determined (Callon 1999). While this hypothesis has opened the social sciences to non-humans it also entails a number of difficulties. The techno-science approach ends up presenting an actor which is an anonymous, ill-defined and indiscernible entity.

Indeed, the inquiry into the technical black boxing of controversies seems to leave out problems of cognition and intentionality. This may foster the idea that actors are mere agents devoid of the ability to think. By being almost mechanically enrolled in controversy-based processes, they become hostages of a network of transactions and translations. Finally, the notion of seamless webs and actor-networks raises the issue of boundaries to knowledge creation. In other words, the assumption of the indeterminacy of the actor leads to a more general indeterminacy principle underlying the development of scientific facts and technological artefacts, and ultimately any knowledge-creation process.

In sum, the techno-science approach oscillates between two forms of determinism. On the one hand, it attempts to ground science and technology in society and to address the context in which technical and scientific knowledge are produced. On the other hand, as Latour (1999*b*) has pointed out, the formulation proposed by such an approach leads to a form of dissolution of humanity into a field of forces where morality, humanity, and psychology are absent.

2.6 Conclusion

Taken individually, the four perspectives discussed above are characterized by distinctive strengths and weaknesses. The cognitive approach stresses the linkages between action and cognition and therefore offers the insight that knowledge is mobilized in the form of representations. At the same time, emphasis on cognitive processes leads to a reification of the mind based on the antithesis of inner and outer worlds. As a result, knowledge is defined in abstract as a representation of an objective world existing 'out there'. Furthermore, the focus on individual mental processes overlooks the collective, public dimension of knowledge.

The knowledge-based perspective probably offers the most consistent conceptualization of knowledge, which is reflected in the attempt to build a knowledge-based theory of the firm. It provides a sound vocabulary for the study of knowledge-related dynamics in organizations while stressing the critical linkage between knowledge and competitive performance. On the other hand, the conceptualization of knowledge as a factor of production or commodity can lead to a functional vision of knowledge creation where knowledge itself is turned into a utility function.

The situated perspective's major strength lies in its relational focus. Knowledge is conceptualized in a holistic fashion stressing the linkages between action, context, and processes. The situated perspective is also strong in its empirical tradition, characterized by interdisciplinary focus and reliance on case studies as the main source of empirical evidence. On the other hand, the descriptive focus of organizational studies highlights problems of theory building. In this respect, the situated approach seems to be characterized by a certain resistance to generalizations and by a difficulty to elaborate a solid theory of knowing and organizing.

Finally, the techno-science approach highlights the controversial, socially constructed nature of scientific facts and technological artefacts. Its focus of inquiry is on the chain of transformations that knowledge undergoes over time and on the conditions that lead to the institutionalization of knowledge outcomes, rather than on finished products *per se*. The empirical focus, combining ethnography and history as methods of inquiry, is the distinctive trait of this perspective and its main point of strength (e.g. Knorr-Cetina 1981; Latour 1987; Pinch and Bijker 1989). On the other hand, certain variants of social constructionism (e.g. actor-network theories) seem to display a tendency towards total relativism, which denies the existence of an objective reality and therefore overlooks the material, content-related aspects of knowledge creation.

In the remainder of the book I shall draw on the complementarities of the four perspectives outlined above in order to develop an empirical study on knowing and organizing which is epistemologically, ontologically, and methodologically grounded. My position is in line with the recent debates on issues of incommensurability in organizational analysis (see Organization 1998). In particular those debates have highlighted the importance of relying on pluralist epistemology (Spender 1998) and paradigmatic pluralism (Kaghan and Phillips 1998) as ways to capture knowledge-related phenomena in a more holistic and systemic way. Inevitably, there are also dangers related to the adoption of a pluralist perspective. Namely, the tendency towards pluralism, eclecticism, and integrationism can lead to excessive drifting and indeterminacy. This could result in the development of an indistinct viewpoint where 'anything goes' and the author is not accountable for his/her position. Taking into account this limitation, I believe that the adoption of a holistic standpoint allows the researcher to engage in an exacting conversation between literatures, rather than assuming an ideological stance. In the pursuit of knowledge, pluralism stresses the value of difference, variety, and heterogeneity as resources for inquiry. To be sure, the above features should not be accepted uncritically. Rather they should promote the elaboration of more thorough and comprehensive strategies of inquiry through which the strengths and weaknesses of different theoretical perspectives are systematically exposed.

3

Studying Organizational Knowledge

3.1 Introduction

The current debate on organizational knowledge has highlighted the difficulty of documenting empirically the processes of creation, accumulation, and maintenance of knowledge in organizations. With some notable exceptions (e.g. Leonard-Barton 1992*a*; Inkpen and Dinur 1998), the few existing studies on knowledge have focused on the possibility of measuring the transfer of discrete knowledge flows by relying on quantitative methodologies (e.g. Szulanski 1996; Mowery, Oxley, and Silverman 1996; Appleyard 1996; De Carolis and Deeds 1999). While the contributions of these studies are valuable insights into the performative aspect of knowledge-related dynamics, the methods deployed somewhat neglect the qualitative nature of the phenomenon under investigation. This chapter sets out to develop the epistemological, methodological, and operational assumptions underlying an inquiry into organizational knowledge. Such apparatus includes phenomenology as the overarching intellectual perspective, ethnography as the strategy of investigation, and a set of methodological lenses as operational tools to gain empirical access into knowledge-based processes.

The epistemological underpinnings of this book have partly been discussed in the introductory chapter. They fall within the tenets of the phenomenological method, emphasizing the inquiry into the structure of everyday life. The essence of such method lies in the detailed analysis of human experience as a way to rescue the tacit, unstated, and taken-for-granted assumptions underlying our everyday dealings with the world. In doing this, phenomenology takes the problem of pre-interpretation seriously and attempts to produce disclosures of human modes of knowing and understanding

On the other hand, phenomenology as an intellectual perspective requires a strategy of investigation for studying empirically the interconnected processes of knowing and organizing. According to Bate (1997), a valid model for a phenomenology of organizations can be found in anthropology. The ethnographic quest revolves around the everyday experience of a society or organization. Indeed, the whole thrust of anthropology is towards accessing 'mundane systems of reason and behaviour' (Pollner 1987), and 'penetrating the intimacy of life' (Latour and Woolgar 1979: 17, quoted in Bate 1997).[1] The intellectual posture of the anthropologist is informed by a kind of 'skilled naivety'; that is, the ability to capture incipient, elementary forms of social phenomena without preconceptions of what constitutes valid knowledge. Accordingly, anthropology stubbornly denies the obviousness of the obvious and deliberately focuses on the details of everyday life. The aim of ethnographic accounts is to disclose the world by simply describing the unfolding of everyday phenomena.

While insightful, the anthropological method has been widely criticized for being unstructured and highly subjective. Indeed, anthropology is more a broad stratagem than a detailed method (Bate 1997). A further step is required in order to reduce the complexity of knowledge phenomena. This involves devising tactical tools able to render operational the methodological principles provided by ethnography. In this chapter, I develop a three-lens framework to conduct description and observation of knowledge-based phenomena in a systematic fashion: time, breakdowns, and narratives. The three lenses provide operational devices to disentangle organizational knowledge from the tacit background against which it is utilized on a day-to-day basis.

The chapter contains five sections. The next section outlines the main issues related to the application of interpretative, ethnography-based approaches to the study of organizations. The analysis is based on a critical discussion of Geertz's notion of thick description (Geertz 1973). Section 3.3 provides an illustration of how thick description generates interpretation. Section 3.4 presents the three-lens framework deployed in this research to study knowledge as an empirical phenomenon. The concluding section addresses issues of validity and rhetorical representation of theory. It suggests that most of the difficulties encountered in articulating interpretive theories are related to the language and discursive paradigms adopted by the analyst. Interpretation is seen as an imaginative act, while the task of writing highlights the identity of the researcher as an author.

---

[1] On the use of ethnography in organizational analysis see also Van Maanen (1979) and Hammersley (1992).

3.2   'Thick description': in search of a strategy of inquiry

In *The interpretation of cultures* (1973), Clifford Geertz provides a brilliant example of interpretive anthropology in practice with his 'thick
description' of the Bali cockfight. Starting from a local episode, the cockfight, and describing how this event is dramatized within the Balinese
community, he is able to trace back the fundamental institutional forms
of Balinese society. In closing his essay, Geertz observes: 'Societies,
like lives, contain their own interpretation. One has only to learn how
to gain access to them' (Geertz 1973: 453). The above statement contains
a fundamental methodological question for the present study: how do
we access knowledge systems, since, as we have seen in Chapter 1,
they are made of assumptions which are mostly taken for granted?
Admittedly, knowledge structures do not exist outside the practices
and behaviours that they govern; rather, they are 'immanent' to them.
Knowledge is embodied in praxis and it is organized according to
complex architectures that the researcher needs to decode and uncover
starting from their visible elements.

In presenting the basic principles of the ethnographic method of
inquiry, Geertz seems to suggest that it is precisely the vividness of
description that provides access to interpretation. In other words, interpretation is embodied in thick description. Accordingly, the task of the
ethnographer is to construct a reading of what happens within an
organization, community or knowledge system, and disclose the basic
structures of signification underlying their functioning. In doing this,
ethnographers play on their unfamiliarity (something of a therapeutic
distance) with the context under study, which provides them with a sort
of privileged observational perspective. In fact, the ethnographer's
description is informed by his/her belonging to a different cultural context. It is precisely this contextual gap that makes interpretation possible:
'the famous anthropological absorption with the exotic is essentially a
device for displacing the dulling sense of familiarity with which the
mysteriousness of our own ability to relate perceptively to one another
is concealed from us . . . Understanding people's culture exposes their
normalness without reducing their particularity. It renders them accessible: setting them in the frame of their own banalities, it dissolves their
opacity' (Geertz 1973: 14). Reading some of Geertz's brilliant prose, the
method appears to be quite suggestive. However, as the author himself
points out, it also hides a number of important methodological problems, closely related to each other, that the present study will have to

address. These problems include: the scope of the description, the relationship between description and interpretation, and the resistance to generalizations and theory construction.

(a) The description is microscopic A common trait of ethnographic studies is the movement from detailed, protracted descriptions of small matters to large-scale interpretations. In doing so, abstract concepts take on a lively, homely form in the rich and circumstantial accounts of the ethnographer. On the other hand, there is a risk of letting the description linger at a local level—incidents, anecdotes, episodes—thus failing to offer a holistic picture of the phenomenon under study. The problem of how to move from local truths to general visions is a major methodological issue.

(b) Impossibility of divorcing description from interpretation Ethnographic description is interpretive. Since ethnographic accounts are normally presented in the form of an actor's-eye description, however, the line between the description of a natural fact and its interpretation tends to get blurred. A researcher has to make sense of how other people make sense and accordingly always deals with 'interpretation of interpretations'.

On the other hand, any attempt to 'artfully' disentangle empirical facts from the material complexity in which they were located—'from what, in this time and place, specific people say, what they do, what is done to them, from the whole vast business of the world'—and then attribute their existence to some autonomous principles or meta-categories would considerably impoverish the relevance of any descriptive account (Geertz 1973).

This embeddedness of social practice explains the impossibility of severing interpretation from the immediacy of detail. It is then necessary to redefine interpretation as a form of inscription: 'Interpreting consists in trying to rescue the "said" of social discourse from its perishing occasions and fix it in perusable terms. The ethnographer "inscribes" social discourse, he writes it down. In so doing he turns it from a passing event, which exist only in its own moment of occurrence, into an account, which exists in its inscriptions and can be reconsulted . . . He observes, he records, he analyses—a kind of *veni, vidi, vici* conception of the matter. However, distinguishing these three phases of knowledge seeking may not, as a matter of fact, normally be possible; and indeed, as autonomous "operations" they may not in fact exist' (Geertz 1973: 19–20).

(c) Resistance to generalizations and theory Lack of categories, rhetorical limitations and the peculiar relationship between the observer and

the interactionist field explain why interpretive approaches tend to resist conceptual articulation and thus escape systematic modes of assessment. Unlike those sciences that can rely on more abstract modes of theoretical formulation, for anthropology description—in the sense of narrative—is the only possible form of representing theory. Furthermore, from the analyst's perspective, there is a problem of how to disentangle him/herself from his/her own accounts. In fact, the analyst him/herself is in a condition of being-in-the-narrative: 'The tension between the pull of this need to penetrate an unfamiliar universe of symbolic action and the requirement of technical advance in the theory, between the need to grasp and the need to analyse, is, as a result, both necessarily great and essentially irremovable. Indeed, the further the theoretical development goes, the deeper the tension gets' (Geertz 1973: 24).

If what has been sketched above is a fair account of how theory functions in an interpretive science, then there is a need to redefine the conventional distinction between description and explanation. According to Geertz, theories generated from thick descriptions proceed through cycles of 'inscription' and 'specification': the double task of the ethnographer consists in setting down the meaning that particular social actions have for the actors whose actions they are, while stating, as explicitly as he can manage, what the knowledge thus attained demonstrates about the society in which it is found and, beyond that, about social life as such (Geertz 1973: 27).

The above considerations about the limitations of the ethnographic method emphasize the fundamental issue of the validity of a study and raise some serious problems of verification and appraisal. These issues will be tackled in Section 3.6 of the chapter.

3.3 Thick description at work: the subtleties of interpretation

My initial reaction when I first entered the shop floor of a car manufacturing plant was one of wonder, puzzlement, and estrangement. Indeed, when entering a shop floor one is faced with an array of tools, machines, and strange artefacts: coils, blank metal sheets, pallets, presses, dies, forklifts, cranes, sample parts, containers, car bodies, robots, production lines, and so on. As a first-time observer I was struck by the mesh of men and machines at work, the mesmerizing movement of the assembly line, the synchronized flow of car bodies, and the occasional irruption of different types of noises and alarms into the smooth functioning of the production lines. Admittedly, the shop floor appears to the visitor as a buzzing yet coherent whole; it functions like a city. However, the purpose of each item of equipment, and the relationship linking different items in a whole is not immediately obvious. As an observer I was in constant search of points of reference, signposts, and regularities enabling me to make sense of the surroundings. Functions and categories gradually emerged as a result of sense-making endeavours. For example, equipment making up the shop floor of an automotive plant could be classified according to four production categories: materials (coils, blank sheets, and components), processing (dies + presses + robots = production line), material handling (forklifts, cranes), and storage (pallets, containers). In turn, those categories could be connected to each other and thereby reveal a practical context defining the activity of assembling and against which equipment functions.

Carrying on the description, it would have probably been possible to achieve further levels of generalization. Roles, division of labour, tasks, operations, routines, standard operating procedures, and the whole activity system of the plant—what we normally infer from organizational charts—would materialize from the unfolding of practical activity in the work setting. In a subsequent phase, the activity system of the factory could be related to the narratives gathered from the shop floor operators, to the tradition of the company, to the differences and similarities with other companies operating in the same sector, and so on. But, at this point, I also realized that my description could generate a huge number of relationships and my problem now was where to stop the narrative.

The above phenomenological, camera-eye description of the shop floor at Mirafiori, provides a good example of how thick description generates interpretation. It also illustrates the kind of puzzlement that a researcher has to face when entering the interactionist field. The first thing to notice is that thick descriptions disclose the world as a web of references. Namely, it is through this reference game, of something referring to something else that relationships are constructed, pictures emerge from backgrounds, and small matters speak to grand realities. Secondly, thick description, like any other type of description, implies the presence of a director behind the camera, deciding about focus and close-ups, back-stage and front-stage, establishing linkages and connections between objects, people and events, hinting at meanings. Each time a new object, event, or character is brought into the picture, it needs to be characterized in order to ensure that its meaning is grasped by the reader. In other words, each element of the description is linked to other elements that are normally taken for granted by the community under study, but are not obvious for the non-natives. It is the task of the researcher to establish a conversation between the two worlds: that of the natives and that of the readers.

Interpretation is fundamentally about choice, it is a problem of judgement. The interpreter, far from simply describing a reality 'out there', is constantly engaged in deciding what meaning should be attributed to what he/she is describing. Furthermore, thick description is not a seamless account of the reality in front of the observer—a list of things, a stream of consciousness—but it has a purpose and is therefore interpretive. In analytic terms, it is possible to distinguish three moments in the interpretation process, each embodying a problem of choice/judgement:

1. *Selection*: Selecting the relevant features of a situation, its characters, and objects. Scanning and sectioning the interactionist field. Defining the relationship between foreground and background.
2. *Emplotment*: Generating references by following the unfolding of action. Establishing linkages and connections within situations and between situations. Creating a perspective by locating action in space and time, thus bringing the observed phenomenon to life. Building a plot through sequencing and punctuating events.
3. *Closure*: Very often phenomenological accounts display a resistance to closure. Thick description can generate a huge number of relationships and thereby produce phenomena of drifting. A last fundamental problem of judgement for the researcher is deciding where to stop the description and accordingly how to frame the phenomenon under study.

To conclude, interpretation is a process of discovery as well as invention (a fiction according to Geertz), a quest for meaning, whereby a picture gradually emerges from a background. To be sure, the author is able to exercise control over the research process, but his/her primary task is simply to let relationships emerge by means of thick description. The tension between discovery and control is the creative engine of any research process.

3.4 Three lenses to study knowledge empirically

The methodological framework adopted in this book provides a composite tool for gaining empirical access to highly idiosyncratic knowledge systems. As we have learned from the work of Polany (1966), Nelson and Winter (1982), and Nonaka and Takeuchi (1995) a major issue in the study of knowledge-oriented dynamics is the distinction between tacit and explicit knowledge. From a methodological point of view this distinction poses a major challenge for the analyst. In fact, while we have access to the explicit, formalized features of knowledge, it is not possible to get the same insight into the tacit, experience-related side of it. In order to tackle the problem one has to find a way to operationalize tacit knowledge. This implies addressing two main questions: (a) what are the ontological foundations of tacit knowledge? (b) what are the factors affecting the degree of tacitness of knowledge?

Tacit knowledge is much more intricate than the reductionist treatment offered by the managerial literature. It is not just a property or a convertible steady state. Rather, the tacit nature of human and organizational knowing is related to problems of pre-interpretation. Reality is necessarily apprehended through socially constructed lenses that have sedimented over time. This leads to a sort of ontological blindness whereby social phenomena become gradually entangled in the structure of everydayness and evade notice. Indeed, the notion of pre-interpretation is paradoxical in nature. Human knowing occurs against a practical background that is transparent to the user and therefore not accessible for inquiry. However, such background is itself a human construction, it is the effect of humans' everyday coping with the world. It incorporates a history of experiences, consolidated habits, and structural repertoires, which over the years have provided successful responses to the emergence of problematic situations. In other words, existential backgrounds presiding over the practice of everyday life are both the source and the outcome of human knowing. If pre-interpretation provides the ontological foundations of human knowing (and therefore tacit knowledge) then we need to redefine the distinction between tacit and explicit knowledge in terms of a dichotomy between background and foreground. In the light of the redefinition the two questions above can be rephrased as follows:

(a) How can we disclose the particular configuration of background and foreground within a given setting?
(b) What are the factors that affect such configuration?

Taking a phenomenological perspective, our operationalization is based on a theory of the actor and on the existential background surrounding the actor's everyday coping with the world. In particular, I suggest that there are at least three important factors that affect the particular configuration of background and foreground knowledge in organizations. The first is history: knowledge recedes to the background as a result of the sedimentation of learning experiences over a time span. The second is habit: when knowledge is deeply internalized and institutionalized we tend to use it in an almost automatic and irreflexive way. The third is experience: by definition tacit, background knowledge is experience-related. The above factors identify three 'lenses' for studying knowledge processes as an empirical phenomenon: time, breakdowns, and narratives.

Time concerns the dynamics of social becoming which underlie processes of knowledge construction in organizations. It points to the sedimentary nature of knowledge and to the deep structures that govern daily practices in the work setting. Breakdowns call into question our habitual way of doing things and thereby bring out the patterns of routinization underlying the smooth functioning of human activities. By interrupting the ongoing sense-making activity of organizational actors, breakdowns also disclose the thematic content of intentionality and highlight the cognitive dimension of organizational knowledge. Finally, narratives provide distinctive modes of knowing through which experience-related knowledge is articulated into some form of organizational discourse. The focus on narratives allows the researcher to gain an insight into how organizational actors represent and make sense of their everyday coping with the world.

The three methodological lenses can be seen as specially crafted tools for studying such relational phenomena as societies, cosmologies, organizations, institutions, cities, knowledge systems, and so on. The main assumption underlying the proposed framework is that social phenomena become conspicuous under special circumstances: for example, when they are in their incipient phase (e.g. witnessing a phenomenon for the first time). What today appears to be invisible and taken for granted, must probably have been apparent in a previous time. Time allows the researcher to trace back the origin of a complex phenomenon (e.g. noise as a proxy for modernity) by providing a formidable travel machine. Or, when there is a disruption of an established order. Breakdowns provide a way of voicing a background that is taken for granted. In this regard, breakdowns and disturbances have the same function as noise in a world of silence. A third strategy of investigation suggested by the above discussion consists in the patient piecing together of evidence and clues. This involves reconstructing past or present experiences through the narratives of the actors involved. The focus on narratives presupposes treating reality as a text unfolding as a story (Geertz 1973; Ricoeur 1981).

Organizational Knowledge in the Making

Table 3.1 *Three lenses to study knowledge empirically*

Lens	Focus	Process
Time	Discontinuities in time	Sedimentation of knowledge-based patterns over time
Breakdowns	Discontinuities in action	Routinization of successful responses to problematic situations
Narratives	Discontinuities of experience	Embodiment of notable experiences into some forms of organizational discourse

This strategy derives from literary criticism. It amounts to deconstructing a text, as Kundera does with the novel by John.

Taken as a whole, the three lenses represent modes of de-institutionalization of knowledge (see Table 3.1). They look at knowledge-creating dynamics in reverse, so to speak, by focusing on discontinuities in time, action, and experience. Each lens provides a distinctive angle, or mode of access, to the tacit features of organizational knowledge systems. Specifically, it is possible to identify three distinctive but interrelated processes to which each lens directs our attention:

- the sedimentation of knowledge-oriented patterns over time (time);
- the routinization of successful responses to problematic situations (breakdowns);
- the embodiment of successful practices into some forms of organizational discourse (narratives).

Under these circumstances, the three lenses also provide a form of methodological triangulation. The triangulation of multiple sources of evidence is a common strategy in qualitative research aimed at improving the richness of the data while reducing the risk of interpretative biases. The three-lens framework presented below extends the principle of methodological triangulation to a higher level of complexity encompassing issues of meta-level perspective and ontological significance. In the following section each lens is discussed in greater detail in order to assess its methodological relevance and distinctiveness.

3.4.1 *Time*

The centrality of time in strategy and organizational research has been underscored by those scholars who have conducted longitudinal and processual studies on such phenomena as change and innovation (e.g. Pettigrew 1985, 1987, 1990, 1997; Whipp and Clark 1986). Other scholars have adopted a historical perspective to interpret the evolution of organizational structures and behaviours as a result of culture-specific historical developments (Chandler 1990; Kieser 1994).

The use of the historical dimension as a methodological lens raises important issues relating to the type of approach and the corresponding conceptualization of time adopted by the researcher. Traditionally, the epistemologies underpinning the historical method have oscillated between the so-called analytical and narrative approaches. The analytical approach refers to a positivist tradition privileging explanation and the identification of law-like causalities. Accordingly, this perspective tends to deny the importance of events in favour of more generalized patterns and structures. In its most radical formulation, known as the 'cover law model' (Ricoeur 1984), the analytic approach aims to develop predictive models of historical evolution and therefore to endow history with the same status as science. A typical application of the analytical approach is Marx's notion of historical materialism as used in his analysis of capitalist societies. Despite the strong criticism levelled at the analytical approach, its added value lies in the possibility of identifying patterns and regularities and therefore connecting organizational phenomena to some kind of causal explanation. At the other end of the spectrum, the narrative approach denies any causality in favour of the objectivity of the plot (i.e. how one writes history and tells the story). For narrativists, the point-like event constitutes the minimal unit of analysis. The historical account relies on the construction of a plot out of a collection of equivocal events. In this respect, the work of the historian is sense making rather than tracing back patterns and regularities. The craft of the historian lies in his/her capacity to cut out the field of events in order to build a meaningful plot (Veyne 1971). Plausibility and probability are the criteria of validation of the historical account.

A critical point of synthesis between the above perspectives is provided by the Annales School (see Bloch 1953; Braudel 1972–74), which attempts to integrate the contributions of history and sociology. Representatives of this School tend to deny the singularity of the event and the role of the individual in favour of holistic notions such as social facts. History is not made of heroes and battles. In this regard, the Annales School is close to the positions of the analytic approach, although within an anti-positivist orientation (Ricoeur 1984). At the same time, the Annalists recognize the importance of human understanding advocated by the narrative approach. Most of the recent approaches in organization studies have tended to set themselves in some sort of intermediary position. For example, the historical account of the dynamics of change and innovation at Rover provided by Whipp and Clark (1986) can be defined as an 'analytically structured narrative'.

When applied to the study of knowledge-related processes in organizations, the rationale for the use of this dimension reads as follows: if the sedimentation of idiosyncratic stocks of knowledge occurs over time, the solution devised to deconstruct knowledge that has become tacit and mostly taken for granted relies on the possibility of manipulating time. Admittedly time exists in different forms. Chronological time emphasizes linearity and provides a trajectory in the sequencing of events (a time span). Knowledge systems are unravelled through the identification of discrete phases, seizures, and breakpoints, which identify evolutionary paths. Sedimentary time (Latour 1999*a*) allows the researcher to develop an appreciation of the processes of inscription and stratification by which knowledge becomes progressively institutionalized. The multiple strata identify distinctive knowledge contents evolving towards increasingly complex forms of organizing. Narrative time (Ricoeur 1984) provides organizational actors with a structuring device that punctuates the unfolding of action according to distinctive plots. It focuses on processes of collective remembering (Middleton and Edwards 1990) surrounding the creation and institutionalization of organizational knowledge. Time as commodity directs our attention towards the ways in which the equivocality of action is harnessed in stable temporal structures (e.g. work shifts, production cycles, deadlines, and so on). Time as tense implies the notion of 'pastness', that is, the idea that the past exerts an important influence on the present and over the future. The theorization of the influence of the past on organizational performance can be connected to theories of imprinting (Stinchombe 1965), according to which the explanation for the current performance of a firm or institution can be traced back to its foundation. Likewise, the notion of path-dependency connects the idiosyncratic knowledge base of a firm to specific learning trajectories developed over time. Finally, social time calls into question the 'facticity' of knowledge (Knorr Cetina 1981). It provides the analyst with a time machine for deconstructing facts that have become taken for granted within a given community (Latour 1987). The journey in space and time allows the analyst to follow the characters involved in situated processes of knowledge construction 'while they are busy at work', and to trace back the network of events, decisions, physical artefacts, and institutions surrounding the 'making' of things. In this respect, emphasis is placed on 'knowledge in the making' rather than on ready-made knowledge (Latour 1987). The use of time as a travel machine points to the ubiquity of the researcher; that is, to the possibility of being in different places at the same time. This possibly redefines time as a spatial dimension.

3.4.2 *Breakdowns*

Breakdowns, in the form of discontinuities, interruptions, and so on, create a cleavage between organization and disorganization, and therefore can be fruitfully deployed for an empirical investigation into knowing and organizing. Indeed, the need to capture relations between flux and stability, practice(s) and narratives, order and disorder are central to the nature of organized activity. There is a considerable body of literature dealing with disruptions and sense making (Weick 1988, 1993; Perrow 1984; Shrivastava et al. 1988). These studies emphasize the cognitive implications of major events such as crises, accidents and failures, often within the context of high-risk systems. Typically, the crisis literature tends to focus on low probability/high consequence events that jeopardize the mission of the organization. Furthermore, given the unpredictability of a crisis, research deals with situations of high discretion in which the cognitive/emotional responses of individuals faced with a breakdown will ultimately prevail over the structural properties of the organization. In particular, the nature of the task at hand is such that a serious disruption could result in a 'collapse of sense making' (Weick 1993) and lead to the disintegration of organizational structures.

To be sure, breakdowns are 'accidental', unexpected, related to the performance and the reliability of a system; they can be more or less serious, local or systemic. More fundamentally, as the literature on situated cognition (Winograd and Flores 1986; Suchman 1987) has pointed out, breakdowns relate to the domain of everyday life and to our way of encountering things. In other words, breakdowns pinpoint the disruption of a pragmatic connection with tools and equipment. They express discontinuities, mismatches, disjunctions, seizures between knowledge and experience, representations and praxis, and between the obvious and the concealed. This view is in line with socio-technical analyses of disruptions in the workplace. In particular, studies of socio-technical systems (e.g. Trist 1981) have looked at how organizations react to breakdowns as a way to explore such issues as the robustness and reliability of a technology in relation to the work organization. From a socio-technical perspective the focus on breakdowns provides a means for testing the resilience of a given organizational setting. As Akrich has pointed out:

A breakdown can only be understood as part of practice—that is, as the collapse of the relationship between a piece of apparatus and its use. A breakdown is thus a test of the solidity of the socio-technical network materialized by a technical object. The rapidity with which the search for the causes of breakdown can be completed is a measure of this solidity. (Akrich 1993: 224)

The use of breakdowns in the present study is informed by the following assumptions. First, breakdowns are treated as pervasive, everyday phenomena that organizations are able to absorb and to harness thanks to their repetitive pattern of recurrence. In other words, the focus of the research is on low-risk breakdowns in large organizations. Second, sense making is not considered a mere psychological process, but is anchored to the phenomenon of organizing. Third, the conditions whereby breakdowns produce a disclosure of the tacit features of organization are connected to the borderline location of breakdowns in the organization–disorganization opposition.

As a tool for inquiry, breakdowns draw on discontinuities in action as a mode to disentangle knowledge from consolidated work practices and routines. In so doing they point to the processes whereby order is disrupted and eventually recomposed within organizations. At the empirical level, the organization–disorganization dialectic translates into the dynamic interaction between routines and breakdowns. Routine and breakdowns identify alternative modes of knowing pointing to different types of intentionality (Dreyfus 1991; Louis and Sutton 1991). In routine situations, organizational actors are absorbed in coping with business as usual. The content and the context of the task at hand are somehow enfolded in a single knowledge system which makes the task itself transparent to the user. In other words, when things are functioning smoothly, organizational knowledge is experienced as something 'ready-to-hand' and used almost unreflectively. On the other hand, when disruptions occur, the coherence of the task (what Heidegger (1962) would call the constitutive assignment of the 'in-order-to') is called into question because the functional relationship between action and goals, activity and context, has been disturbed. As a consequence, the obviousness of daily routines becomes problematic (Ciborra and Lanzara 1994; Ciborra, Patriotta, and Erlicher 1996). Since, in those situations, knowledge needs to be applied in a deliberate way, the ongoing flow of action and sense making is articulated in the form of narratives, moves and decisions, while projects emerge as they are interrupted. In order to restore normality, organizational actors need to explicitly interact with the tacit background against which knowledge is used. As a consequence, knowledge references to the context of use are disclosed and emphasized. In this respect, breakdowns bring tacit knowledge to the fore by exhibiting it as 'present-at-hand'. This has two major consequences for the disclosure of tacit knowledge. Firstly, breakdowns produce a de-coupling of action and cognition and thereby reveal the projects behind the execution of a task. Secondly, practical knowledge is disentangled from its context of use and is de-situated. The analysis of breakdowns provides, then, a useful method for reflecting upon the organizational context 'hosting' a particular knowledge system and opens up the possibility of deconstructing the meanings embodied in organizational artefacts, routines, and other knowledge-based activities. In this regard, breakdowns provide a window through which it is possible to access the organizational reality as they put the organization in a situation that requires deliberate attention.

3.4.2.1 *Routines and breakdowns*

The discussion carried out above raises the issue of whether breakdowns can be distinguished at all from organizational routines. For instance, Nelson and Winter (1982) contend that breakdowns are absorbed by organizations through their incorporation into some kind of problem-solving routine. They provide the following example:

Consider the foreman of a work team responsible for a particular operation (set of routines) who observes that a machine is not working properly. He routinely calls the maintenance department, which in turn routinely sends out a machine repairman. The machine repairman has been trained to diagnose in a particular way the troubles that such a machine might have. He goes down a list of possible problems systematically, and finds one that fits the symptoms. He fixes the part so that the machine again plays its role in the overall work routine. He may also, however, report to the foreman that this particular kind of trouble has become very common since the supplier started using aluminium in making the part in question and that perhaps the machine should be operated in a different manner to avoid the difficulty. (Nelson and Winter 1982: 129)

The authors suggest that 'the responses described fall into the typical pattern in which a crisis or "exception" condition in one part of the organization is part of the routine content of jobs of other personnel. On the other hand, it is significant that the problem-solving responses routinely evoked by difficulties with existing routines may yield results that lead to major change' (Nelson and Winter 1982: 130).

From a phenomenological perspective routines and breakdowns have to be seen as alternative modes of encountering things. Namely, while routines relate to things functioning smoothly, breakdowns point to the temporary collapse of a pragmatic relationship with things. Another way to understand the difference is to locate the interplay of routines and breakdowns within a broader epistemology of action. In this sense, it is possible to think of action as an ongoing flow of routine and breakdown events unfolding in time and space. Following this line of reasoning, routines do not include breakdowns; rather, they embody the possibility of disruption in the smooth flow of action. As Winograd and Flores (1986) have pointed out, 'things' do not exist in the absence of a concernful activity with its potential for breaking down. Of course, the entity of the breakdown affects the extent to which order is interrupted and eventually recreated.

Taking such perspective, the example provided by Nelson and Winter highlights precisely how organizations attempt to anticipate action in space and time by means of absorptive mechanisms. Here we have an exemplification of how the routinization of activity allows organizations to harness the occurrence of disruptions. Echoing Cooper and Law (1995), problem-solving routines are 'a matter of constructing the future so that it looks like it's always been there'. Secondly, the above example illustrates how breakdowns can provide an insight into the purpose of routines. In fact, the actors involved in the solution of a problem are forced to articulate knowledge through a series of 'organizing moves' (Pentland 1992), decisions, narratives and so on, which enact certain structural features of organization (the division of labour, the application of problem-solving procedures, and the deliberate use of equipment and work tools). Finally, when the occurrence of a breakdown does not enact an automatic, routinized response, the observation of the dynamics triggered by the disruption points to specific learning requirements and reveals stocks of knowledge that have not been institutionalized and embodied in organizational artefacts. This is controversial knowledge that still needs to be confronted with the organizational reality. It could lead to innovation or, conversely, it could be abandoned with surrender to the existing state of affairs.

Through the mechanism of repetition, routines characterize organizations as quasi-liturgical entities. Within this framework, the role of breakdowns is similar to that of social dramas as dissected in the work of Victor Turner (1974). In Turner's words, social dramas are public episodes of tensional irruption. They refer to a situation of obvious opposition in the interests and attitudes of individuals and groups within a community. Therefore, social dramas point to discordant phases of the ongoing social process. However, as routines, social dramas are characterized by a 'processional' form which is aimed at remedying the schism produced by their occurrence. It is thus possible to say that, to some extent, breakdowns are part of the liturgy.

The 'dramatic' character of organizational action suggests that the disclosure of the tacit features of organization does not occur in a straightforward manner. Rather, it is mediated by processes of *mise-en-intrigue* (emplotment) (Ricoeur 1984) whereby disruptions are socially dramatized in order to help organizational actors make sense of the situations they encounter. It is only then that knowledge is expressed in a deliberate way and becomes visible to the researcher. For this reason, in order to empirically observe how organizations create, use and disseminate knowledge, we have to look for disruptive events conceived as turning points in an ongoing flow of activities. We have to observe the discontinuities and asynchronies, even local or temporary, that breakdowns cause in the smooth functioning of everyday practice, and to follow how they affect the fluid unfolding of action in space and time. The above observations reinforce the argument against the risk of treating critical incidents as isolated episodes occurring at specific points in time. Since, in order to become meaningful, disruptions need to be contextualized through the construction of narratives, the researcher should be able to avoid that risk by systematically linking sense-making dynamics occurring around breakdowns to the broader organizational context.

To conclude, breakdowns do not destroy organizations, let alone routines. Rather, they help us understand why and how certain strands of knowledge have become tacit. Once a specific routine has been invented, the problem addressed by it simply stops being a (conscious) problem. Echoing Latour's terminology, it is possible to argue that breakdowns constitute an alternative way to open organizational black boxes and uncover concepts that have become tacit. The close examination of disruptions takes us back in space and time and, hopefully, leads us to understanding the organizational devices designed to anticipate them. To use an analogy, just as in science a fact or a paradigm is challenged by the emergence of counter-evidence that leads to a controversy, so in organizations the concept of organizing is challenged by the occurrence of disruptive phenomena.

3.4.3 *Narratives*

Narratives deal with the vicissitudes of human intentions (Bruner 1986). They can be seen as a form of problem-solving in our everyday coping with the world. In a sense, narratives provide access to the world conceived, in William James' terms, as 'a buzzing, pulsating, formless mass of signals, out of which people try to make sense, into which they attempt to introduce order, and from which they construct against a background that remains undifferentiated' (James 1950, cited in Czarniawska 1998). The significance of the narrative approach to the study of contemporary organizations has been widely recognized in the literature. For example, Boland and Tenkasi (1995) consider narratives and storytelling as the basic organizing principle of human cognition. They believe that explicitly recognizing the narrative mode of cognition is important for understanding how perspective-making and perspective-taking occur within a community of knowing. In a similar vein, Weick (1995) contends that stories simplify the world by providing cognitive devices to guide action. Brown and Duguid (1991) have connected the narrative process to a situational view of organizational knowledge and learning (Lave and Wenger 1991). Narration is seen as a central feature of the *modus operandi* of informal communities-of-practice, reflecting the complex social web within which work takes place. Accordingly, the practice of creating and exchanging stories has two important aspects. First of all, storytelling allows organizational actors to keep track of their behaviour and of their theories; secondly, stories act as repositories of accumulated wisdom (Lave and Wenger 1991). At the empirical level, Orr's (1990, 1996) ethnography of photocopy repair technicians (reps) probably provides one of the classic applications of the narrative approach. By following in detail the technician's 'talk about machines', Orr discovers that the practices enacted by the reps in their everyday coping with troubled machines is much richer and more complex than the prescriptive documentation provided by the company manuals would suggest. Narratives appear to be fundamental diagnostic devices, enabling operators to perform a coherent description of machine breakdowns. In addition, they maintain the stability of the work setting by fostering the circulation of organizational knowledge within the community of workers.

Narratives connect modes of knowing with modes of organizing. On the one hand, it is possible to say that narrating is organizing (Czarniawska 1997). Indeed, organization itself can be regarded as a story, as a social construction that is interactionally relevant and constraining. At the same time, narratives identify a distinctive mode of thought (Bruner 1986). They point to the cognitive processes by which people in organizations engage in debate, dialectics, and collective inquiry. From a phenomenological perspective, narratives provide access to the controversy-based dynamics through which organizational actors deal with the equivocality of everyday action. They unfold the features of knowledge-making processes in terms of an internal dialectic between text and action. According to Ricoeur (1981), action may be regarded as a text; it is a meaningful entity which must be constructed as a whole. However, this construction is subject to conflict of interpretations that can be resolved only by a process of argumentation and debate. Like a text, human action is an open work, the meaning of which is 'in suspense'. In this regard, narratives turn action into text and text into action. Through the institutionalization of meaning, action is temporarily fixed, it turns into a textual artefact that can be dissected by using the methodology of text-interpretation. In turn, by connecting event and meaning, the text becomes a script to be acted upon, a prompt for *ad hoc* performances. Ultimately, texts provide a guide for conduct and thereby link action to cognition and sense making.

The dynamic interplay between text and action portrays narrative as encompassing both the process and the content of organizational knowledge. In fact, narrative knowing highlights the fundamental sense-making processes leading to the enactment, punctuation and retention of organizational action (Weick 1977). Through narratives, occurrences are located in space and time and translated into meaningful events by organizational actors. Emplotment is the process whereby actors impose a logical structure (a beginning, a middle and an end) upon a flow of equivocal happenings through processes of ordering and sequencing. Time plays a critical role in conferring consistency on the plot and thereby promotes sense making. In fact, the strength of narratives as interpretative devices stems precisely from their ability to link the present to the past and the future, anticipation to retrospection and repetition.

The above considerations bear important implications for knowledge, knowing, and organizing. Firstly, narratives show how knowledge in organizations is mobilized through discourse, and therefore highlight a distinctive mode of knowing related to the everyday coping with the world. Because of their connection to experience, narratives display common-sense wisdom—in the form of anecdotes, jokes, and war stories—in organizational discourse. Common sense is based on unspoken premises and therefore underscores the tacit aspects of knowledge in organizations. Narratives, articulated as plots, are the carriers of such a deep-seated, sticky, commonsensical stock of knowledge. Furthermore, because of their commonsensical nature, narratives point to shared worldviews, that is, to the meanings that the members of a given community have come to take for granted. The deconstruction of organizational narratives should therefore allow the analyst to look at how individuals in organizations articulate knowledge by weaving webs of signification (Geertz 1973). Secondly, narratives emphasize the processual nature of knowing and organizing. Like routines, they act as carriers of tacit knowledge as well as storage devices. However, while routines refer to organization as a clockwork governed by mechanisms of repetition and standardization, narratives exhibit organizations as enacted through discourse and characterized by ongoing processes of transformation and social becoming. The text metaphor reinforces the idea of narratives as instances of knowledge in action. Narratives, articulated as texts, can be seen as material traces of learning and collective remembering processes, social imprints of a meaningful course of events, documents, and records of human action.

Within the framework depicted above, the task of the researcher is simply to describe in detail how organizational actors make sense of equivocal happenings in the work setting while attempting to identify emerging patterns and regularities of action. On the other hand, the focus on narratives has important consequences as far as the relation between actors and observers is concerned. In fact, the observer is him/herself involved in the construction of narrative accounts in order to make sense of certain patterns of behaviour. He/she too engages in the construction of plots (texts) out of equivocal events and in so doing he/she deals with 'interpretation of interpretations' or texts about texts. In this respect the relation between actor and observer may become self-referential in so far as the distinction between the actor and observer's accounts gets blurred. Narratives are a sense-making device in a two-fold sense: they allow actors to articulate knowledge through discourse; and they provide the observer with access to tacit stocks of knowledge that have been externalized in a text-like form. It is therefore important to distinguish between narratives as a methodological lens (focus on actors) and the narrative voice of the observer in describing certain organizational phenomena (see Hatch 1996). The latter relates to issues of rhetoric of representation and will be discussed in Section 3.6.

3.5   The research setting

This research provides an empirical illustration of the three-lens framework based on an in-depth case study conducted at Fiat Auto, Italy. Two organizational settings—a greenfield site and a brownfield one—pointing to different cultural traditions, knowledge, skills, and possibly attitudes towards breakdowns, were considered. Three case studies (two of which concerned the greenfield site and the other the brownfield one) were conducted in two major Fiat plants: 'Mirafiori Presse' in Turin and 'Fiat SATA' in Melfi. The two field sites display a number of differences including the nature of the workforce, the technology deployed, and the factory sub-culture. The Mirafiori Presse plant is an old pressing plant located in the company's headquarters (Turin) and set up in the 1950s. Its highly institutionalized context is characterized by an experienced workforce, often with low levels of education and mostly composed of migrants who came up from the south of Italy during the 1950s and 1960s. In the past, the plant has been notorious for its high levels of conflict in industrial relations and hierarchical managerial practices. Fiat SATA Melfi is one of the most avant-garde assembly plants in the world. The factory, situated in the south of Italy, is a 'green field' site, set up at the end of 1993 and, after an experimental phase, opened officially in October 1994. Melfi's green field can be described as an emergent context, characterized by a young and highly educated workforce recruited from a homogeneous cultural and geographical background. Finally, since its opening Melfi has been the factory with the lowest level of conflict in industrial relations amongst Fiat plants. The two factories also differ in the type of technology/production system employed. The Mirafiori Presse plant produces car parts, the Melfi plant produces cars. The batch production system typical of pressing plants can be seen as a discontinuous system which in theory should display a better tolerance of disruptions and breakdowns. The assembly line that we find in the Melfi factory can instead be characterized as a continuous production system which possibly exhibits a lower tolerance of breakdowns. Production systems can be seen as knowledge systems which have a strong influence on how time is structured, action is punctuated, and, more generally, on how people make sense of their working environment. The two factories were followed throughout a major reengineering process undertaken by the company at the beginning of the 1990s. As mentioned above, this period marked the shift from total automation to a new organizational model known as the 'integrated factory' and designed according to the lessons of 'lean production'. Figure 3.1 summarizes the rationale behind the choice.

At the synchronic level, the selection of the cases is aimed at gaining insight into the multiple faces of knowledge-related phenomena. The design of the three lenses responds to this need. More specifically, the variations in context offered by the cases allow the researcher to gain access to different modes of knowledge creation, utilization, and

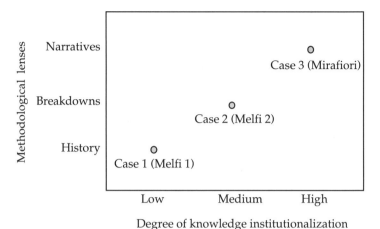

Figure 3.1 *Selection of the cases*

institutionalization. At the same time, the study treats knowledge as a dynamic phenomenon. In this respect, it takes a diachronic perspective in order to follow the transformations that knowledge undergoes over time. The three case studies can be placed on a continuum characterized by increasing levels of knowledge institutionalization. In particular, the distance that separates case 1 from case 3 highlights the presence of polar situations. The latter has been emphasized by the literature (e.g. Pettigrew 1990) as a fundamental requirement for studying processes of change and knowledge transformations over time. The characteristics of the settings illustrated above are consistent with this need. Admittedly, the construction of the Melfi factory from the greenfield takes into account the 'industry recipes' (Spender 1989), and the stock of idiosyncratic knowledge developed by the company over the years. At the same time, the rationale behind the strategic choice of a greenfield site points to crucial dynamics of innovation, namely the need for a fresh start as a pre-condition for implementing a new organizational model. On the other hand, the Mirafiori pressing plant operates according to the principles of the integrated factory model. However, the factory clearly possesses the characteristics of a brownfield, as reflected in the nature of the workforce and the technology used. Finally, the purpose of splitting the Melfi case in two was to assess the process of institutionalization of knowledge during the period that runs from the induction phase of the factory to its operation at full capacity. The position of case 2 on the continuum ideally links the other two cases by stressing elements of change and continuity in the process of knowledge institutionalization. In so doing it points to possible trends in the evolution of organizational knowledge over time.

3.6 How do we write the story: rhetoric of representation and the problem of validity

In this concluding section, I shall go back to the methodological problems highlighted at the beginning of this chapter in order to analyse the relationship between the rhetorical forms of representation of theory and the problem of validity. I will argue that most of the difficulties in articulating interpretative theories are related to the language and discursive paradigms adopted by the analyst. I will then reconsider Geertz's account of the Bali cockfight and suggest that its narrative structure could provide a template for the cases contained in this book.

Recent years have witnessed a 'silent qualitative revolution' (Denzin and Lincoln 1994). The growing popularity of qualitative methodologies has mostly derived from the numerous attempts to structure and systematize the basic rules of method while defining (nebulous) criteria for assessing interpretative validity. Admittedly, the validity of a given empirical study and of the method informing it rests on the use of shared interpretative categories that have been legitimized within a certain community. These categories are socially constructed and reflect the institutional canons whereby knowledge is produced, codified and transferred in a given environment. However, the presence of institutional canons of appraisal have brought important consequences for the modes of representing theory in qualitative research. Interpretation, far from being an imaginative act (a fiction, a 'making'), has become, in some cases, almost mechanical.

Let us consider the conventional way of writing down or presenting a research study.[2] We normally use frameworks, variables, and conceptual categories to circumscribe our descriptions and render them meaningful to the scientific community. In doing so, we also expropriate our account from its value for the community under study ('natives'). We artificially divorce description from interpretation and elevate the order of the latter towards the abstract. It this precisely at that moment that the narrator is detached from his/her own account. He/she no longer speaks with the voice of the characters; instead an institutional voice

---

[2] Another good example is the quasi-compulsory use of slides in conference presentations. Here the mere use of the medium is a way of legitimizing the value of a study.

bursts into the picture. The narrator has stopped conversing with the natives and is now addressing his/her words to the broader academic community, matching the institutional canons of his/her research environment.

The heavy reliance on abstract categories and the tendency to set clear cut distinctions between description and interpretation, data collection and analysis, may at times render the phenomenon under study almost transparent. In the field of organization studies, this may lead to a situation where all organizations look the same no matter what their activity is. They become dead entities and their uniqueness is lost. The above considerations emphasize the need for bringing to life the entity under study and letting the phenomena speak with their own voice. Ideally, the interpretative account should give the reader the feeling of being there.[3]

Let us go back for a moment to the Bali cockfight and to its narrative structure. The thick description of the event involves speaking about the cocks and their sacred value, the spectators, the rules of the game, the homology between the betting system and the class system in Bali. It is by introducing new elements and new relationships into the picture that the social system of Balinese society is gradually uncovered and disclosed to the reader. We have also seen that one of the major problems that the observer has to face is how to harness the complexity of the relations generated in the description and eventually decide where to stop the narration. In fact, the construction of a plot and its closure are vital for interpretation.

Following Geertz, it is possible to depict the narrative structure of the Bali cockfight as a web of signification (see Figure 3.2). The storyline is developed by drawing concentric circles that move from the particular towards the general, from description towards interpretation. The circles are held together by rays departing from the core event (the cockfight) and moving outwards. The narrative texture is such that the conceptual world of the Balinese community is gradually disclosed to the reader.[4] More importantly, the verisimilitude of the account seems to rest on the author's ability to clarify what goes on within the community under study, to reduce the puzzlement of the reader in the face of an unfamiliar world: validity becomes a matter of authorship and difference (Geertz 1988).

---

[3] An outstanding example is Latour's (1987) description of laboratory life where the author imagines conversations going on between scientists and creates semiotic characters that serve the purpose of the narration.

[4] The same narrative structure applies to the example of the shop floor provided earlier.

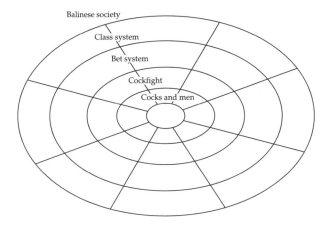

Figure 3.2 *Narrative structure of the Balinese cockfight*

Undoubtedly, problems of generalization and theoretical formulation are strongly related to the nature of interpretative sciences. However, they also depend on the rhetoric of representation of a given phenomenon within different sciences. Typically, positive sciences find articulation through scientific essays, whereas humanities refer to literature. The interdisciplinary nature of social sciences generates a fundamental ambiguity between their ambition to be exact sciences and the objective limitations stemming from the nature of the phenomena observed. In the field of organization studies this ambiguity is reflected in two distinctive modes of representation. On the one hand, the geometrical-positivist way of representing organizational phenomena, with tables, matrices, circles, boxes, and arrows, Cartesian axes, and bullet points; on the other hand, the post-modernist way, with its minimalist argumentations, its loose and cryptic accounts, whose purpose is often difficult to grasp. This tension points to the need to combine different modes of representation.

To some extent, thick description can offer a satisfactory solution to the problem of rhetorical representation. As I have shown above, the major strength of thick description lies in its ability to generate references, to penetrate the boundaries of any organized form of activity, thus providing rich accounts of social actions. It is the task of the researcher to decide in which directions to point the description and to provide a holistic picture of the broader phenomena in which a small fact is inscribed. Like a captain, he/she needs to be in control of drifting and keep his/her ship on course. He/she needs to find a balance between creativity and authority, govern the tension between discovery and appropriation. Thick description is about patiently weaving webs of signification, drawing concentric circles by moving from small matters to general truths, creating interpretative structures which, like a spider's web, are difficult to spot and easy to break.

To sum up, a writing strategy should serve the purpose of addressing the main research questions of a study in a coherent way by combining inductive and deductive lines of reasoning. In other words, any 'argument building strategy' aimed at detecting patterns, categories, and analytical reasoning needs a 'text building strategy' which makes the construction of the argument possible. For example, the text building strategy of the Balinese cockfight analysed above allows the author to uncover 'deep' social structures. This is achieved through a web-like construction moving in a centrifugal manner towards deeper structures of signification. As I mentioned earlier, such a strategy presents the difficulty of reaching a closure which basically rests upon the craft of the author rather than the presence of objective boundaries.

Part Two

Organizational Knowledge in Action

4

Tradition and Innovation at Fiat Auto

4.1 Introduction

This chapter intends to set the background to the description of the case studies by providing a brief outline of the firm's origins, business activities, and organizational model. Specifically, the chapter relies on longitudinal analysis techniques combining business history (the evolution of management composition and organizational models) with labour history methods (the relationship between company and labour movements). On the one hand, it outlines the evolution of production systems and organizational models within the company. From this vantage point, three main organizational phases are considered: (1) the early introduction of mass production systems after the Second World War, acting as a backbone for the company's expansion throughout the 1950s and 1960s; (2) the investments in heavy automation during the 1970s, leading to the adoption of a high-tech factory model at the beginning of the 1980s; (3) the paradigm shift from Fordism to lean production at the beginning of the 1990s epitomized by the introduction of the so-called 'integrated factory' model. At the same time, the chapter analyses the historical background against which organizational change takes place. Here, the main line of argument revolves around the presence of conflict, both in the form of strikes and militant antagonism, as a pervasive feature of the history of Fiat. Admittedly, the vicissitudes of Italian industry have mirrored the tensions, contradictions, and radical conflicts characterizing the economic development of the country since the Second World War. Under these circumstances, Fiat seems to embody the archetype of industrial conflict. Significantly, Mirafiori, the largest factory in Italy, has been defined as the 'factory of factories' (Berta 1998*a*) in order to stress its archetypal nature so ingrained in the cultural identity of the country. As Berta (1998*b*) has observed, the imprinting underlying the relations between work and the company seems to be characterized by supremacy games occurring against a background of high instability and conflict rather than being governed by procedures of reciprocal legitimization. Under these circumstances, beyond destructive effects, conflict acts as a phenomenal catalyst for change, affecting both the strategy and the management's composition of the company. The next section outlines a profile of the company by describing its main business operations as well as by providing a series of significant performance indicators. Sections 4.3–4.5 analyse the distinctive chronological phases characterizing the development of the company. Finally, Section 4.6 presents the main structural principles underlying the organizational model currently adopted by Fiat at the plant level, and hence in the plants considered in this study.

4.2   General: The Fiat Group

Fiat—an acronym for Fabbrica Italiana Automobili Torino—was founded in Turin in 1899. By the first decade of the new century, with the industrialization of its manufacturing processes, it had become Italy's most important car-making concern. Initially created to build cars, it immediately diversified production into the fields of commercial vehicles, ships, airplanes, trains, agricultural tractors, and construction machinery. The development of its production was soon followed by expansion abroad. From the 1950s, a new burst of international development took the company into more than 180 different markets. In the past twenty years, the Fiat Group has expanded into new manufacturing areas linked to its original activities by industrial, commercial, and financial synergy.

Today, with revenues of more than Euro 57 billion, Fiat is one of the world's largest industrial groups, operating in 61 countries with 1063 companies that employ over 223,000 people, 111,000 of whom outside Italy. The Group runs 242 manufacturing plants (167 abroad) and 131 research and development centres (61 abroad). 46 per cent of production is generated outside Italy, while exports account for over 67 per cent of sales. Fiat Group companies are organized into 10 operating Sectors: Automobiles, Agricultural and Construction Machinery, Commercial Vehicles, Metallurgical Products, Components, Production Systems, Aviation, Publishing and Communications, and Insurance and Services.

Fiat Auto manufactures automobiles and light commercial vehicles. Currently, the automotive division employs about 74,000 people and sells its products in the international markets under the Fiat, Lancia, and Alfa Romeo brands. Fiat's car business has been traditionally based on small cars and on the Italian market. Some observers have seen the narrow focus of the firm's operations as a source of competitive disadvantage. For example, Camuffo and Volpato (1994) have observed that Fiat's two-fold strategy entailed a specialized stock of competencies, narrowing the scope of future strategic options. However, in the past decade, Fiat Auto has been implementing a purposeful strategy of globalization aimed at strengthening its manufacturing presence in the fastest growing markets. The company is directing its efforts to emerging countries with the highest potential for the growth of demand in the medium and long term (e.g. Brazil, Argentina, Russia, China, and India) although initiatives are undertaken with a policy of modular investment in order to limit possible risks.[1] Globalization activities at Fiat Auto focus primarily on the production of models in the World Car family (e.g. the Fiat Palio). Since its launch the Palio has given Fiat the lead over Volkswagen in the Brazilian market, which accounts for 70 per cent of all the South American sales (Economist 1998). The Palio won the 'Caro de ano 2001' prize in Brazil.

In 2000, Fiat Auto sold 2,439,000 cars in the world and achieved net revenues of Euro 25,361 million. Customers outside Italy purchased approximately 60 per cent of the total output. Car sales were split roughly three ways between Italy, Europe and the rest of the world. During the same year, Fiat entered into an important industrial alliance with General Motors, which led to the creation of two 50–50 joint ventures in the areas of purchasing and powertrain production. Following this agreement the Sector was reorganized, a new parent company, Fiat Auto Holdings B.V., was created (80 per cent Fiat, 20 per cent General Motors (GM)), and Fiat acquired 6 per cent of the American company. And in June 2001 the Sector's powertrain activities were transferred to the Fiat–GM Powertrain joint venture.

Since its founding, Fiat has manufactured over 70 million vehicles, many of which represent milestones in the history of automobile development. During the last four years, three Fiat Auto models have been selected as Car of the Year: the Fiat Punto (1995), the Fiat Bravo/Brava (96), the Alfa Romeo 156 (1998), and the Alfa Romeo 147 (2001). The Fiat Group's portfolio of automotive brands also include Ferrari and Maserati.

4.3   The years of perennial conflict (1919–79)

Fiat automobiles were initially conceived as a luxury item designed for a consumer elite. The early history of the company saw the gradual

---

[1] The recent economic crisis in Argentina is an example of such risks.

introduction of mass production schemes. This approach reflected the vision of the founder Giovanni Agnelli, who was already planning methods to strengthen the production system. The result was the Lingotto Project—in its day, the biggest automotive complex in Europe—which came on stream in 1922. The project was based on a specific strategy: to transform the automobile from a product for the elite to one available to the steadily growing mass of ordinary consumers. This was accomplished thanks to the new principles of industrial organization based on the assembly line.

Since its early days the history of Fiat was punctuated by high levels of conflict unfolding in parallel with the two world wars. Up to the 1950s, conflict was partly a continuation of the social agitation following the Second World War, which gradually led to the emergence of a highly politicized labour movement. This period was characterized by strikes, struggles, and reciprocal opposition between the unions and the company management. As Berta (1998*b*) pointed out, the two parties seemed to perceive the contest in the workplace as an exclusive match played out against the backdrop of the Cold War (Berta 1998*b*: 14).

In the post-war period, with Vittorio Valletta replacing Giovanni Agnelli at the top of the company, Fiat fully developed mass production schemes, drawing on the booming Italian economy and the unions' weakness. A key element in this expansion was the Mirafiori plant, inaugurated in 1939 to enlarge production capacities. Fiat's strategy based on high production volumes, cost efficiency and Fordist work organization, required strict control of workers' behaviour (Camuffo and Volpato 1994). In this respect, the 1950s were characterized by a systematic repression strategy pursued by the company to weaken the organizational roots of the labour movement. In the course of the cold war fought within the factory, the scales seemed to tilt towards the company. However, a reversal occurred in the following decade, leading to the so-called 'hot autumn'. The 1960s inaugurated a phase of predominance by the unions that would last until 1980. The high levels of conflict through the 1960s and 1970s marked the pinnacle of the union's power. In the face of the increasing power of the unions, Fiat decided to engage in an open confrontation in order to restore the authority of the company within the production sites. The period 1968–80 comprises the extremities of the major phase of conflict in the company's history, conveying an image of industry as a source of unbearable social contradictions. A few significant features are indicative of the scale of the conflict. During the 'hot autumn' of 1969, strikes amounted to 9 million hours, the equivalent of 270,000 cars lost. This level remained constant throughout the 1970s: 4 million hours of strikes in 1970; more than 3 million in 1971; 4.5 million in 1972; 12 million in 1973; and so on until the end of the decade (Berta 1998*a*). From 1972 terrorist attacks occurred against both union representatives and managers (throughout the 1970s Italy was hit by a strong wave of terrorism). The oil shock reduced the company's capacity for investment, while the introduction of wage indexation (index-linked pay scale) raised labour costs substantially, affecting Fiat's productivity and competitiveness (Camuffo and Volpato 1994).

Berta (1998*b*) describes the conflict cycle characterizing the period 1919–79 as a pendulum oscillating between the company and the workers and periodically redistributing the role of winners and losers. He sees the evolutionary process of Industrial Relations (IR) at Fiat as a sinusoidal movement: the apex corresponds with peak levels of conflict, while the lowest points represent a stasis in the strikes occasioned by a power shift in favour of the firm. Accordingly, collective bargaining activity seems to follow a zero sum game logic dominated by supremacy games. This opposition between Fiat and the labour movement emphasizes a low capacity for the consensual production of shared norms. It also highlights a form of path-dependency where the institutional production structure appears to be precarious and uncertain. In this respect, the 1980s inaugurated a new phase characterized by the end of antagonism and militant confrontation.

4.4   From Fordism to the high-tech factory (1980–89)

After 1980, industrial relations at Fiat seemed to lose much of their militant and antagonistic character. Camuffo and Volpato (1994) have characterized the early 1980s as a phase of managerial unilateralism and union demise. A turning point in this phase was the so-called 'march of the 40,000' in October 1980, during which a 'silent majority' of workers (mostly middle-managers) stood up against the protest strike that had led to the shut down of the firm for five weeks.[2]

The company took this opportunity to adopt a tough line against the unions and the state in negotiating the labour implications of the process of restructuring. Total automation was one of the pillars of the restructuring process. Admittedly, the adoption of the Fordist paradigm at Fiat

---

[2] The strike was called by the unions in response to the management announcement of an imminent layoff of 14,469 workers.

had been characterized by the presence of high levels of automation since the 1970s. According to Camuffo and Volpato (1994), the automation choice, at least initially, was part of a defensive strategy enacted in response to the increasing levels of conflict within the company, which had led to conspicuous losses in productivity (see Section 4.3). In this way, the company aimed to reduce conflicts by improving ergonomy and working conditions, while making production less dependent on workers' consent and participation. The same strategy was conceived as a means of bypassing union control on work organization. The technology strategy was successfully pursued throughout the 1980s, becoming a sort of organizational paradigm.

In fact, at the beginning of the 1980s, Fiat embarked on the high-tech factory concept which privileged intense automation to yield high productivity and quality, while reducing the role of human work drastically. The high level of investment in so-called 'flexible technology' was supposed to compensate for the rigidities of the Fordist production system and to adapt to the fluctuations in the market. Termoli and Cassino, the first examples of high-tech factories, were considered at that time to be the most technologically advanced plants in the world.

At the same time, total automation was part of a labour saving policy aimed at the substitution of human labour with machines. In the years between 1980 and 1986 the workforce was reduced by 57,000 employees (42 per cent of the total workforce) (Cersosimo 1994).

The high-tech factory model brought positive effects in the short term by yielding higher productivity and a decrease in production costs. Productivity per employee rose from 15 to 28 cars, bringing a simultaneous decrease in labour costs from 28 to 17 per cent of the company's turnover. In 1989 Fiat, the only Italian car manufacturer, reached a record production level of 1,971,969 cars, placing Italy fifth in the world rankings (Cersosimo 1994). Given the outstanding performance of the Italian company throughout the 1980s, the crisis that was about to hit the European and American automotive sector did not seem to be perceived by the Fiat management. However, the flaws inherent in the high-tech factory model emerged dramatically in 1990, when the effects of a worldwide crisis in the automotive sector together with the success of Japanese car manufacturers brought radical changes in the strategies and organizational models underlying the traditional mass production systems.

Fiat's two-fold specialization, which had represented a source of competitive advantage until that moment, turned into a 'core rigidity' (Leonard-Barton 1992*a*) highlighting the incapacity of the company to penetrate foreign markets and to respond to the trend towards integration and globalization of the market.[3] The same fate befell the marketing policy based on high production volumes and low prices, and supported by Fordist mass production systems. This strategy, which prioritized quantity over quality, was supplanted by the new way of producing and selling cars put forward by Japanese companies, based on customer orientation and commitment to high quality standards.

At the organizational level, Fiat's technocentric approach revealed some crucial mismatches. Technological investments had not been supported by innovation in managerial and organizational models. In fact, the high-tech factory was still operating within a Taylorist–Fordist paradigm. The dominance of the 'hardware' (technology) over the software (organization) led to increasing difficulties in the capacity to harness the complexity of the technical system. Technology was supposed to govern the production system, but no mechanisms had been devised to govern the technology. Technological rigidities quickly started to emerge: the highly sophisticated technological system was not able to cope with continuous disruptions and, although non-conflicting, even robots did not seem to be reliable. As a result, the quality of the cars decreased without a simultaneous increase in productivity.

At the end of 1989, in a dramatic speech at the annual company convention, the Chief Executive Officer (CEO) of Fiat Cesare Romiti recognized for the first time the superiority of the Japanese production system. His analysis of the state of the company highlighted the need to raise overall levels of efficiency, improving the quality standard of the products and reducing time to market. On that occasion he announced Fiat's new commitment to total quality and to the principles of lean production. This was the prelude to the 'integrated factory' model, which would put an end to the Taylorist–Fordist phase at Fiat and bring in a new production paradigm informed by the principles of Toyotism and lean production. As we shall see in Chapter 5, this paradigm shift entailed renegotiating the existing IR policies. The pillars of the reengineering process are illustrated in the next section.

4.5 The integrated factory model (1990s)

The deceptive results delivered by the high-tech factory concept and the lessons learned from 'lean production' (Womack et al. 1990) have led

---

[3] It is important to remark that throughout the 1980s Fiat had pursued a policy of disinvestment in overseas markets, which were considered not profitable, leading to the closure of overseas plants. This stands in sharp contrast to the current strategy of Fiat overseas.

Fiat to the implementation of a new production concept known as the *integrated factory*. The Melfi plant, described in the next two chapters, is the first example of this organizational revolution. The apparent shift from automation to integration, from flexible to lean technology, is attributable to the management's newly acquired awareness that quality cannot be the outcome of sophisticated technology alone, if there is little or no involvement of the workforce. The new philosophy of integration tries to reconcile a high-tech infrastructure (including extensive use of robotics) and the rigid synchronization of the assembly line, with elements typical of the job shop (such as working in teams).

Lean technology means, first and foremost, less technology. Admittedly, the backbone of the integrated factory is still the traditional assembly line, which makes it possible to transform a sequence of orders as specified by the market into a linear, sequential production process. What really changes is the interface between man and machine, which involves a shift in the concept of automation from substitution to delegation: within the flexible technology model the professional capabilities of the workforce were subordinated to the governance of the technical system; with lean technology, the technical system is explicitly designed in order to promote the development of the potential capabilities of human capital.

The new model required consensus. This led the company to define IR policies characterized by a new attention to Human Resource Management (HRM). A number of accords with the unions at the beginning of the 1990s created the conditions for the institutionalization of a collective bargaining framework. Camuffo and Volpato (1994) have identified four emergent themes in the bargaining process:

- work hours and shifts;
- work organization and cycle times;
- reward system;
- union–management relationships.

The need for higher levels of productivity, quality and efficiency required negotiating new work schemes. For instance, in the new Melfi plant work hours were based on three daily shifts, six days a week, eight hours per shift. Another important innovation regarded the flexibility of cycle times. In the light of the accord of June 1993, line speed could be increased up to a maximum of 10 per cent to allow for recoveries of productivity levels in the face of line stoppages.

The higher level of flexibility on the part of the workforce was compensated by the creation of new performance-related incentive schemes based on suggestion systems and competitiveness rewards. Likewise, IR policies were re-designed according to collaborative patterns, thanks to the introduction of bilateral union–management committees at the plant level.[4] Although the above policies did not define a fully-fledged participatory model (unions were just consulted on decisions taken by the company), they recognized an important institutional presence of the unions within the process of change and innovation that Fiat is still undergoing.

Overall, the above innovations seem to have promoted a better climate in the workplace by fostering communication and information sharing, improving trust relationships among different organizational actors, and framing the complexity of the production process in a common language.

4.6   The crystal pipeline: Principles and structure of the integrated factory

The integrated factory is divided into Operating Units (OU) responsible for the different stages of the production process. For example, the typical assembly plant comprises four stages: Stamping, Body Welding, Painting, and Assembly. The OUs co-operate in defining the daily production plan, monitoring the advancement of production, and managing critical situations. The longer term production plans are defined at Fiat's head office in Turin. Each OU is divided into a number of UTEs (Elementary Technical Units).[5] The UTE, which comprises between 80 and 100 workers and supervisors spread over three shifts, is the basic production structure of the integrated factory.[6] It can be seen as a semi-autonomous minifactory managing a whole segment of the production process. Specific objectives and results are assigned to each UTE, such as productivity, quality, budget, mix, and quantity. A UTE has a head supported by a staff of technical specialists

---

[4] Here, two major innovations have been introduced: (a) consulting committees, where the firm reports to the unions about the results on quality and productivity; (b) participation committees, which team-up plant managers and union representatives in order to facilitate workers' participation (Camuffo and Volpato 1994).

[5] Throughout the study I will maintain the Italian acronym UTE, which stands for 'Unità Tecnologica Elementare'.

[6] The above figure represents the average size. The size of UTEs varies according to the OU in which they are located and the nature of the tasks performed at that production stage. For example, UTEs in the assembly unit are characterized by manual operations and accordingly employ more operators than highly automated units.

dedicated to repairing and maintenance tasks (the 'technologists'). The institutional nucleus of the UTE also includes a group of specialist and generic workers, whilst a number of *ad hoc* figures can be called upon to intervene in the event of a concrete problem. Finally, co-ordination among the different UTEs is entrusted to the Operations Manager, who also acts as the hierarchical chief of the UTE heads. Typically, a UTE controls one or more production lines, which are split into a varying number of workplaces occupied by one or two workers (or robots in the automated OUs). The number of workplaces depends on the number of elementary operations which have to be carried out in order to complete a given production sequence.

The organizational principles of the integrated factory model stress the importance of the production process over functional specialization. Decisions are taken where problems arise and where specific competencies exist for their solution. Accordingly, problem-solving and the management of the workflow are delegated to the work team, which stays at the core of the production process. Interestingly, the UTE can be considered as a socio-technical system in that it connects two distinct elements: a socio-organizational one—the 'team', a collective way of working, collaboration, the intimacy of staying together and sharing; and a technical one, the world of machinery and equipment (see Ciborra 1996). The delegation of decision-making to work teams makes it possible to run factory operations with a reduced number of hierarchical levels. In fact, the integrated factory presents two fewer hierarchical levels with respect to the previous organizational structure (see Figure 4.1). A quick look at the two figures highlights the leaner structure of the new organizational model. First of all, the governance of the production process is simplified with the decentralization of previous organizational functions at the level of OUs and UTEs. In addition, the adoption of team working practices leads to the elimination of the traditional foreman figures.

The modular organization fosters fluidity and integration of production processes and ensures a high degree of flexibility. The various units composing the organizational structure are linked according to an *internal customer model*, which means that each UTE must think of the next process as its 'customer'. More generally, the whole production system is organized as a customer-driven market in which activities are structured as a network of flows and transactions among semi-autonomous units. The lean production logic implies producing only the amount required by the customer, at high quality, low cost, and at the time needed. The production lines are organized in a way

Traditional high-tech factory

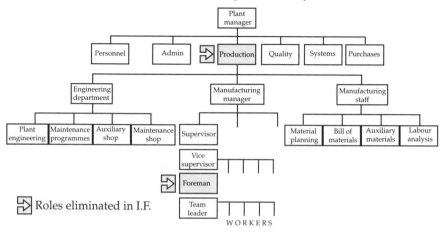

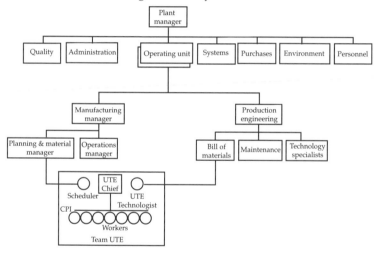

Integrated factory

Figure 4.1 *Changes in Fiat's organizational structure at the plant level*

that allows every workplace (and therefore UTE) to receive and pass on a 'finished product' that can be judged for its quality.

The information system reproducing the production process in the smallest detail is built according to the logic of 'systemic visibility'. Rather than depicting the status of local workstations or operations, emphasis is placed on systemic implications: it is information about the causal relationship between what is happening in one point of the work flow and the production process as a whole. Through the public diffusion of information the production process is rendered transparent.

Within the logic of lean production and just-in-time (JIT), systemic visibility should bring the inconsistencies in the production process to the surface and lead to solutions aimed at maintaining a dynamic equilibrium among the different parts of the organization's techno-structure (Cerruti 1994).

Bonazzi (1993) has described the integrated factory model as a 'crystal pipeline'. The pipeline represents the continuous flow as it was originally conceived: a simple, linear structure in which work-in-process flows. The pipeline is open to market demand and the workflow is structured by a rigid orders schedule, which is imposed from Fiat headquarters according to the productive mix required by demand. The image of the pipeline that portrays lean production indicates a rigid synchronization of all the processes occurring inside it and a high level of collaboration among the different units. But the pipeline is made of crystal, material that evokes the idea of transparency and fragility. Transparency means first eliminating waste and defects. Second, avoiding informal stocks and slack, and thus curbing shirking and other forms of opportunistic behaviour. Third, making all available knowledge explicit: work is made transparent and 'textualized' (Zuboff 1988) by representing all relevant aspects of the workflow through a *visual control system*. The fragility of the pipeline is related to the rigid synchronization of the workflows and to the lean production concept. Since bottlenecks and the piling up of inventories can disrupt the flow and break the pipeline at any moment, everything in the plant has been synchronized with the purpose of avoiding bottlenecks, work-in-process inventories, and buffers.

4.7   Conclusion

The beginning of the new millennium marked a period of transition for the Fiat Group. A shortfall was particularly evident at Fiat Auto, which suffered from a tough cashflow situation and strong competitive pressures—particularly in the intermediate segment, where its products were reaching the end of their life-cycle. The reasons for the crisis were manifold and included among other factors the worldwide recession and the consequent downturn in the auto sector; the collapsing markets in Brazil, Argentina, Poland, and Turkey, where Fiat had big operations; and the mixed success of Fiat's latest medium-sized model, the Stilo, which was falling short of its sales targets.

The financial crisis called into question the overall strategy that Fiat had pursued throughout the 1990s, especially in relation to diversification, strategic alliances, globalization policies, brand management, and product innovation. Fiat attempted to respond to the challenges that existed within its organization and to the deterioration of the business climate by pursuing a radical process of strategic renewal. A key step in this process was the industrial alliance with General Motors in 2000, which created a unique business model in the international automobile industry. The alliance contract allowed GM to acquire a 20 per cent stake in Fiat Auto and included an option to sell Fiat Auto to GM after 2004. The agreement would enable Fiat Auto to benefit from economies of scale made possible by a twofold increase in the manufacturing base, while at the same time gaining access to the global resources—especially R&D—of the world's largest car maker and maximizing its distinctive competencies. This relationship with General Motors opened up interesting prospects for the re-entry of Alfa Romeo into the North American market.

However, the financial crisis escalated in 2002 and brought Fiat to the brink of collapse. As a result of the factors discussed above, Fiat's market share worldwide (and especially in Europe) has continued to be eroded and sales have dropped from 2.6 million cars in 1997 to 1.7 million in 2002. The car business is losing money at a rapid pace while worries over Fiat's debts have driven down the share price of the group. Fiat's European factories are working below their production capacity and the company has recently announced 8,100 job cuts across the group's car factories. Despite the desperate measures taken to save the car business, many analysts think that this is Fiat's worst ever crisis and predict that the group will be forced to exercise the put option with GM before the 2004 deadline.

Under these circumstances, the distinctive industrial heritage and structural repertoire of the company will affect the new strategic development of the Fiat Group and impinge upon the very survival of its car business.

5

Knowledge-In-The-Making: The 'Construction' of Fiat's Melfi Factory

5.1 Introduction

The purpose of this chapter, the first part of a double length case study, is to analyse the action-based processes of knowing and organizing surrounding the coming into existence of one of the most advanced car manufacturing plants in the world: Fiat's Melfi assembly plant.[1] This new 'green field' factory features a lean production organization, work flow based on assembly lines and teams, advanced applications of IT (Information Technology) to production management and control, and extensive reliance on total quality management (Ciborra, Patriotta, and Erlicher 1996). Beyond technical specifications, however, the most interesting feature of the plant is that it has been built with the active involvement of the workforce. Indeed, the Fiat management conceived the whole Melfi project as a learning experiment based on a greenfield strategy where the future workers would literally build the factory, including the place and the setting where they would be assembling cars. The experiment had no antecedents in Fiat's history and the whole project relied on a young and inexperienced workforce.

The deliberate strategy of Fiat's management was that a human-centred design would ensure workers' participation and consensus and thereby have a positive impact on the overall performance of the factory; and indeed everything in the present situation of the factory seems to confirm the soundness of such theory. Still, together with intended ones, emergent phenomena were also produced in the course of factory construction which turned out to be crucial for the success of the Melfi project. The distinctive character of the factory was the outcome of an endogenous process of institutionalization of collective

---

[1] Melfi is the largest greenfield plant in Europe (Production 1995). In 1998 Melfi ranked third in Europe in terms of productivity, according to a table published yearly by the Economist Intelligence Unit. In 1999 productivity fell slightly—moving the plant into fourth place—owing to the introduction of the new Punto model. In 2000, despite a further drop, Melfi still ranked in the top ten.

action which seems to have been largely invisible to the designers of the Melfi project, and to the workers themselves. Building the factory involved a kind of learning that went beyond resource development, skill acquisition and workers' participation. In a way, such learning transcended the problems of performance and consensus that were at the core of the HR-based strategy, and more significantly had to do with a knowledge-making endeavour that touched the deeper domains of value and identity. If we take this perspective on the design experiment, the factory becomes different things at the same time: it is an artefact to be assembled, a tool to be used in assembling the car, a medium for knowing and interacting, a formative context (Unger 1987; Blackler 1992; Ciborra and Lanzara 1994).

This chapter is an effort to understand the many facets of the Melfi project. Particularly, I am interested in exploring the foundational and generative mechanisms underlying the making of the factory. Drawing on the time lens, I want to track the process whereby a complex manufacturing machine and the associated institutional order of the factory came into existence in a relatively short period and were encoded into stable organizational structures, procedures, and other artefacts. In the remainder of the chapter I tell the story of the Melfi project as it unfolded over time. Following Latour (1987), the strategy of investigation adopted in the case study will be to follow the characters on the 'construction site' while they are 'busy at work'.[2] A short journey in space and time will take us to the Melfi greenfield at the moment when the construction works of the factory are about to begin. Here, we will follow the phases from the design concept of the factory to its formal opening. The latter marks the technical black boxing of the original nucleus of organizational knowledge developed on the greenfield and, at the same time, provides the 'closure' point for the analysis.

The longitudinal study of the knowledge-creating processes surrounding the making of the factory emphasized the presence of systemic capabilities through which workers and managers were able to connect the details of production to the original experience of building the factory from the greenfield. The progressive appropriation of the factory by its final users resulted in the acquisition of distinctive competencies

---

[2] The analysis focuses on the role of young managers, middle managers and technicians in the process of learning and knowledge acquisition over the greenfield. The choice of the sample is justified by the fact that these profiles were those most closely involved in the training process surrounding the coming into existence of the factory. In particular, given their connecting function within the new integrated factory model (i.e. 'being in the middle'), middle-managers are considered by the company as a crucial asset in the process of knowledge creation and transfer.

based on a pervasive identity between the experience of assembling the factory on the construction site and the task of assembling the car on the shop floor. Under these circumstances, the ability to grasp the inner workings of the assembly line seemed to be grounded on the experience of having built it, rather than on a mere technical understanding of the equipment itself.

At the overarching meta-level, the study highlighted a distinctive pattern of knowledge creation and transfer relating to the content and the process of the learning experience. Learning seemed to occur in the form of progressive ownership processes connected to different aspects of work: the role, the task, the product and production process, and most importantly the workplace itself. Rather than a sheer knowledge transmission model, going from a knowledgeable source to a passive recipient, ownership processes imply taking a pro-active role on the part of the learners. As a consequence, knowledge creation appeared as the outcome of interacting forces working according to 'specification–delegation' chains. The latter underscores the interplay between top–down and bottom–up processes, planned and emergent factors involved in the design and implementation of the Melfi project.

This chapter is organized as follows. Section 5.2 elaborates a conceptual framework for the case study based on a review of two conflicting perspectives on organizational learning. Section 5.3 describes the main phases characterizing the unfolding of the Melfi project, identifying knowledge sources and outcomes, learning settings and organizational actors involved in each phase. Sections 5.4 and 5.5 review the chronological advancement of the Melfi project in order to identify both the learning-specific outcomes relating to each phase, and the pervasive patterns of knowledge creation underpinning it. The chapter concludes with some considerations about the sedimentary nature of competence and the importance of approaching knowledge-related phenomena from the point of view of knowledge-in-the-making.

5.2   Two perspectives on organizational learning

Conventional learning and training theories are based on a pedagogical perspective which sees learning as the outcome of a knowledge transmission process between a knowledgeable source and a passive recipient. Within this perspective, the details of practice, the communities of practitioners, and the setting in which the learning experience takes place are specifically excluded (Brown and Duguid 1991). Interestingly, training in the work situation seems to fall within this instructional paradigm, as the following definition, quoted from a glossary of training terms, suggests: 'a planned process to modify attitudes, knowledge or skill behaviour through learning experience to achieve effective performance in an activity or range of activities. Its purpose, in the work situation, is to develop the abilities of the individual and to satisfy the current and future manpower needs of the organization' (quoted in Jones 1994).

More recent theories have rejected transfer models which isolate knowledge from practice and emphasized the social, situated nature of the learning experience. A chief claim of situated learning theories is that knowledge is embodied in praxis (Pentland 1992) and that learning takes place through participation within 'communities of practice' (Lave and Wenger 1991). Rather than being a passive recipient, the community of learners is constantly engaged in sense-making and interpretation activities whereby knowledge is appropriated out of a wide range of materials. The latter include 'ambient social and physical circumstances and the histories and social relations of the people involved' (Brown and Duguid 1991). Accordingly, what is learned is profoundly connected to the conditions in which it is learned. Importantly, learning is about identity construction through engagement in social practices, including the construction of diverse social bonds with other participants or co-workers. The identity building aspect of the learning experience is captured by the notion of legitimate peripheral participation (Lave and Wenger 1991) according to which learning involves becoming an 'insider', acquiring a particular community's subjective viewpoint and learning to speak its language. Finally, the situated approach is consistent with adult learning theories. In his extensive review of the literature on the topic, Jones (1994) emphasizes the importance of self-directed learning and active participation in the construction of learning events, as opposed to the traditional teacher–learner principle. For example, adults seem to learn most effectively through experience, and by means of actual day-to-day jobs and routines (learning by doing) rather than from formal and structured training programmes. In this regard, meaningful adult learning occurs when it is based on problem-solving and connects with a person's general life events and activities. Accordingly, adult learning is seen as a lifetime process continually shaped by the experience of the past.

The two paradigms described above are characterized by Jones and Hendry (1994) as 'hard' learning, which is pragmatic, formal and brought about through prescribed training, and 'soft' learning, which has a more subtle nature and is concerned with the social context which shapes the learning process. Accordingly, they imply different perspectives on the agents of the knowledge-creation process and the learning path underlying this process. Schematically, the instructional paradigm emphasizes the planned factors of the training process and the fact that knowledge transmission occurs in a top–down manner. Situated learning, by contrast, seems to view the dynamics of knowledge creation through learning as a bottom–up process shaped by those factors emerging along the way.

As we shall see, besides being a physical location, the greenfield site here under study represents a particular situation, a learning setting characterized by distinctive contextual features, where a community of learners is undergoing a peculiar experience. In order to convey the uniqueness of this experience, the case described below adopts a situated perspective, focusing on two important aspects of the appropriation and learning processes surrounding the coming into existence of the new factory. The first emphasizes the holistic character of the learning experience. As Winograd and Flores (1986) have pointed out, any technological artefact is situated or dwells in a heterogeneous network that includes other equipment, materials, institutional arrangements, practices, and conventions. Accordingly, any learning process is shaped by the encounter between heterogeneous sources and multiple outcomes. The second concerns the sense-making and interpretation dynamics underlying the learning experience. The construction of the factory can be compared to the introduction of an 'alien' object which has to be 'metabolized' and placed into context by the community of practitioners in order to represent and understand events related to it.

5.3   The making of a factory

The SATA plant at Melfi is one of those exceptional plants—like the Toyota-managed NUMMI plant in California (Adler 1993) and Volvo's small scale Udevalla factory (Berggren 1994)—which have recently attracted the attention of the media for their outstanding levels of performance and innovative learning methods (e.g. Fortune 1994; Economist 1998). The plant produces the leading Fiat model, the Punto, today one of the best selling cars in Europe. The factory, situated in the south of Italy between Naples and Bari is a greenfield site set up at the end of 1993 and, after an experimental phase, opened officially in October 1994. Melfi is the world's first car factory capable of running flat-out three shifts, six days a week. With a production capacity of 1600 cars a day (450,000 per year) employing 6300 people, the factory holds one of the best productivity records in the world. The Melfi industrial district covers a surface of 2.7 million square metres, including the plants of 16 suppliers. Their location, close to the main assembly plant, makes possible the reduction of suppliers' lead times. Lean production and Just-In-Time (JIT) are applied as a method of organizing the work cycle. The workforce in Melfi belongs to a homogeneous cultural and geographical background. The local identity is quite pronounced: workers, managers, and employees are young and mostly from the South (98 per cent), often in their first jobs (the region where the plant is located, like the rest of the South of Italy has a very high level of unemployment).

The factory—what today appears as a ready-made product, a black box—is the main visible outcome of a construction process involving the future workforce. The chronology of the design and implementation of the Melfi project reveals six main phases underlying the construction of the factory and progressively leading to the sedimentation of a core nucleus of organizational knowledge:

1. the design concept;
2. recruitment;
3. formal training;
4. construction work;
5. learning to (dis)assemble;
6. full production.

The following sections portray the chronological advancement of the Melfi project through the phases defined above. In particular, I briefly review the design strategy of the Melfi factory and discuss the premisses underlying the coming into existence of the factory. Then, I examine the major building operations through which the factory is constructed. I show how each building step results in an inscription of agency, knowledge and social interaction into organizational artefacts to which technical, cognitive, and social complexity is delegated.

5.3.1 *The design concept*

The Melfi project is part of a broader strategy formulation process aimed at re-establishing the competitive position of Fiat worldwide. The genesis of the project lies in the increasing attention devoted by the company to the emergence of the lean production paradigm in Japan and to its diffusion in Europe, and especially in the United States. For

Fiat the successful experience of the Japanese transplants in the United States was a clear signal of the need to break with the Fordist cultural tradition. Since the mid-1980s Fiat had been carrying out a series of benchmarking activities on Japanese automotive plants and especially on US transplants. These activities gradually led to the elaboration of a new work organization, known as the integrated factory. However, for some years the change process was at a standstill. Only in 1989, when the Punto was conceived, was there a physiological convergence between the above reasoning and the new productive needs.

In an effort to come to terms with chronic problems in production, in industrial relations, and, particularly, in the management of human resources, the design concept of the factory was informed by two fundamental assumptions. The first was the need to break with the cultural tradition of the past, which had led to the crisis of the mid-1980s. This implied the choice of not transferring the 'Headquarters culture' or at least minimizing the transfer. The second was the intention to build a learning organization characterized by high levels of commitment of the workforce. This addressed the need for training a group of knowledge workers and promoting a systemic understanding of the work process:

It is the peculiar quality of work in Melfi that it requires an extended training program, specifically aimed at competence acquisition, one that does not only imply learning how to do things, but also looking at the other segments of the production process. In order to put into practice a form of training that makes one aware of the lateral whereabouts, one needs to know the boundary, that is, what is going on in the upstream and downstream processes; furthermore one needs to know how to work in a team, to control certain variables previously uncontrolled, to develop a financial sensitiveness towards the cost of the product. (Former Fiat Personnel Director, quoted in Donzelli 1994)

As Donzelli (Donzelli 1994) has rightly pointed out, given the complexity of the new work organization, the most challenging task Fiat had to face in the training of the new workforce was to devise specific learning paths. In other words, the challenge did not seem to lie so much in the 'what' of training as in the 'how': how to convey the awareness of the boundary; how to foster a systemic orientation towards work while learning how to do specific things; and how to equip the newly hired workforce with cognitive tools able to support this systemic orientation.

The design of the plant had a major impact on the company's existing culture, since it raised traditional controversies such as the opposition between North and South, novices and experienced, and engineers and Human Resource Management (HRM) managers. Interviews with the former Plant Director and the Personnel Director highlighted four major controversial issues related to the design of the plant. A first point of controversy concerned the governance of the socio-technical system. There was a presumption of conflict related to the history of the company, especially as far as IR practices were concerned. In the past, this problem had been dealt with through massive investments in technology to be used as a defensive strategy against social conflict. As we have seen in Chapter 4 the technocentric approach was only partially successful. The alternative position was represented by those who believed in the role of HRM policies and the partial involvement of the trade unions as a strategy to gain consensus on such an ambitious project. Second, there was a debate about the new production system. The lean production philosophy, the adoption of JIT, the presence of suppliers on site, involved eliminating all those forms of external warehouses which served as the backbone of the traditional mass production systems operating in Fiat's plants. The 'crystal pipeline' concept, that is, the idea of a rigid production flow with no buffers, was more than a technological challenge as it affected the company's traditional culture on production methods. Third, the new team-based organization and the delayering of the traditional organizational model were at odds with the company's deeply hierarchical tradition. Finally, the greenfield concept and the involvement of a green workforce in the realization of the project were a major question mark. Some managers believed that the lack of experienced people would impede the project and that at some point the company would be forced to call back the old 'cavaliers'.[3]

The company board, in charge of the direction of the operations, acted as a sort of tribunal engaged in settling controversies between innovators and the so-called 'cavaliers'. The board assessed the proposals brought forward by the committee in charge of the implementation of the project. It selected between alternative choices by endorsing the entrepreneurial risk behind each option. As mentioned earlier, Melfi certainly represents a breakthrough and a paradigm shift within the Fiat world. It is therefore sensible to imagine that the decision-making process underlying the design of the new factory was characterized by

---

[3] Within Fiat, the term 'cavalier' refers to powerful, charismatic figures who have served the company for long periods of time. It also points to a conservative mode of thinking deeply grounded in the old company's tradition.

strong negotiation if not open conflict between 'innovators' and 'conservatives'. However, we do not possess any evidence to document the details of this conflict. What can be said here is that the Melfi project was driven from the outset by the idea of radical innovation related to the survival of the company in a fierce competitive environment. The mission, imposed in a top–down manner, set the background against which decisions would be taken within the board.[4]

5.3.1.1   *The greenfield*
The policy decision to go ahead with the Melfi project was made by Fiat senior executives in December 1990. The recruitment of the workforce and construction work commenced almost simultaneously in September 1991. It took 24 months to complete the construction work and the first car body rolled off the line in September 1993. The implementation of the project was initially entrusted to a group of 50 young managers, all in possession of a university degree, highly trained, with two to three years of managerial experience within the company's production plants. Their mission, as defined by the company headquarters, was to build one of the most competitive automotive factories in the world, which would be erected on a greenfield site. This high profile group was in charge, amongst other things, of the recruitment and training of the new workforce. The group of hired employees initially comprised approximately 1000 workers, engineers, middle managers, and technicians in possession of a high school diploma or university degree. The bulk of the generic workers (approximately 5000) was hired subsequently and put into training.

Questions of site location, building construction, and plant layout were crucial for the design concept of the Melfi factory. The adoption of a greenfield strategy was a core design specification and a fundamental pre-condition for successful implementation of the whole project. Figure 5.1 illustrates the greenfield area selected for the construction of the SATA plant in Melfi.

---

[4] Here it is important to reiterate that the research is not concerned with the paradigm shift *per se*, which remains in the background providing a context for description. Specifically, in my account I chose the design concept of the factory as a point of departure, without questioning the decision-making process upstream of it. It should be noted that the process under consideration—unfolding according to chronological/thematic phases—is delimited by the presence of black boxes: it starts with a project on paper (a script) and ends with the physical factory. From the above consideration it is possible to derive the following proposition: in a process of social construction, the status of an object or artefact depends on the arbitrary decision to question it or conversely treat it as a final product or black box. It is a matter of where one sets the boundaries of the description. The latter raises an important methodological issue and highlights the role of research design in cutting up the interactionist field.

Figure 5.1 *Melfi's greenfield site (June 1991)*

The rationale behind the choice of Melfi included at least three major reasons. The first was its strategic location within the wide network of Fiat's plants already existing in the south of Italy. Secondly, Basilicata—the region where the plant is located—can be considered a 'green area' in its own right, not contaminated by pre-existing industrial models and yet characterized by the local population's positive attitude towards industry and new work opportunities. Finally, the same region is distinguished by high levels of schooling—a knowledge asset in itself, and therefore offers an ideal recruitment basin.

The strategic implications of greenfield sites for the management of innovation and change have been widely recognized in the literature.

A number of authors have emphasized the systemic features of greenfield sites and the holistic character of design connected with the adoption of a greenfield strategy. For Clark (1995), the structural features of greenfield sites allow for the design of systems where all parts of the organization are consistent and the multiple facets of the design concept fit together. Important areas in which greenfield sites offer the opportunity for innovation include building design, internal plant layout, technology, relations with suppliers, customer relations, and distribution and communication networks.

The notion of greenfield stresses the experimental character of a new plant within a network of existing plants (Beaumont and Townley 1985). In turn, the design of innovation processes associated with greenfield sites is made possible by distinctive structural conditions. These include, amongst others, geographical isolation from a major manufacturing district and cultural distance from industrial communities. Greenfield sites are often located in less-developed regions characterized by high levels of unemployment and by a lack of socially embedded knowledge about industry. Furthermore, those regions are usually eligible for grants from local governments or supranational bodies like the European Union. The presence of new work practices and new employee relations bears crucial implications as far as HRM and industrial relations policies are concerned (Newell 1991). For example, the choice of a greenfield can be instrumental in reducing the potential level of conflict within the new plant and possibly bypassing the unions' control of work organization. As we have seen, a similar strategy had been adopted by Fiat in the past although using different instruments (e.g. automation as a defensive strategy). This time, however, the deal with the unions played a critical role. To a certain extent, the deal was constrained by the very idea of providing a major employment opportunity in a depressed area, which ensured consensus (and major incentives) at the political level, while limiting the bargaining power of the unions. For example, the unions were deliberately excluded from the decision-making process related to the design of the factory. On the other hand, they were crucially involved in the implementation phase through participation in bilateral commissions specifically designed to monitor the advancement of the project. As Rieser (1992) has observed, the main role of the unions in Melfi was to provide feedback in the set-up process and thereby absorb the potential sources of social conflict inherent in the implementation of the new organization model. In other words, they were part of the company's strategy for building consensus around the project (the Melfi workforce is highly unionized, although non-conflictual).

More generally, greenfield sites provide an opportunity for managers to make a philosophical break with the traditional ways of doing things and to experiment with untried systems or practices (Clark 1995). Beaumont and Townley (1985) have clearly explained this point:

The green field site offers the prospect of a *tabula rasa*, . . . the possibility of establishing work organization, job design, personnel and industrial relations policies afresh rather than attempting to tackle these issues on an *ad hoc* basis in existing plants. It provides the opportunity to experiment with the development of a coherent 'green field philosophy'. (Beaumont and Townley 1985: 189)

In its connotation of *tabula rasa* a greenfield site provides a background for learning and knowledge creation which is characterized by a low level of knowledge institutionalization. In other words, it provides a context where it is possible to create not only a new factory but also new modes of organizing, and new ways of doing and seeing things. To a certain extent, the structural features of greenfield sites allow a company to keep the learning and knowledge-creation processes under control. For example, the absence of a sedimented industrial tradition associated with greenfield sites may facilitate the 'schooling' of the workforce and the transfer of knowledge in a top–down manner. At the same time, the low degree of institutionalization of the initial stock of knowledge creates the conditions for the emergence of unforeseen facts which may challenge the original design concept, enrich its scope and act as new knowledge-creation forces. The design concept of the Melfi plant embraces many of the ideas connected to the choice of a greenfield strategy. However, the implementation of this strategy, especially as far as training and learning dynamics are concerned, also presents many aspects that are unique and possibly explain the stunning performance of the factory.

5.3.2 *Recruitment*

The selection process was designed following a benchmarking activity on Japanese automotive plants scattered around the world. A threshold of 10 per cent had been identified as the ideal ratio between selection and recruitment. Consequently, almost 100,000 people were interviewed in order to select 7000 workers:

We designed a selection system before a training system. We wanted to select people not only in possession of a theoretical background, but also with a positive attitude towards work, in particular towards teamwork; people willing to put themselves at stake, with a sense of challenge; people with whom it would be possible to build a new factory model, far from the traditional one. In sum, people with a strong personality. (Former Personnel Director)

As stated above, the original core group of hired workers can be seen as a group of novices. The basic stock of knowledge they possessed came from formal education. What was the nature of this first minimal nucleus of knowledge? It was formal, non-experience-related knowledge; it was explicit knowledge, easily detectable since it coincided with a specific school qualification; more importantly, as we shall see shortly, it was knowledge that could be manipulated and put to use. Another important factor was the homogeneity of the workforce and the cultural values related to the particular area where the plant is located. The workforce embodied the cultural values typical of a rural community, such as the importance of the family, sense of belonging to the territory, honour and accountability, tinkering, and the art of 'managing to get by', inclination towards mutual help, and readiness to 'give each other a hand'. Although those values may seem in sharp contrast with an avant-garde industrial project, the production reality within the Melfi plant offers a different picture. In order to function effectively, a factory like Melfi needs consensus. Hence derives the importance of a healthy cultural environment, where local values can be re-invented and turned into a valuable resource for the company. Today, those values find original applications in key areas such as quality control, teamwork, problem-solving and organizational learning.[5] On the other hand, in order to be successful, an ambitious project like Melfi had to be contextualized. A number of sociological studies aimed at assessing the core cultural features of the local population, the local sub-cultures, and the potential impacts of the new plant on the local cultural context were undertaken on behalf of the company as part of the design activity. For example, the presence of a strong local identity and the importance of maintaining close social bonds, suggested recruiting people living within a range of 30–60 kilometres (one hour's drive) from the factory, in order to facilitate commuting to work. In this way, workers could keep living in their home towns and carry on their social activities, without having to move closer to the factory. As a consequence the construction of the factory did not produce a dramatic impact on the territory, as had been the case with previous industrial installations in the south of Italy. The contextualization strategy achieved two important results. First, as explained by the former Personnel Director of the plant, it contributed to building consensus and reduced the level of conflict of the workforce:

Melfi represents an innovation even with respect to the other company experiences in the south, characterized by high levels of conflict in the initial two to

---

[5] During the interviews some operators described the experience of assembling a Punto as building their own car; others often referred to the team as a family.

three years of operations. Many people wonder why Melfi did not have to pay this price. I think that a novice who does not find certain cultural references for his working condition will end up rejecting it. With Melfi, we have tried to understand the needs, the motivations and the experience of the individual and to harness these traits for the benefit of the company's performance.

Second, as we shall see in the following sections, the 'protection' and reception of the local values fostered a crucial process of knowledge creation from the bottom.

5.3.3 *Formal training*

Having gone through selection sessions and been tentatively assigned to a role, the freshly recruited workers were subsequently put through intense formal training. One thousand people from Southern Italy spent a year at the Fiat headquarters in Turin. There, undergoing a sort of full immersion in Fiat's industrial cosmology, they acquired knowledge about the company, the production process, and the basic principles underlying the new organizational model. Professional profiles, learning programmes, and career advancement tracks were tailored according to their different educational backgrounds, and the individual attitudes that emerged during the selection process. The training period in Turin encompassed both classroom sessions and simulation exercises in laboratories. Knowledge acquired in the classroom would be continually tested and put to work through rotation in other Fiat plants. The latter provided the first contact with the production reality. Here the training consisted of operational simulations where the newcomers would take part in shadow teams working side by side with experienced operators along the assembly lines. In a subsequent phase, while the new plant was still not available, a real simulation of the production process at Melfi was undertaken in the Fiat factories scattered around Italy. The future workforce was organized in virtual teams and assigned to specific UTEs, with each member taking up the position corresponding to his/her future role at Melfi. The training experience in Turin also provided a golden opportunity for socializing the future workforce. For more than a year, the trainees lived as a community in the residences provided by the company. The company also arranged cultural and leisure activities, tours at weekends, and trips back home once a month. Then they were sent back to the greenfield at Melfi, where, at the construction site, they engaged in the construction of the plant in which they would finally end up working.

5.3.4   *The construction work*

On the building site, 3000 people belonging to the contracting firms in charge of the construction of the plant were at work. The entire operation was supervised by an interdisciplinary group that involved automotive production specialists from Fiat Auto working side by side with the civil and structural engineers from Fiat Engineering. From these combined forces emerged the site plan as well as the architectural and structural design of the factory. In September 1991, large-scale construction began on the site. By September 1992, the Fiat Auto engineers could start installation of the production systems. By May 1993, the energy supply systems were ready for testing. By September 1993, the entire plant was ready for operation. To cite just a few figures, the construction site operation amounted to 12 million working hours, 4 million cubic metres of earth were moved, 16,000 metres of foundation were laid, 500,000 cubic metres of reinforced concrete were used, 90,000 tons of structural steel were erected, 5000 tons of pipes, 100,000 metres of insulated electrical wiring, 16,000 metres of high and medium tension power lines were used and 16,000 metres of railway track were laid. Figures 5.2–5.10 depict the advancement of the construction work over the greenfield site.

Figure 5.2   *Construction work: laying the foundations (October 1991)*

Figure 5.3   *Construction work: the stamping shop (January 1992)*

Figure 5.4   *Construction work: the paint shop (April 1992)*

Figure 5.5   *Construction work: the body welding unit (September 1992)*

Figure 5.6   *Construction work: initial assembling of the plants in the body welding unit (September 1992)*

Figure 5.7   *Body welding unit: production lines (November 1992)*

Figure 5.8   *Body welding unit: overview (August 1993)*

Figure 5.9   *Closing the box*

Figure 5.10   *The Melfi plant (September 1993)*

The strict deadlines foreseen in the project plan schedule made it necessary to start construction site work concurrently with project development, thus breaking with the traditional procedure of one phase following the other. This innovative methodology required close co-ordination among project partners. More importantly, it allowed for the crucial involvement of the future workforce of the factory in the construction work. As soon as the new hired workers completed the formal training period in Turin, they were sent in small contingents to the greenfield site in Melfi, where an *ad hoc* training centre had been set up.

The objective of the participatory strategy pursued by the company was twofold: to adapt the new socio-organizational model of the integrated factory to a complex technological system in order to accelerate the operations of debugging the production apparatus; and to create a political and professional avant-garde, highly motivated, integrated in the company culture, carrying deep knowledge of the factory and its inner workings, and able to lead the remaining workforce on the principles of the new production policy. As a result, the building site experience promoted within the workforce the development of a sense of belonging to a community of 'pioneers and constructors' (Cerruti 1994). Working on the greenfield soon assumed the meaning of a founding experience for the novice workforce involved in the construction of their 'own factory'. In the recollections of the core group of hired workers the greenfield site personified the myth of genesis, a *tabula rasa* where nothing existed before their arrival:

When I arrived here, in May 1992, there were only a few pillars and the roof. One of the first things we did was to involve our work force in issues related to the set-up of the assembly unit. They *assembled* this unit [the Assembly unit], together with the other companies which were here. (Production Engineering Manager, Assembly Unit)

I was one of the first to arrive here in October 1992. Nothing existed here, not even the shell of the building. Although I had been hired as a member of maintenance staff, I did my first work experience as a surveyor (that is my educational background) working with the firms in charge of the construction work. So I was involved in heavy construction jobs before setting up and testing machinery. (Technologist, Body welding unit)

I have been here since May of last year. Now it is difficult to explain. There was nothing here: the plants were here but they were not operational; there was nothing on the (shop) floor, we designed the workstations, we built our boxes: none of this furniture was here, there were no desks, we built them on our own, we cut the iron, painted it, built poles, we did a bit of everything. We could not believe that in a few months all that was going to become operational; and yet it happened. We like to think that it is our achievement too. (Head of UTE, Assembly Unit)

During the first few months, since there was nothing here, we would act as operators of the firms which were supposed to build the plant; therefore we would do nothing that was related to our future work, apart from studying the production cycles on paper. (Head of UTE, Assembly Unit)

For the young work force the experience of the construction site was a sort of rite of initiation or passage—a ceremony—that might have possibly played the same role that formal co-optation or professional socialization play in more established professional communities (Van Maanen 1984; Beyer and Trice 1987).

5.3.5 *Learning to (dis)assemble*

As a result of Fiat's initial choice, the original 'green field' was transformed into an industrial landscape in a relatively short time. Buildings, equipment, machinery, various implements, and all sorts of industrial paraphernalia were placed and lined up on site according to a pre-designed plan. The complete factory materialized as it was simply 'unfolded'. Within the building site, the core group of hired workers was organized into Work Breakdown Structures (WBS) responsible for the development of the multi-faceted aspects of the avant-garde factory: monitoring the construction of the plants, testing the machinery, and adapting the new socio-technical system to the specific context of the Melfi factory. Each WBS would act as a start-up team directed by a team leader, and was encouraged to submit written proposals to the newly formed steering committee of the plant. The management structure of the plant was rather loose at the time, with the steering committee comprising a group of 22 managers recruited from the original group of 50. The evolution of the training process was kept fluid, grounded on the solutions proposed by the start-up teams and on the critical issues emerging along the way. Follow-up decisions were kept on stand-by, awaiting new developments. WBS provided the core operational units of an architecture of complexity whereby organizational tasks were 'broken down' into elemental components. The following example illustrates the functioning of a typical start-up team engaged in setting up the presses within the stamping shop, while stressing a crucial learning pattern based on a comparative experience surrounding the appropriation of the machinery:

For assembling the presses, we formed two work teams including both internal personnel and members of the supply companies. As you may know Schuler and Komatsu make the presses we use. The Japanese team was in charge of assembling the large presses, while the German team took care of the medium presses. The Japanese team had managed to rationalize its activities up to a point where, in the face of a sudden disruption, they were able to suspend the job and keep going somewhere else. They had disassembled the press as if it were Lego; they had numbered the containers; in each container there was a set of inferential moves, the so-called 'ifs' of a project, representing variations or possible ramifications within a planned activity. The Japanese never opened more than two containers at the same time, and therefore utilized a minimal amount of space. They were able to complete the assembling job and test the machinery three months before the deadline. On the other side, the Germans had very loose planning, and accordingly each single problem encountered while assembling would disrupt their work. The Germans were just on the deadline, but they occupied the entire shop floor, with parts scattered everywhere. Our engineers were involved in both experiences and clearly they learned something about their own work method. They would not make any move without planning, without assessing the possible consequences of their actions. 'What happens if ...' and they would start assessing the 'ifs'. (former Plant Director)

The shift of the activity from assembling the plant to assembling the car was a gradual one. It happened through a phase where the car was repeatedly disassembled, laid out on the ground in thousands of separate pieces, and then re-assembled. What in the early stages was the explicit focus of attention and construction later became the implicit background and equipment for the car manufacturing operations on the shop floor. Thus, practical knowledge about assembling learned at the construction site was transposed to the shop floor:

In order to familiarize themselves with the list of components, the young engineers were asked to develop it physically. Basically, they took all the parts of a specific model as listed on the bill of materials, and spread them over a surface of about 800 square metres. Subsequently, they developed all the Punto's product range by separating the common parts from the specific ones. (former Plant Director)

The induction phase that followed the construction work was aimed at making shop floor operators familiar with the details of the product and the intricacies of the production process. In the body welding unit car bodies were dissected and inspected again and again in order to understand the interfaces between the different car parts. In the assembly unit a number of simulations were carried out off the line as a way to convey a practical mode of thinking and knowing:

Later on, the UTE leaders arrived, then the technologists and the line workers, all of them after a training period in Turin. Those people were introduced to the product by working on a stock of cars provided by the Mirafiori plant. On those cars we did some training, by disassembling and re-assembling them again and again. We were asked to come up with a 'disassembling' cycle for the car. Although those people had already gone through operational simulations in other plants, they now had the opportunity to have some 'hands on' experience. (Production Engineering manager, Assembly Unit)

In a subsequent phase, the 'ownership' of the product became a vehicle for transferring a stock of practical knowledge from a core group of knowledgeable workers (namely UTE leaders and technologists) to the newcomers:

Having learned how to disassemble and re-assemble those cars, the UTE leader and the technologist had become 'owners' of the product. They were now in the position to transfer their competence to the line workers. Starting from this training exercise, we moved to the actual production of the car within this plant. Those cars were used to show our people how a car is assembled and produced. Since then we have only built cars that could be sold. (Production Engineering Manager, Assembly Unit)

The above examples highlight a well-known image, typical of mechanical manufacturing, which portrays the organization as a sort of LEGO-like composable and decomposable system. Just like a child exploring the content of a new toy, the act of disassembling becomes a distinctive mode of knowing aimed at understanding the relations between parts and whole. More importantly, through disassembling exercises a work pattern emerged based on the possibility of building rules of method 'empirically' by drawing on concrete occurrences and continuous improvement activities. The resulting patterns of work would be repeatedly tested until they were eventually stabilized at a later stage. Through the endless repetitions of the Disassembling/Assembling (D/A) task, the workers would simulate the functioning of the assembly line. Interestingly, the training provided through this type of simulation was centred around the task (building the car bit by bit), with shop floor operators moving from one work station to the next while the production lines stood still. Only after they had appropriated the practice of manually assembling the car did the workers delegate it to the moving line, which thus inscribed the agency and the task (time and motion, functions and operations). In the process of appropriating the work method a major anchoring role was played by the car and its physical components. Through the repeated hands-on procedure of breaking down the car into separate pieces and then remaking it by putting the pieces back together, the structure of the task was revealed and the logic of manufacturing was appropriated. Thus the car, in addition to being the thing to be manufactured (the product), also became a cognitive tool—a medium—for understanding and institutionalizing the method of manufacturing.

A major outcome of the D/A exercise was the production of empirical know-how and rules of thumb which were eventually capitalized and crystallized into explicit rules. A crucial feature of Melfi's general-ized work method, at least in that early stage, was the capacity to systematically formalize emerging stocks of empirical knowledge by letting it come to the surface. Under these circumstances, the work method became a virtuous force for generating new knowledge:

Melfi represents a bit of a paradox. Since the start-up phase the Melfi plant has been very successful and today it is one of the most competitive automotive plants in the world. Yet, since the very beginning the factory has been gov-erned by a group of young novices who were on training. Where did such a complex system find the power to sustain itself and become more and more productive? In my opinion the secret of the success of this plant lies in the abil-ity to sustain its growth through method. The major strength of a UTE leader, a technologist or a line conductor was not his/her knowledge. Certainly, a sound knowledge of the integrated factory model was paramount and it had been transferred through the formal training in Turin. On the other hand, that knowledge, albeit important, could not be exhaustive because of the lack of experience. What was crucial was the transfer of a method for handling prob-lematic situations. This has made possible the accumulation of further know-ledge about the factory both during the start-up phase and at full production. Method implies very practical questions such as: how to solve a problem? How to organize a job? How to plan? How to take action? How to control? How to question? The methodological capacity of this organization has been a major success factor. (former Plant Director)

The induction phase of the factory came to an end one year later, with the formal opening of the plant in October 1994. This moment repres-ented the closure of the black box as well as the termination point of this part of our analysis. The factory then gradually moved towards its full production capacity and other stages in the knowledge-creation and institutionalization process.

5.4   Learning as appropriation: building identity through ownership processes

The chronological advancement of the Melfi project and the know-ledge sources associated with it highlight knowledge-specific outcomes related to each phase, which have been described in the previous sec-tions. The results are summarized in Table 5.1.

At the outset of the knowledge-creation process lies the encounter between the factory's design concept—laid out in detail by the top man-agement of the company—and a group of young and highly educated novices carrying a stock of core values typical of the area where the

Table 5.1 *Phases, sources, and outcomes of the knowledge-creation process*

Phase	Knowledge source	Knowledge outcome
1 Design concept	Benchmarking, company values	Integrated factory model
2 Recruitment	School education, local values	Degree-specific knowledge
3 Formal training	Classroom, rotation in other plants	Ownership of the role (e.g. professional profile)
4 Construction work	Building site	Ownership of the factory (e.g. activities, territory, equipment)
5 Learning to (dis)assemble	Simulation exercises on the shop floor	Ownership of the task/product (e.g. work method)
6 Full production	Factory operations	Routines

greenfield is located. The greenfield strategy is instrumental towards the fulfilment of one of the two main assumptions stated in the design concept: to break with the cultural tradition of the past. The second objective specified by the top management, the acquisition of a holistic vision of the work process, relates explicitly to organizational learning, and is to be achieved through an intensive training programme (phases 3–5). Although the outcomes of the training process are manifold, encompassing both theoretical and practical aspects of work, it is nonetheless possible to identify a pervasive learning strategy underlying the long path preceding the formal opening of the factory. Learning seems to occur as a form of situated appropriation or progressive ownership of different aspects of work: the role, the task, the product and production process, and most importantly the workplace itself. The ownership strategy characterizes the overall organizational learning process in at least two ways. First, it emphasizes the proactive role of the learners: becoming owners does not imply a mere knowledge transfer. Rather, it involves filling a gap on the part of the learners, becoming users and accordingly re-inventing the task at hand. In a sense, even the benchmarking activities performed by the company and leading to the design concept of the new factory can be seen as a process of appropriation and re-invention of concepts invented elsewhere, namely in Japan and filtered by US car manufacturers. Second, the concept of ownership is closely related to identity building. When looking at the larger picture, the learning processes described in the previous section depict an impressive socialization endeavour aimed at the construction of a distinctive identity of the workforce as 'pioneers and constructors'. Entering the work environment implies taking up a role within a community of practice. Accordingly, the training phases described in the previous sections portray the progressive development of individual (role), collective (community), and corporate (product) identities. The evolution of the training process also highlights a move from a narrow focus (the role) to a holistic vision of the production process, with crucial implications for sense-making activities. This is particularly visible in the construction work, where the appropriation of the factory requires the characters involved to relate the task at hand to a broader network of equipment, practices, and institutions. Finally, it is precisely the constitution of a distinctive identity that explains how the workforce came to accept the apparently 'onerous' deal proposed by the company. In fact, a striking characteristic in the evolution of the Melfi project is the considerably low level of conflict and controversy around the knowledge-creation process. For example, how did the company manage to convince the 'green' workforce to spend a large amount of time on training, away from their homes, and even get involved in the building works of the factory?

A major source of identification of the workforce with the objectives of the company and acceptance of the conditions imposed by the implementation process was certainly the conceptualization of the factory as a public good, whose construction required a collective effort. The symbolic value of the involvement of the workforce in the construction work was very strong, stressing the sense of belonging and ownership of the workplace. First of all, the young workforce was asked to work for a 'greater' good, that is to create its own job opportunity in a traditionally depressed area. Secondly, building the workplace was different from just walking into a ready made one. It emphasized the notion of familiarity as opposed to alienation. Within this conceptualization, the potential sources of conflict were subtly absorbed through a variety of social mechanisms intended to build consensus around the project, maintain the commitment of the workforce, and prevent opportunistic behaviour and free-riding. The deal with the unions, the contextualization strategy, and the socialization of the workforce as part of the training programme, exemplify some of these mechanisms.

5.5 Specification–delegation chains: planned and emergent factors in the knowledge-creation process

The Fiat Melfi case shows in a straightforward manner what knowledge making entails as a unique, history-dependent mix of purposeful design and unintended, endogenous processes. The chronological advancement of the Melfi project clearly illustrates the above argument. A first thing to be noted is that the process of knowledge creation and transfer was bi-directional. In the recollection of one of the managers involved in the project, the striking characteristic of the decision-making and implementation processes was the degree of discretion left to the decision makers at the lower levels:

I would say that the ratio between planned and emergent factors in the design of Melfi was 50–50. Based on benchmarking activities and a feasibility study, the headquarters had defined the rationale for a project aimed at building one of the most competitive automotive factories in the world. We were assigned specific key targets and excellence standards (organizational model, production, ergonomy, working time, etc.). However, we were autonomous as far as how those targets were to be accomplished. The same applied to the start-up teams that were in charge of the set-up of the production system and the training of the generic workers that were eventually hired. (former Personnel Director)

This finding is consistent with the adult learning theories presented earlier for at least two related reasons. On the one hand, the role of the workers' background (including lack of work experience) was a critical feature selected by the company to implement the training process. On the other hand, the learning dynamics observed on the greenfield and during the induction phase, seemed to possess an element of autonomy and self-directedness stressing a learning-by-doing pattern.

The implementation process of the Melfi project seemed to unfold according to a specification–delegation pattern. The original plan was encapsulated in the design concept of the factory. Based on benchmarking activities (a knowledge-creation process in itself) the company defined the strategic mission of the project (to build one of the most competitive factories in the world), outlined the main specifications of the design concept (location of the plant and nature of the work force) and provided a cutting edge tool kit for the new factory (organizational model, technology, and production system). Also the selection process and the initial training of the workforce, based on pre-existing training modules, was very much under the control of the company headquarters. However, since the early stages, the implementation of the project was characterized by a considerable degree of delegation and consequently by a significant process of knowledge creation from the bottom. As Donzelli put it, 'Melfi has a degree of autonomy, a philosophical independence from the Headquarters, that perhaps escapes even its designers' intentions' (Donzelli 1994: 19). The people chosen to make the project happen were young and highly educated. They can be seen as carriers of 'fresh' knowledge and new values. The more the project moved forward, the more the influence of the company values got diluted. This fact became particularly conspicuous once the operations were transferred to the greenfield site. Here, the Melfi workforce—knowledge builders and construction workers at the same time—was actively involved in 'making the project happen'. The community of 'builders' operating on the greenfield was constantly engaged in a sense-making activity whereby the cognitive and material resources at hand were assembled in original ways. In other words, the construction site provided the locus for the encounter of formal and practical knowledge. The factory itself represented the visible and measurable outcome of this collective effort, the hard product born of a process of social construction. In addition, the advancement of the project was not always smooth: the construction site raised continuous challenges, forcing the different teams at work to adapt existing solutions or to devise new ones. The context shaping the development of the Melfi project was constantly shifting as the multiplicity of implementation phases, training venues, learning settings, and knowledge sources demonstrate. The dynamic character of the knowledge-creation process over the greenfield has been stressed by one of the managers who took part in the Melfi steering committee:

The evolution of the training process in Melfi has been incessant. While the factory was growing, the training programmes and methods were constantly reviewed in accordance with the evolution of the context, the suggestions gathered from the trainees, and the emerging training needs. (former Personnel Director).

Furthermore, the scope of the project required the management of the factory to co-ordinate with the broader network of organizational actors operating in the immediate environment: for example, synchronizing the advancement of the construction work with the suppliers who were constructing their own plants; lobbying political actors at the local and national level in order to get concessions and build infrastructures; and dealing with utility companies to get the necessary connections.

In sum, the construction site embodied the characteristics of a 'formative context' (Ciborra and Lanzara 1994) providing a mixture of opportunity structures and structural constraints. At the same time, the advancement of the construction site described a highly situated process of knowledge creation and accumulation, while emphasizing the provisional character of that knowledge (knowledge in the making).

The learning process on the greenfield relied on a collection of multi-faceted sources which were originally combined in the implementation process in order to serve the performance of the newborn factory. Training of the workforce and investment in HRM were critical factors. Teamwork, socialization programmes, respect and protection of the local cultural values, and definition of the project as a collective effort were the multifaceted aspects of a human-centred design concept. However, the expansion of the core stock of knowledge governing the functioning of the new factory was based on a pervasive strategy of delegation: knowledge transfer occurred top–down in the form of guidelines and specifications; bottom–up in the form of finished products that could be capitalized as consolidated knowledge assets. Method played a major role in keeping creativity on course. On the one hand, it made up for the lack of experience of the novice workforce by providing a shared framework. At the same time, method provided a strategy for the capitalization of knowledge, that is, its transformation into a corporate asset: knowledge creation had to be institutionalized in the method in order for successful experiences to be repeatable. Consider the disassembling exercise. The exercise was aimed at transferring knowledge (top–down) about the product and the production process. At the same time, operators were asked to devise a disassembling cycle and suggest the best way for re-assembling the car. In other words, knowledge appropriation was closely linked to practice and institutionalized in the method. As we shall see in Chapter 6, the disassembling/assembling exercise also bears important cognitive implications which emerge in the resolution of breakdowns along the assembly line.

5.6   Concluding remarks

What has been the meaning of letting the workers build their own factory from scratch? What have been the knowledge implications of such a move? Why was the greenfield crucial for establishing the technical and institutional order of the factory, from the overall manufacturing system down to the shop floor level? How might such a complex manufacturing system be built?

The construction of the plant from the greenfield represented a unique experience for the original core group of workers. It stood at the heart of a highly situated learning process which carried crucial cultural, organizational, and epistemological implications. Bringing the plant to its full production took two-and-a-half years, which still counts as a significant proportion of time for a young factory like Melfi. Moreover, it consisted of an intense and emotional experience, one which was to remain imprinted in the memory of the participants. Just imagine a group of young people, coming from a rural community to their first work experience, who are actively involved in a major re-engineering process on behalf of the most important Italian company. As we have seen above, the interviewees proudly refer to the greenfield as a unique experience, emphasizing the emotional implications of 'being there'.

Certainly, this knowledge-creation process seemed to be character-ized by low levels of conflict, thanks to the participatory strategy of implementation promoted by the company. On the other hand, the advancement of the Melfi project was controversial in that it was con-stantly subject to shifting trajectories and contrasting forces (top–down and bottom–up), albeit within a planned and very structured design concept. In this respect, the 'construction site' became the emblem of knowledge in the making. It provided a competence/identity building space, characterized by the encounter between the avant-garde design concept of the factory, the company culture and the values embodied by the green workforce. The building site was a learning laboratory, a training yard, where experiments and simulation exercises could be tried out without any pressure stemming from production plans. It also conveyed the idea of gradualness of the learning process: as in construction work, competence building took place step by step, gradually moving the workforce towards higher levels of understand-ing. Yet, this learning process was highly situated and never detached from practice. For the above reasons, I argue that the initial stock of knowledge embedded in the design of the Melfi factory probably represented the most crucial knowledge asset for the company. It can be seen as a distinctive feature of the way the factory operated and therefore regarded as a source of competitive advantage. I have also contended that it is precisely here, in the experience of building the fac-tory from scratch, that a great deal of tacit knowledge lies, and it is here that we need to look in order to explain specific organizational dynamics.

In sum, what emerged from the Melfi building site was a process of social construction of corporate knowledge, rather than a mere top–down transfer of knowledge. The factory gradually took shape with the fundamental contribution of the workforce. The development of oper-ators' competence went hand in hand with the physical construction work, highlighting the processual and sedimentary nature of organi-zational knowledge.

At the methodological level, the strategy adopted in the present case reminds one of the work of an 'archaeologist of knowledge' engaged in a process of discovery and delayering the multiple strata in which knowledge has been sedimented and institutionalized over time. My analysis, based on the use of the time lens, has identified six phases/sources of knowledge creation and institutionalization of core competencies. By the time construction work is completed and the factory runs at full production, knowledge too seems to become fully institutionalized. The factory and the core stock of knowledge underlying its functioning have finally been sealed, transformed into black boxes, and manifold experiences have been concealed in a protected nucleus. From now on, it will be more difficult to access tacit knowledge, except on those occasions when knowledge is displaced and somewhat disclosed. In the next two cases, therefore, we will focus more explicitly on breakdowns as a way of exposing the tacit features of organizations.

6

Breakdowns and Bottlenecks: Capturing the Learning Dynamics on the Assembly Line

6.1 Introduction

In Chapter 5, I contended that the appropriation of the workplace by the novice workforce, through progressive ownership processes, was the main outcome of a highly situated learning process occurring at the Melfi greenfield site. A few years since it was officially opened, the Melfi plant presents a quite different picture. To start with, the complexity of shop floor operations has increased considerably: the factory is now running at full production speed, whereas during the induction phase the lines would only operate at half-capacity load. Today, given the impressive rhythm of the production lines, and the exceptional levels of productivity, the Melfi plant is often referred to as a 'steamroller'. Secondly, the 'learning laboratory' is facing new challenges stemming from the fact that business operations are now carried out in a competitive environment. Managers and operators in Melfi are confronted with a number of issues related to dealing with changes while keeping pace with production targets and maintaining the organizational identity, which is increasingly taking shape. A third element of novelty is that the original management group of the factory has been completely replaced. Most of the young managers (today in their early forties) who were in charge of the start-up of the factory have followed brilliant career paths at the corporate level, with some of them holding key positions within the company. Paradoxically, while Melfi is attempting to build its past, the competitive challenges and the related dynamics of change seem to keep the organizational context of the factory still 'in flux'.

More generally, now that the induction phase has terminated, the factory has entered a new phase—one in which knowledge has been deeply transformed. At the shop floor level, the move to full production involves shifting from a non-routine situation to one where work has become routinized. A new institutional order has been created in which knowledge has been handed over to impersonal mechanisms: routines, standard operating procedures, organizational artefacts, and technology. The factory as a whole has been transformed into a clockwork device epitomized by the presence of the assembly line and characterized by mechanisms of repetition. Finally, at the cognitive level, the move towards a situation of 'business as usual' points to a kind of transparent intentionality which makes knowing processes less accessible.

Taking into account the above considerations, this chapter aims to assess the process of institutionalization of knowledge within the Melfi factory now that the plant had reached its full production capacity. More specifically, the case study presented below attempts to test how the competencies acquired by workers and managers on the greenfield site are applied in the practical context of the production process. In order to 'scratch' the stock of tacit knowledge that had sedimented within the factory over time, the case study relied on the use of breakdowns as a methodological lens affording empirical access to the dynamics of learning and knowledge acquisition. Detailed observations were carried out on how operators and managers on the shop floor behaved when faced with a variety of minor and major breakdowns by enacting different sorts of problem-solving procedures, computer-mediated communication, and learning strategies. The analysis revealed a widespread isomorphism between the physical infrastructures through which factory operations were performed (e.g. layout and assembly line), and the cognitive frames governing the execution of those operations. More specifically, I found that the standard problem-solving routine applied on the shop floor was based on a generalized capability to (manually and mentally) disassemble/reassemble (D/A) the car. As a consequence, the D/A template seemed to connect the way operators think at work with the piecemeal nature of the task (building the car bit by bit) and the assembly line concept. At first glance, this may appear an obvious finding: it could be argued that a factory like Melfi ultimately embodies the old principles of mass production here revived in the traditional image of the assembly line concept. However, a careful consideration of the Melfi workforce and the core capabilities underlying the factory operations highlights profound discontinuities with respect to the old production paradigm. A first point of divergence concerns the nature of the Melfi workforce and the intense training process that it underwent during the greenfield phase of the factory. Unlike traditional unskilled Fordist workers, the Melfi work-force consists of knowledgeable workers, highly educated and highly trained. Secondly, the capacity to disassemble/re-assemble the car as a problem-solving strategy seemed to be grounded on a holistic picture of the product and the production process. In particular, evidence suggests that the cognitive template detected in Melfi was directed at capturing the fundamental relationship between parts and wholes by conveying a virtual image of the production process. As a result, the systemic features of the assembly line concept (the chain of transformations along the pro-duction process) were emphasized, rather than the narrow focus on the single operation characterizing the traditional Fordist 'formative con-text'. Finally, in accordance with the company's commitment to quality, the task of building the car bit by bit—at the core of the assembly line con-cept—was redefined as a craft activity carried out by semi-autonomous teams, and sustained by a general capability for tinkering.

This chapter contains 8 sections. Section 6.2 outlines the production process within the body welding unit, where observations were car-ried out, and describes in some detail the sophisticated information system that controlled production operations along the assembly line. Sections 6.3 and 6.4 depict a number of scenes observed on the shop floor in relation to the solution of breakdowns and bottlenecks, stress-ing the knowledge implications underlying the way operators dealt with disruptions. Drawing on the above episodes, Sections 6.5 and 6.6 highlight the main learning processes dedicated to the control of local and systemic breakdowns. Section 6.7 identifies the main outcomes related to the above process. The learning dynamics observed on the shop floor highlight the distinctive features of Melfi's production sys-tem as opposed to the traditional Fordist model. Crucially, this distinc-tion is grounded on knowledge-based rather than technology-based factors. The concluding section highlights the implications of the Melfi case for knowing and organizing.

6.2 The body welding unit

The body welding unit within the Melfi plant is a small technological jewel, worth more than 1000 billion lire (about $ 600 million), and featur-ing the most advanced technology available today in car manufacturing. With 100 per cent automation and 233 robots it is the epitome of the concept of the high-tech factory. The body welding unit consists of seven Elementary Technical Units (UTEs) (1–7) integrated according to the internal customer logic and linking the stamping shop with the paint shop. Car bodies flow along 19 automated lines, stopping at the different workplaces where robots perform most of the operations. The workers' role, in most of the UTEs, is to monitor the process through information systems and visual control tools. The skills required by operators are mostly technical and concern the governance of machines. The UTEs are small and there are few blue-collar workers.

The work flow is characterized by the presence of two kinds of lines: production lines on the shop floor are utilized to assemble the car body; overhead conveyors consist of a sequence of aerial hangers on which car components are accumulated and transferred from one process to the following one. Aerial lines have a dual purpose: besides moving car parts between processes, they serve as dynamic inventories where parts are temporarily stored before reaching the next process. A system of elevators, situated at the extremities of each production line, makes it possible to load and unload the car components and to transfer them between production and transportation lines. The final assembly of the car body is the result of three synchronized flows (under-bodies, sides, and roofs) joining in a specific work station of UTE 5, where a 'robo-gate' performs the 'marriage' between the three components. The 'marriage' of the car body is the most spectacular operation in the unit, requiring a high level of synchronization among different production processes. In order to be successfully assembled the components must have the same sequence number; that is, they must belong to the same customer's order.

When entering the body welding unit, the first question that a visitor may ask himself/herself is 'where are the workers?' In fact, a visitor is shocked by the fact that there are no workers around, the UTE offices are usually empty, and one only sees the car bodies flowing along the lines and being assembled by robots. Occasionally, some workers appear, moving by bicycle along the lines; another small group goes back to the UTE office and does some work on personal computers (PCs), or controls monitors, or fills charts, or makes calls. Other small groups talk along the lines, then go back to work. The body welding unit is the realm of machines and geometry, of measurement and exactitude. Technology plays a dominant role. As the head of the OU put it: 'technology provides visibility'. The seven UTEs in the unit have been designed according to a clear-cut definition of the boundaries among the semi-finished products which compose the car body. In this regard, boundaries promote an unequivocal demarcation of responsibilities in case of anomalies or breakdowns.

The capacity to govern the technological system and keep the production process on course is crucial. Unlike the assembly unit, where the bulk of car parts are assembled, here knowledge of the process (the sequence of operations) is more important than knowledge of the product (the different car sub-components). In fact, only 200 parts out of about 10,000 are assembled in the body welding unit. Machines provide automatic measurements and reports on the state of production and the quality of the product. Echoing Zuboff (1988), it is possible to say that they automate the production process as well as 'informate' it. The task of operators involves making sense of the data provided by machines and using them in a purposeful way. Accordingly, knowledge of the machinery, method, and inferential capabilities are very important. Also, taking care of machines by performing constant maintenance operations accounts for a substantial part of the routine within the body welding unit. The production process is backed up by sophisticated information systems, which are supposed to 'textualize' work and render it transparent (Zuboff 1988). The information system architecture in Melfi is articulated into three levels mirroring the production process described above. Level 1 comprises machine software or task automation. Each machine on each workstation is operated and controlled by a specific piece of software which recognizes the local operation to be performed at that work station. Level 1.5 controls the system of elevators, located at the beginning and at the end of each line, which lift the semi-finished products from one process and unload them for the next one. Level 2 is responsible for workflow management, highlighting the interdependence among different UTEs. Basically, this level controls the flow of the overhead conveyors which transport car parts in the form of semi-finished products from one process to the following one. Level 2 is the systemic level of automation governing the synchronization of the different processes and the consistency of the different parts composing the car body. A typical example of level 2 in action is the 'marriage' between under-bodies, sides and roofs, which implies ensuring that all the components assembled belong to the same customer's order. Level 3 controls the mix of orders from the customer and sets the production sequence. The system is connected to the network of Fiat dealers and to the headquarters in Mirafiori. A fourth level should be added to the three above and seen as a sort of meta-level which makes the Melfi plant visible to the Fiat headquarters.

The three levels described above reflect the hierarchical division of labour within the plant; that is, 'where control is located' Level 1 is visible at the UTE level: UTE members are entitled to perform modifications on the machines' software whenever that would improve the production process. For instance, UTE members may decide to modify the production cycle by eliminating a superfluous operation. Level 2 is still visible at the shop floor level, but any modification of the software is entrusted to specialized offices (e.g. production analysis); level 3 is operated at the plant level (top management). In organizational terms, the three levels can be named 'local', 'systemic', and 'strategic', reflecting both the division of labour and the articulation of knowledge within the plant. In other words, the system's architecture mirrors both the organizational structure and the knowledge architecture of the plant.

6.3   Men and machines

The concept of automation is conventionally defined as the substitution of human labour with machines. Although this definition is certainly correct, it seems to overlook some important aspects of human–machine interaction. For the purpose of my analysis, and in order to reach a better understanding of the knowledge implications of technology, I will conceptualize automation as the delegation of certain functions normally performed by humans to non-human actants. From this perspective, automation is a modification in the pragmatic relationship between humans and equipment. Delegation to non-human actants (Latour 1993) pinpoints the notions of knowledge transfer and knowledge embodiment. As for humans, automated tasks are grounded on a stock of knowledge that has been delegated to machines and is embedded in the software in the form of a set of operating instructions. According to this perspective, machines are not mere instruments; rather, they are entities endowed with the ability to perform certain actions. When a breakdown occurs, not only is the functionality of the machine questioned, but also the original delegation mechanism gets disrupted. Humans need to re-appropriate the machines in order to restore a situation of normality. In other words, recovering from disruptions implies a re-appropriation of the task from technology.

The knowledge implications of a pragmatic definition of technology are far reaching. The body welding unit is the realm of automation and machines, while the role of humans is closely related to the governance of the automated workflow. Shop floor operators are separated from machines along the lines by means of transparent gates which are supposed to render the production process visible at any moment and allow the human eye to follow the car bodies along the lines. In addition, the workflow is monitored through the data produced by the sophisticated information systems attached to the machines. The ability to make inferences from numbers appearing on print-outs in order to monitor the 'drifts' of the production system is part of routine work in the body welding unit.

As we saw in Chapter 5, the training of the workforce during the induction phase played a crucial role. Core competencies were transferred through the active involvement of the new workforce in the physical construction of the unit, the set up of machinery, and a series of 'hands on' exercises on real cars. Besides the disassembling exercise, the training included dissecting the first set of cars produced on the assembly line by performing a sort of appendectomy on each of them. The principal aim of the 'dissecting' exercise was to transfer diagnostic skills to technologists, UTE leaders and other technical figures within the unit. The pervasive influence of the induction phase of the factory and the importance of diagnostic skills becomes apparent in the way operators deal with defective components. Within UTE 5 there is a small display area where defective car bodies are exposed so that in-depth analyses can be performed on anomalies generated by the body welding unit in the production process:

This is the display area where we look over the waste generated in the production process. Typically this is a gathering point where UTE members or external suppliers convene to take note of waste generated by them. There you see two of our suppliers who are examining some waste for which they are responsible. (UTE technologist)

The area resembles a 'mortuary' where 'dead' car bodies are waiting to be dissected before being definitively discarded. Not surprisingly, the role of the technologist within Fiat is defined as that of a 'physician' who is in charge of detecting anomalies, working out the causes, and coming up with solutions:

We have had to discard this one (car body) ... Now it is going to be dissected and opened; basically we perform a few cuts in order to understand what happened. (UTE technologist)

The car body mentioned by the technologist has been sent back by UTE 6, which had discovered the anomaly while operators were performing a particular welding operation. The body has a fault on the left side, which is one millimetre lower than the other one. Although the magnitude of the default could make it acceptable, the car body has been discarded so that diagnosis of the problem can be performed. The problem seems peculiar because it did not recur over time. This fact makes the diagnosis particularly difficult and provokes a dispute over attribution of the anomaly to a particular UTE. At first glance the source of the anomaly may be UTE 1 (sides), but this hypothesis has already been discarded. Also UTE 5 has been exempted from any responsibility. The candidate 'culprits' appear to be UTE 2 and UTE 3:

The only thing that can give us a response is to dissect the body, i.e. take out the side and analyse it; if that is not sufficient we will have to disassemble the car bit by bit. (UTE technologist)

The dissection of car bodies possibly represents a variation of the 'disassembling' exercise (see Chapter 5) and accordingly carries important knowledge implications. Dissecting bodies is a way of dissecting knowledge; it is a fundamental diagnostic practice underlying the way operators make sense of disruptive occurrences within the body welding unit. The case reported above portrays an unusual situation, where an anomaly eludes both automatic measurements (because a small deviation from the standard is tolerated by the system or because the point of anomaly is not subject to measurement) and human control. Interestingly, it is precisely automation which makes it difficult to 'see' the problem; as a consequence the anomaly can be detected only when the car body re-emerges from the automated flow and reaches a point where manual operations are performed (UTE 6 in the above case). In general terms, problem-solving activities are triggered by the appearance of anomalies which can be detected either by human or non-human actants. When a breakdown occurs, the interaction between man and machine is called into question, and humans are confronted with the complexity of machines:

The first thing we do when an anomaly is detected is to stop the line and go to see. If the problem is serious, we open the gate, enter the line and perform the operation manually in order to make sense of the problem. Normally we try to repair the machine, if that is feasible; otherwise, we perform a 'rough and ready' intervention and postpone the repairing to the end of the shift. As a general rule, we try to avoid 'rough and ready' solutions because with three working shifts there is not much room left for maintenance or repairing interventions. (UTE technologist)

Typically, operators in the body welding unit are confronted with dimensional anomalies. Such anomalies are related to the geometry of the car body and are detected by automated measuring devices (MAC).

A MAC operates as an electronic finger, touching the car body in different areas and comparing the values detected on each measuring point with standard quality values predetermined by the company. Whenever there is a deviation from the standard, the MAC people inform the UTE responsible for the anomaly detected. The measurements are performed every hour or every 50 car bodies produced and take about 20 minutes. However, anomalies which elude measurement, as in the case reported above, are difficult to detect.

As shown by the episode described above, automation may render the production process quite transparent, since the complexity of the task is hidden in the complexity of the machine. As a consequence, when things go smoothly operators are absorbed in the business as usual of daily routines and the task is encountered as something ready-to-hand. On the other hand, when machines break down, humans are confronted with the complexity of the task while the technology becomes problematic. In order to perform a diagnosis of a problem, operators are often induced to stop the lines, open the gates, perform operations manually, and dissect car bodies. In other words, recovering from disruptions implies a re-appropriation of the task from technology. Furthermore, by temporarily excluding the mediation of technology, disruptive events emphasize the role of the body, since they restore physical contact between workers and product. In dissecting car bodies or performing operations manually, operators act as craftsmen (physicians, surgeons, mechanics, and so on). Mastering the machines means being able to establish a sort of 'dialogue' with them. In other words, machines need to be humanized in order to be harnessed and mastered. Knowledge of the machines is developed through practical involvement with them and through the experience of successful problem-solving. Another important source of appropriation is the knowledge of the 'non-visible' aspects of machines (history and design). At Melfi this appropriation occurred through the active involvement of the workforce in the setting up of machinery. In this respect, the behaviours observed above seem to be consistent with the findings presented in Chapter 5, highlighting the effectiveness of learning based on ownership processes.

6.4 Breakdowns and bottlenecks

In the best of all worlds, the line never stops. Unfortunately, the lean production concept is a source of unexpected events. At any moment the mechanical synchronization of the operations can collapse for various, unpredictable reasons: process/product anomalies, machine breakdown, lack of materials, quality problems, lack of workforce, and so on. When the line stops work-in-process piles up quickly, bottlenecks may occur, and UTEs can be kept on hold, unless workers intervene. In some cases the causes of bottlenecks can be very complex, since they are related to the constantly changing product mix, and not to a specific breakdown. That is, even if the factory as a whole may have enough capacity, there is a mismatch between the line balance and the product mix being pushed through. Such bottlenecks highlight the key role of capacity planning.

Bottlenecks may also have a more 'abstract' origin related to the opacity of human behaviour, to the tendency to focus on individual interests and to 'manage one's own position' (Senge 1990). For example, the customer–supplier concept implies that UTEs co-ordinate activities as transactions between semi-autonomous units. In this 'co-ordination game', instances of 'local sub-optimization' and opportunistic behaviour may arise; that is, activities are executed in order to optimize a given UTE's performance rather than the plant production. In its turn, local sub-optimization may lead to the building up of inventories along the lines. Often, opportunistic behaviour may be fostered unwittingly by company values. For example, at Melfi *quality* is a pervasive concept throughout the production process, manifest in multiple organizational artefacts. Quality is both a *technical requirement* (absence of faults; reduction of waste and 'demerits') and a *cultural value* (responsibility; collaboration; commitment and motivation; identification with the customer, the product, and the company). In order to 'measure' it, quality has been defined in terms of 'demerits' (i.e., number of faults). The demerits system sets visible targets for continuous improvement and enhances the levels of care and attention to the product and the process. However, as each demerit is ascribed to a UTE (or better, a work station), supposed to be at the origin of that demerit, a negative measurement may be perceived as a punishment and be frustrating for particular individuals and UTEs. As a result, the demerits system may represent a barrier to the achievement of full transparency of behaviours, since it induces workers to enact defensive behaviours, face-saving, scapegoating and other tactics that ultimately interfere with effective problem-solving and learning (Argyris 1993). Finally, bottlenecks can be traced back to the coupling between the sheer complexity of the production system and the actors' bounded rationality. The new assembly line and the system of exchanges between customers and suppliers can be compared to a network of concurrent events which is impossible to fully control, as opposed to the traditional, sequential assembly line. Sometimes a corrective action performed at one point of the system can generate a problem at another (distant) station along the line. As the relationships between different processes are very complex and cannot be properly handled, bottlenecks can be generated without awareness as a result of a lack of 'systems thinking' (Senge 1990). At the same time, bottlenecks also present opportunities for problem-solving and learning. Effective intervention requires an ability to discern their sources and causes, lest corrective routines be adopted that lead to further propagation of mistakes and disruptions, and to very little learning.

6.4.1 *Systemic breakdowns: analysing bottlenecks*

Bottlenecks are the most frequent manifestation of both local and systemic breakdowns. Car bodies that have undergone a certain processing are lifted up from one production line and moved to the next stage. Overhead conveyors serve as dynamic points of accumulation, where the car bodies in transit, waiting to reach the next process, are stored. Given the tight nature of the production flow, the aerial inventories can be seen as buffers. If a line stops as a result of a breakdown, the upstream processes keep going until the inventory closest to the problem is full. At this point a bottleneck may arise and the upstream lines must be stopped (thus creating work-in-process inventory). The downstream processes, in turn, stop receiving cars and, once their upstream inventory has been emptied, they must be halted too. When the problem causing the bottleneck is solved, the line is able to receive the bodies and the flow can restart. If it is solved before the formation of bottlenecks along the line, it will remain at a local level. Otherwise, it will affect the whole system. The longer the duration of the halt, the higher the number of parts accumulated and the greater the imbalance caused to the flow. Keeping the 'metal' moving is a matter of line balance and absence of breakdowns. Furthermore, the customer–supplier model requires having general knowledge of the upstream and downstream processes in order to make sense of the unfolding of the production flow and figure out the potential causes of a problem when breakdowns occur.

A new 'radar system' has been installed for workflow management (level 2 of automation). It consists of *Andon* boards displaying data about the amount of parts produced, the daily production target, and the inventory build-up in the upstream and downstream flows (customers' and suppliers' inventories). A number of coloured lights provide additional real time signals about the current status of the production process: a green light stands for 'in production' and indicates absence of problems; a red light signals machine breakdowns. A yellow light followed by the message 'loading/unloading failure' indicates the presence of a bottleneck. More specifically, it refers to two possible scenarios: either the upstream inventory is empty and parts cannot be loaded on the line (loading failure), or the downstream inventory is full and parts cannot be unloaded on the line (unloading failure). Electronic notice boards provide shop floor operators with a rich, albeit stylized, description of the current status of the production flow. Furthermore, they are conceived as predictive tools: by reading the electronic boards UTE members are in a position to make inferences about the immediate future and the possible developments of the current production situation. Therefore, the radar system can arguably be seen as a decision-making support system based on information technology (IT).

The following episode depicts UTE 5 in its interaction with customers (UTE 6) and suppliers (UTE 1, UTE 2, and UTE 3). More specifically, the scene portrays the UTE leader as he explains how to read the data displayed on the electronic board. By 'reading' the board, the UTE leader detects a breakdown in the upstream process (sides) and makes conjectures about what might happen next:

Let's start from the left side of the board. That number refers to the pairs of sides which are flowing towards our UTE from UTE 1. In this case there are three of them; the number below refers to the under-bodies which are in the queue, 22 on the left production line; next we have the flow of roofs; and finally the flow of assembled bodies which indicates the number of car bodies, 30 at the moment, which are flowing in the downstream production lines (UTE 6). The current situation indicates that the UTE producing the sides is experiencing some problems. However the problem should not be serious, otherwise we would have been informed over the phone.

The current display also highlights a line imbalance, which means that UTEs are running at different paces. It is precisely the lack of balance between production lines which eventually generates bottlenecks:

In a few minutes we are going to see a loading failure, because of a lack of sides. . . In this situation we normally go to have a look at the problem upstream (sides) in order to assess the exact nature of the problem and, if the problem is serious, possibly exploit the line stoppage to perform short maintenance jobs. It's one of the few moments we can really exploit.

However, from the interviews and observation carried out on the shop floor, it seemed that team members seldom rely on electronic devices in order to act and make decisions. Rather, most of their work consists of walking along the lines, and listening for unusual noises. As the UTE leader put it:

We prefer to walk along the lines in order to understand in real time what's going on. Data displayed on electronic boards is generally reliable, but walking along the lines gives you a better picture of the situation.

The above quotation is promptly supported by a concrete case:

Now we should have a loading failure (meaning problems in the upstream UTE), but that is not displayed on the board. Shall we check whether that's true? Here you are. My machine is waiting for the sides . . . So there is an inconsistency with the system . . . Basically the upstream inventory (UTE 1) has been emptied and we are now emptying our production lines . . . Now the loading failure has appeared on the notice board. Typically the system would wait for a few minutes before updating the situation, whereas we had already detected the loading failure.

Despite the presence of sophisticated information systems, UTE members prefer to spend most of their time walking along the lines and watching the car bodies moving, in an attempt to detect any possible disturbance. Even sounds or silence on the shop floor are taken as clues to the smoothness of the production flow. In other words operators on the shop floor seem to have developed a certain sensitivity towards the subtle functioning of the assembly line. This highlights the role of perception and the importance of craftsmanship as necessary complements to high-tech devices.

Despite the fact that we have no inventory of sides, the pieces produced have gone from 45 to 50. It means that we are emptying the line. We still have about 30 bodies to send forward. Once our line has been emptied we will probably have around 80 bodies in our inventory. That will take about 15 minutes if things go smoothly. If the problem upstream is not solved within this lapse of time, the production level will start to decrease since we won't be receiving components from the upstream processes (in this case sides from UTE 1). (UTE leader)

The UTE leader glances at the aerial lines:

Look there are two more pairs of sides arriving, let's go and check what's going on at the UTE 1 . . . You see, it's the left side which is in trouble, but now the line is producing . . . there are nine sides in transit . . . now look at our production level, we have reached 55 pieces, despite the lack of accumulation in the upstream inventory.

The problem at UTE 1 on that particular day persisted for a whole shift. The UTE was beset by an impressive number of micro-stoppages. This type of breakdown is very difficult to handle and does not leave any room for performing alternative operations (e.g. maintenance). Micro-stoppages normally last for less than three minutes but nonetheless they disrupt the smoothness of the flow and are difficult to diagnose:

Micro-stoppages are problems which are not real problems. They take up a lot of time. If you have a breakdown, you can understand what is causing it and therefore perform an intervention and solve the problem. With micro-stoppages you are always short of breath, it is not easy to recover from them …

Despite this problem, UTE 5 was able to carry on without particular problems and meet the daily production target. The above episode suggests some important implications about the nature of knowledge in the Melfi factory. Notice boards can be seen as sense-making devices. As is apparent from the description of the way operators use the system, electronic boards act as systemic maps enabling operators to make sense of what is going on in the immediate surroundings of their UTE, and to take action on the basis of if-then inferences. In other words, the numbers and messages displayed on electronic boards have important cognitive implications for shop floor operators. The capacity to read the data displayed on electronic boards and make inferences from them indicates the presence of systemic maps at the cognitive level. However, as the above quotes suggest, these maps seem to have been acquired through experience, rather than being derived from the information systems architecture. Operators do not necessarily trust or rely on electronic devices. The radar system seems to be there to reinforce rather than guide the way people think. In other words, notice boards seem to expose the systemic features of the production process and the assembly line rather than provide handy information. As an artefact, they convey the idea of transparency and systemic visibility of the production system.

6.5   Trouble-shooting at Melfi

The problem-solving routine most frequently observed in the plant operations is based on an incremental feedback model. Whatever the breakdown, the routine seems to consist of the following 'moves' (Pentland 1992; Ciborra *et al*. 1996):

- 'see' a problem (e.g. a building up of the work-in-process inventory);
- 'search' for the station where the cause of the problem may originate, based on knowledge of past bottlenecks; work stations and relevant

operations characteristics; information received or gathered from other points on the line;

- 'go to' the station held responsible for the breakdown, or communicate with operators there (depending on the proximity of the station);
- 'disassemble/reassemble' a part or a component of the car or the production machine in order to fix the problem (e.g. dissect a car body, perform automated operations manually);
- register intervention and solution for future memory.

The striking characteristics of such a problem-solving procedure, which I have called the 'Disassembly/Assembly' (D/A) problem-solving routine because of its 'routinized' or repetitive nature (Pentland and Reuter 1994), are its ubiquity, concreteness, 'situatedness', and high level of consistency.[1] As my previous analysis of the building site illustrates, I found instances of its application even in areas distant, at least conceptually, from the car manufacturing process. Today, the application of the D/A routine is evidenced by a number of problem-solving and continuous improvement activities, from Total Quality Management (TQM) to phasing of new car models, where the D/A concept works as a primary sense-making mechanism:

The final quality control procedure performed on each is based on a retroactive mental process, whereby defects (in the form of demerits) are assigned to a specific UTE. (Quality manager)

During the phasing of the Lancia Y we would invite our operators to disassemble a car that had just been completed on the line and then re-assemble it. Then we would ask them which was the best method for re-assembling the car and what their suggestions were about the method (former Plant Director).[2]

More generally, the D/A routine seems to point to the tacit stock of knowledge governing the execution of work operations on the shop floor. In this regard, the D/A routine appears to be grounded on a knowledge template that provides a master or pattern from which other similar

---

[1] A typical instance of this attitude towards disruptions is the very popular problem-solving procedure imported from Toyota and known as 'the five whys'. Production workers are taught to systematically trace every error back to its ultimate cause (by asking 'why' as each layer of the problem is uncovered), and then to devise a solution so that it never occurs again. This strategy, which is widely adopted in Fiat factories, most of the time leads to good and 'clean' solutions, since it tackles the causes generating the problem. The five whys procedure presents many similarities with the D/A routine since both are based on a retroactive mental process aimed at detecting the source of a problem. The efficacy of the latter, however, seems to derive from its meta-routine character (see Adler, Goldoftas, and Levine 1999) governing the shift between routine and non-routine tasks.

[2] The Lancia Y is the second car model produced by the Melfi plant.

things can be made. The idea of disassembling is 'exposed' in a variety of organizational artefacts making up the so-called visual control system: notice boards and panels on the line display the sequence of operations making up the production process, the details of the car components and even the tools that operators are supposed to use in order to carry out their operations. The computer-based information system also reinforces this way of solving problems. In each UTE office, a personal computer (PC) shows screens which portray the relevant segments of the production lines, listing for each work station the number of semi-finished cars entering and exiting the station, together with the levels of in-process-inventories. Other screens display the data in a more aggregate form by identifying the quantitative flows between UTEs. The same network feeds into the big *Andon* boards which show production data for each UTE and all the related alarms. The *Andon* boards reproduce at a higher level the idea that you have to 'see' and 'feel' a problem in order to make it 'really true', and amenable to a 'go to' and 'hands on' solution. Finally, the routine allows for variations, though within the boundaries set by the D/A metaphor. At a cognitive level the whole production process is perceived and thought of as a sequence of operations, the product as an assemblage of parts (see Figure 6.1).

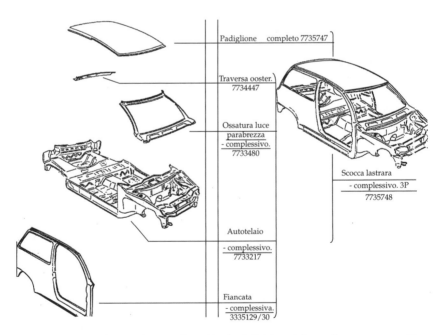

Figure 6.1   *The D/A template is reflected in the definition of the product as an assemblage of parts*

Although knowledge of the global process and product is sometimes necessary to solve 'local' problems or cope with the ramifications of local breakdowns, the procedure followed consistently implies the deconstruction of global problems into lower level ones capable of being resolved through a local D/A intervention. I have observed various instances when a breakdown occurs, or a bottleneck is perceived, in which the worker or the supervisor goes back through the working cycle, and through a *gedanken* experiment disassembles the car in order to search for and identify the potential source of the default: that is, what operation might not have been carried out in the proper way. Thus, once the mental search results in a physical identification of the problem, workers propose a local intervention, try it out and learn.

To conclude, an analogy emerges between the *physical* layout and workflow in the integrated factory, and the *cognitive* strategies present in the problem-solving routines. The way operators think is linear and sequential, thus reflecting the organization of the physical flow of cars along the line.

6.6 Local and systemic breakdowns: cognitive implications of the D/A routine

The cognitive connotations of the D/A routine became apparent through the observation of those situations related to the building up of in-process inventories. Their causes are often of a 'second order' nature as they may stem from local sub-optimization strategies carried out by some UTEs, or they may be unintended side-effects due to the application of a local D/A routine to fix a problem somewhere along the line, or 'systemic' causes linked to the production mix and capacity load. In this respect, bottlenecks confront the work team with crucial cognitive challenges, emphasizing the need for systemic understanding and capability for abstraction. The scenes depicted above seem to confirm a widespread capacity for inferential reasoning (if-then) underpinning the micro decision-making processes at the team level, and highlight a systemic orientation towards the analysis of cause–effect relationships. The following conversation with the technologist is particularly significant, since it refers to a 'hypothetical' and therefore abstract situation, where line stoppages due to the work-in-process inventory are related to machinery maintenance problems.

Let me give you an example: suppose the downstream UTE has 90 car bodies in the inventory (I am calling it inventory, but it is actually a dynamic inventory, a transit), basically 90 bodies in the workflow. At that point the upstream lines will stop; we will then have about 15 minutes before the inventory is emptied and the upstream lines can resume production ... Ideally, in order to keep the flow running, one should have about 70 car bodies in transit; having a high number of car bodies in the inventory (full) allows you to perform maintenance jobs; having 45–50 car bodies means that you can work without having the pressure of constantly monitoring the workflow. Having less than 30 car bodies can be dangerous, because you will start creating production voids in the downstream UTE (UTE 6). With more than 30 they will receive the car bodies one after the other.

As a cognitive resource, the D/A template provides operators with a virtual map of the assembly line and of the division of labour on the shop floor. The map seems to possess a spatial connotation. As for a city, it provides a diagrammatic representation of the whole production process and at the same time it says: 'you are here'. The mental process underpinning the application of the D/A routine instantly tells operators where certain things are happening (e.g. where problems are arising), why (diagnosis) and who is responsible for them. In other words, the D/A template captures the fundamental relationship between parts and the whole, components and systems, which governs the execution of operations on the assembly line. Finally, it offers a conceptualization of the assembly line as a chain of transformations of the product along the production process (building the car bit by bit).

On the other hand, as the analysis of bottlenecks illustrates, the background knowledge required for the resolution of bottlenecks is highly situated and grounded on perception. Electronic boards and IT-based resources provide systemic maps enabling operators to get a snapshot of the current situation on the shop floor. However, the sense-making activity related to the potential build up of work-in-process inventories seems to be based on a deep-seated form of 'circumspection' grounded on the ability to 'see', 'feel', or 'listen'. For example, while notice boards display numbers about the status of the production process, the overhead conveyor—the impressive mechanical infrastructure that dynamically links the different production processes—provides a much more concrete picture of the situation. Likewise, sounds tell operators whether production lines are moving or being idle.

The above analysis shows how, within the notion of an assembly line, hard concepts and soft ones are inextricably intertwined. From a technical standpoint, the assembly line is the basic infrastructure through which the plant organizes its activity. However, the peculiar division of labour underlying the operations on the shop floor (assembling the car bit by bit) is subtly reproduced in the background knowledge (the D/A template) that governs the way operators deal with routine and breakdown events. Thanks to its situatedness, the assembly line becomes part of the background of 'readiness-to-hand' that is taken for granted by the users without explicit recognition or identification as an object. It lies at the heart of the cognitive, social and material background by which people interrelate with organizational practice, and therefore becomes a crucial mechanism for synthesizing knowing and organizing processes.

Finally, if we are to understand the interplay between systems and components, we need to consider the socio-organizational elements which shape them. For instance, the task of building cars bit by bit on an assembly line (governed by the technical sub-system comprising machines and equipment) acquires different meanings according to the underlying production system (e.g. mass vs. lean production), the organizational model (e.g. hierarchical vs. team-based), the cultural values (e.g. quantity vs. quality and the demerits system), the capabilities required (e.g. local vs. systemic), and so on. The lean production concept as applied in the Melfi plant generates an integrated dynamic system connecting interdependent stations which have a certain degree of autonomy in carrying out operations (the customer–supplier model). Accordingly, the smooth functioning of shop floor operations becomes not only a matter of mechanical synchronization, but depends crucially on human behaviour: the trust relationship between internal customers and suppliers, co-operation among teams, the attitude towards the demerits system, and so on. The latter emphasizes the importance of the core values embodied by the Melfi workforce which were discussed in Chapter 5.

6.7   Digging into organizational knowledge

The pervasive influence of the D/A template is apparent at different levels of the organizational knowledge system (Ciborra, Patriotta, and Erlicher 1996). Work practices, both individual and team-based, are aimed at building the car, or deconstructing it in case of breakdowns, bit by bit. In its turn, the D/A work practice becomes a generalized problem-solving capability in use across the whole plant. It is applied to whatever problem emerges along the line. Where distance impedes direct presence 'at the machine', appropriate communication and information mechanisms are set up to handle the problem in a distributed way while preserving the basic approach. The 'skills without a place' character of organizational capabilities is apparent in the conceptualization of the D/A routine as part of a work method. Finally, the piecemeal character of the D/A template is very much alive in the design and implementation of the Melfi project, as discussed at length in Chapter 5. The construction process of the factory and the simulations carried out during the induction phase at the Melfi building site seem to rely on the same core stock of knowledge which today governs the execution of routine operations on the shop floor.

The above considerations invite thorough reflection on the meaning of technology, the task, and the role of human skills in the setting under study. The learning process developed around the task of disassembling, and eventually institutionalized in the D/A template, highlights an important knowledge-based distinction between the traditional mass production system and the new post-Fordist paradigm developed at Melfi. The Fordist model integrates task and technology in the assembly line concept. The skills necessary to perform the task are built into the technology. The Fordist assembly line is based on alienation of the task and the substitution of human labour with machinery. Accordingly, the moving line defines the job of shop floor operators.

On the other hand, the appropriation of the assembly line at Melfi occurs around the task rather than the technology. The initial experience of assembling a car takes place off the line. Certainly, production lines have been set up, but they are idle. Operators, not the technology, are physically moving on the shop floor and this clearly indicates who 'owns' the task. Under these circumstances, the role of the technology emerges only later, when the factory becomes operational and the moving line is brought into the picture. Indeed, assembling is not about craft; it is about speed, time and motion (Benyon 1973; Adler 1993). Finally, even when the technology is operational, the job of shop floor operators seems to be defined by the tension between routine and breakdown events, between separating from and re-appropriating the practice of building the car bit by bit according to the changing circumstances on the shop floor. In this sense, technology becomes a mechanism of delegation of human agency and knowledge.

To sum up, the distinctive features of the production paradigm applied at Melfi can be connected to a different conceptualization of the relationship between four related systems with respect to the traditional Fordist model. These are: the task, the technology, human skills, and the division of labour. Crucially, this is a knowledge-based rather than technology-based distinction. In the Fordist model, the *assembly line* acts as an independent variable driving the execution of the task and dictating the division of labour. The assembly line is a social system in which the distinction between task, technology, and human labour has been somewhat blurred. The model stresses precisely the concept of automation, defined as the substitution of human labour with machinery. Conversely, in the post-Fordist environment observed at Melfi, competence seems to be built around the task. Accordingly, the *task* mediates between human labour and technology. Figure 6.2 illustrates this distinction between the two production paradigms.

Competence at Melfi is developed around a redefinition of the organizational socio-technical system. On the one hand, the D/A template is so powerful in shaping problem-solving and learning throughout the plant because it embeds the 'archetype' of the assembly line (Greenwood and Hinings 1988). The D/A template apparently has been transferred almost intact from the slaughterhouses in Chicago, where Ford first had the idea of the assembly line, to the avant-garde plant in Melfi. At the same time, the knowledge template based on the D/A concept is developed through a historical process related to the greenfield experience. In fact, a crucial knowledge transfer occurred during the intensive training period on the Melfi greenfield site, where the capabilities of the future workforce were developed

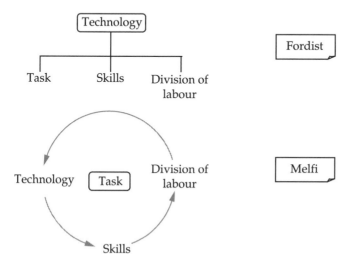

Figure 6.2   *The knowledge implications of production systems*

and fine-tuned, especially during the hands-on sessions that included building off the line a real car 'bit by bit'. The D/A template remains at the heart of Melfi's formative context and exerts a strong influence on the vast array of learning processes which take place in the plant. From the above considerations we can draw the following conclusion: the D/A template does not reside exclusively in cognition, technology, the task or the skills related to its execution. Rather, it can be seen as a distributed knowledge system linking different variables in a coherent whole. The D/A template draws on the semantic overlaps around the concept of assembling, and affects the relationship among task, technology, human skills and division of labour. It is this holistic dimension of the template which makes it work. In this respect, the D/A template gives meaning to factory activities, which become part of a distinctive organizational 'cosmology' (Weick 1993), and thereby acquire both a descriptive and prescriptive value.

6.8 Epilogue: assembling, knowing, and organizing

What makes Melfi a distinctive auto assembly plant? What is the ontological significance of the D/A template? And ultimately, what is the meaning of assembling? Answering the above questions implies addressing a more fundamental query about the meaning of knowing, the purpose of organizing and the linkages between knowing and organizing.

The circumstances surrounding the coming into existence of the Melfi plant represent a unique experience in the world of car manufacturing. The strategic choice of the company to involve the future workforce in the physical construction of the factory played a crucial role in the creation and development of what might be called a manufacturing community. Indeed, in the process of building the plant not only was a manufacturing machine assembled and put into operation, but also an institutional and cognitive order was established, based on an industrial paradigm. Letting the workers build their own factory from the greenfield led to a form of situated appropriation of different aspects of work: the role, the task, the technology, the product and production process, and most importantly the workplace itself. Appropriation emphasizes the notion of familiarity as opposed to alienation; it involves acquiring citizenship within a given community of practice. In this respect, the concept of appropriation is closely related to identity building.

The construction of the factory was first of all a knowledge-creating endeavour through which a community of workers developed a distinctive perspective on the world in which they lived. On the basis of my field observations I argue that by building the factory the workers learnt a practice of assembling that fed into the core competencies on the shop floor—the competencies of assembling a car. Indeed, the Melfi factory as an artefact is a sedimentation and stratification of an ordered sequence of assembling operations which define a collective experience. The knowledge template based on the D/A concept and governing the execution of day-to-day operations on the shop floor was developed through a historical process originating from the greenfield experience. It was then carried forward once the factory had reached the full production stage. The template is built precisely on the identity between learning experiences carried out in different settings and under diverse historical contingencies (e.g. assembling/construction site; assembling/shop floor).

The above considerations highlight the ways in which knowing is related to the experience of time. For the builders, the factory inscribes not only technical and functional requirements, but also a historical dimension. The possibility of referring to the greenfield as the beginning of the Melfi story, generates processes of collective remembering and historicizes the learning experience of the 'pioneers and constructors' around a founding event. In the recollections of the original group of workers the greenfield is turned into a saga, an array of emblematic stories representing instances of exceptional behaviour ('there was nothing here'). Accordingly, the factory becomes something that can be talked about, referred to in the past; that is, 'narrated' through its different stages of construction.

Secondly, the making of the factory was an organizing endeavour. The case study portrays a process of organizational becoming. The construction work proceeded from an embryonic form of organizing—defined by a minimal set of boundaries (the greenfield)—to a sophisticated one (the operational factory) characterized by impersonal mechanisms and complex interdependencies. Once again, the notions of assembling and disassembling provided an overarching principle based on the image of organization as a composable and decomposable system. Indeed, the Melfi factory itself can be seen as an 'assemblage' (Cooper 1998) subject to continuous transformations and reconfigurations. The construction site, with its layers of equipment and machinery, expressed the dynamic character of the assemblage. It conveyed the ideas of work in progress, craftwork and *bricolage*, transience and transformation, underlying the technical black boxing of the factory.

The above discussion leads to our third question about the meaning of assembling. In the context of Melfi's avant-garde factory the notion of assembling, conveyed through the D/A template, pervades the work setting in its smallest details. Overall, what stands out when we 'explode' the micro-dynamics observed in the case study are the distinctive linkages between modes of knowing and modes of organizing in the setting of an avant-garde factory. Paradoxically, the knowledge processes surrounding the construction of Melfi's avant-garde factory take us back to a 'pre-Fordist' age. Before the assembly line was invented, cars used to be hand-built in small numbers by skilled craftspeople (Womack, Jones, and Ross 1990). When the mediation of the assembly line was brought into the picture, the basic task of building the car bit by bit was simply delegated to the technology. Today, despite revolutions and paradigm shifts, the functioning of modern car manufacturing systems is still based on assembly lines, although the heavy reliance on computer-mediated devices to control the production process has rendered the basic task of building the car bit by bit more transparent. Under these circumstances, the D/A template enacts a powerful craft production system, emphasizing the task of building the car bit by bit and allowing shop floor operators to re-appropriate the task whenever a disruption occurs or machinery breaks down. Thanks to the D/A template, the complexity of a modern production process based on assembly lines can be unpacked, reconnected to mechanical operations, and pinned down in the smallest detail.

To conclude, the activity of assembling at Melfi epitomizes the ways in which knowing and organizing are mutually constituted. Echoing Weick (1993), it is possible to say that assembling becomes a 'microcosm for organizing' where a distinctive organizational community can dwell in its everyday dealings with practice. A cosmology is both a way of making things and seeing things. It conveys the idea of knowledge as a totality, of a universe that is taken for granted within a particular community. The findings of the study portray a parallel transformation process of knowledge and organization, a co-evolution of knowing and organizing, which occur over time. The potential implications are particularly relevant in so far as they open up the possibility of relating the evolution of organizations to the knowledge processes underlying their functioning.

7

Sense Making on the Shop Floor: The Narrative Dimension of Organizational Knowledge[1]

7.1 Introduction

This chapter looks at the sense-making processes through which narratives in the workplace lead to the creation and institutionalization of organizational knowledge. The setting is the stamping shop of an automotive plant. The focus of the inquiry is on how a best performing team resolves disruptive occurrences on the shop floor. In contrast to Melfi, the Mirafiori Pressing plant incarnates a highly institutionalized context, characterized by experienced workforce, consolidated and often opaque work practices, and distinctive cultural tradition. In trying to penetrate such a deep-seated knowledge base, the technological discontinuities inherent in the nature of the task and the batch production system provide a fundamental entry point. A typical day on the shop floor seems to be punctuated by the occurrence of interruptions and disruptive events which prompt operators to make sense of the situation and respond through different types of interventions. Precisely because the line between routine and breakdown situations—the cleavage between organization and disorganization—is very thin, the above context offers a privileged observational perspective.

The analysis of narratives on the shop floor highlight a distinctive mode of investigation conceptualized as 'detective stories' because of its analogy with the literary genre. Dramatizing breakdowns as detective cases provides operators with a sense-making strategy for representing equivocal action in a meaningful fashion and achieving epistemological closure. Detective stories generate a repertoire of solutions, notable experiences, and learning examples that can be stored in the organizational

---

[1] An extended version of this chapter has been published in the *Journal of Management Studies* (see Patriotta 2003).

memory and retrieved when disruptive events occur. In this respect, they act as 'templates' for the resolution of future cases. On the other hand, detective stories are deeply entrenched in the social fabric of the shop floor. As a genre, the narrative structure of detective cases involves achieving closure by finding a culprit and attributing blame. In particular, the *modus operandi* of the team members at Mirafiori seems to be based on a compelling system of sanctions and rewards which stresses the core value of taking responsibility for one's own mistakes. The interplay of narrative and social factors highlights problems of blame management, scapegoating, and face-saving in the day-to-day practices on the shop floor.

The main findings of the study seem to be partially consistent with the existing literature. Narratives appear to be essential diagnostic devices, enabling operators to perform a coherent description of troubled machines (Orr 1996). Furthermore, they provide operators with guides to conduct (Weick 1995) or cognitive maps based on the recurrence of histories of disruption. Finally, narratives act as storage devices, providing receptacles for organizational memory. In so doing, they maintain the stability of the work setting by fostering the circulation of organizational knowledge within the community of workers. On the other hand, the narrative form of the detective story have some novel implications for the study of knowledge-making processes in organizations. In particular, detective stories identify an emerging epistemological archetype similar to what Ginzburg (1990) calls the 'evidential paradigm'. The essence of the paradigm lies in the formation of conjectures and the use of common sense as a primary mode of knowing and discovering reality. By relating empirical evidence from the case study to the contributions already present in the literature, the chapter explores the role of narratives as carriers of organizational knowledge. Specifically, the chapter attempts to explain how knowledge is capitalized in a narrative form, and thereby explicitly links narratives to dynamics of organizational knowledge creation, utilization, and institutionalization.

The chapter contains six sections. Section 7.2 provides an overview of the Mirafiori Pressing plant and discusses the organizational and cognitive implications of batch production systems. Sections 7.3 and 7.4 describe instances of disruptive occurrences on the shop floor. The sense-making dynamics underlying problem-solving activities are connected to a distinctive narrative-based process of investigation, conceptualized as 'detective stories'. The analysis shows how sense making is grounded on the core values of the team and how those values affect collective learning processes. Section 7.5 reconsiders the detective method as an archetypical practice or template. It is argued that detective stories define a distinctive process of learning and knowledge acquisition based on the possibility of turning critical incidents into emblematic experiences. The concluding section analyses the implications of detective stories for a theory of knowing and organizing.

7.2 The Mirafiori Pressing plant: production system and cognitive implications

The Mirafiori Pressing plant (Figure 7.1) is one of the largest in Europe, covering an area of 233,000 square metres with about 3000 employees.

Figure 7.1 *The 'Mirafiori Presse' plant within the Mirafiori industrial district*

It is housed in buildings constructed in the 1950s during an extension of the Mirafiori industrial district. The shop floor consists of fifteen Elementary Technical Units (UTE) distributed across two Operational Units. The production process on the shop floor is organized in lots, scheduled according to the customer's requirements. The stamping shop represents the beginning of a vehicle's journey through the production process. The primary function of stamping is to transform coils of steel into sheet metal components and parts for the body shell (e.g. fenders, hoods, and doors). The process starts with steel coils of various sizes and compositions that are delivered as needed to the stamping area. Overhead cranes load the steel coils into a coil cradle. Robots then feed the coils through a series of rollers which clean and straighten the steel. The flattened steel is transported to a large press which cuts the steel into the primary size for the final part. These parts, called 'blanks' are stacked and taken to a temporary storage area. Team members transfer the blanks to a press line (see Figure 7.2) which stamps or shapes them into parts. During this process, dies are used to shape the metal, trim excess, bend edges, and pierce holes. The team members use forklifts to move the stamped parts to a temporary storage area until they are needed by the Body Shop. Once each lot has been completed, the dies are replaced and the presses can start processing a different part.

The essential characteristic of batch production is that to accommodate a product change, the process has to be stopped and reset. Batch production is typically classified as an intermittent system (Hill 1991) because the product/service does not flow through the system but rather undergoes a series of stops and starts. Under these circumstances, time is punctuated by the succession of production lots with changeover operations providing major points of discontinuity: a batch is not simply a production unit, it is also a temporal point of reference. For this reason, die change is perceived as a major technological perturbation, with important consequences on the unfolding of organizational action and sense making. Significantly, one manager remarked that 'each lot tells a different story'.

The production system in Mirafiori provides a crucial entry point for the observation of knowledge-making processes on the shop floor. In fact, technology defines a set of cognitive models and sense-making capabilities which enable its users to represent and understand events associated with it (Weick 1990). In particular, the intermittent nature of large batch production requires switching between continuous flows and discrete events, absorbing interruptions and technological perturbations, coping with disconnections and discontinuities, dealing with

Figure 7.2 *A traditional production line*

trade-offs and tactical choices. As such, the production system requires governance mechanisms partly embodied in the organizational structure (e.g. plans, routines, and procedures) and partly contingent upon the sense-making activities of the organizational actors. In other words, continuity in the performance of the system critically depends on the interplay between structure and sense making (Weick 1993).

By establishing the long-term plans, organization sets the stage against which operations can be performed. However, the way in which plans are to be fulfilled is often subject to interpretation. While production plans act as a basic organizational constraint, the frequency of unexpected events and deviations from standards allows for a certain degree of interpretive flexibility. Scheduling is the activity that translates organizational plans into shop floor activities. It entails converting actual or forecast demand for products or services into demand for time, labour, and plant resources; specifying when particular products or services will be processed with precisely which resources; determining the sequence in which batches are processed. Successful scheduling ensures the smooth flow of products and services through the system. As such it depends on a number of variables/factors that are difficult to control. At the cognitive level, scheduling involves addressing 'what-if' and 'if-then' questions on an ongoing basis.

Notwithstanding the paramount importance of planning activities and the high degree of repetitiveness, a batch production system seems to share some of the characteristics of stochastic events (Weick 1990), since the very distinction between predictable and unexpected is problematic. The repertoire of skills defined by such a production system are indeed those typical of a stochastic environment: 'people are usually on standby, giving special attention to start-up and to anticipating faults that may lead to downtime; the distinction between operations and maintenance is blurred; skills in monitoring and diagnostics are crucial; people must be committed to do what is necessary on their own initiative and have the autonomy to do so; and people have now assumed the role of "variance absorber", dealing with and counteracting the unexpected' (Weick 1990: 9). No scheduling system can accommodate random disruptions. Under these circumstances, organization seems to provide a relatively stable background for the local, often improvised practices of the team members.

7.3   Entering the shop floor

Conversations on the shop floor highlighted the pervasive presence of machines in the daily talks of the team members. The vulnerability of machinery and its tendency to break down exposed the fragility of the work setting: solving problems was an ongoing endeavour for the team:

UTE leader: 'In the course of a day you are confronted with 10, 20, 30 problems, all of them related to your production targets, all of them affecting the number of pieces you have to make . . . whenever you have a setback the line must keep producing pieces. So you try to tame the problem, to find a temporary solution in order to keep the line going. Then the day after you have to go back over the problem, but in the meantime 9 new problems might have cropped up.'

Typically, the actions undertaken by the team were aimed at collectively making sense of disruptions, responding to or preventing the occurrence of technical breakdowns. The 'presence' (real or impending) of a disruptive event emphasized the constraints typical of a batch production system. Batch production is based on intensive exploitation of the machinery and therefore, on completion of a production lot, the dies and machine tools are worn out. Accordingly, product quality was heavily dependent on repair and maintenance activities. When breakdowns occurred maintenance teams were allocated to the problem and their role was to respond quickly and make the decisions necessary to minimize the effect of the breakdown on the operations system. In many instances, temporary repairs were made so that the process could resume as soon as possible. Permanent repairs would be made at a later and more convenient time. Beyond its technical complexity, the production system raised critical cognitive challenges for the team. The need to respond to frequent breakdowns, interruptions, and unexpected events was a dual challenge for sense making: planning (dealing with the unexpected) and diagnosis (dealing with the equivocality of action). The two activities pointed to the interconnected processes of anticipation and retrospection, which are at the core of any sense-making endeavour (see Weick 1995). In the remainder of the chapter I shall present some typical instances of breakdowns on the shop floor, analyse the narratives constructed around them, and draw implications for a theory of knowing and organizing.

7.3.1 *The Panda's dashboard* [2]

I am with the UTE technologist. Yesterday the Mirafiori assembly plant detected a hole off centre on the Panda's dashboard and reported the problem to our UTE. Although the anomaly is limited to 156 pieces, the problem is still important because it has been detected by the assembly plant, at an advanced stage of the production process, and the consequences could well have been more serious. Together with the UTE leader and the technologist we walk to the repair area where the chief repairman, the die maintenance leader and one die operator are waiting for us. We take one of the defective parts from a container

---

[2] The Panda is one of Fiat's car models.

where the faulty pieces are stocked. The group begins to examine the anomaly by touching the component at the point of anomaly.

Since the parts have been returned by the customer, there seem to be only two possible explanations for the problem, both relating to a quality control procedure and both involving a human error (although to different extents): the anomaly could be related to the completion of the lot. Anomalies towards the end of a batch are very common owing to wear and tear of machine tools. In this scenario, operators had completed the lot without noticing the problem (an oversight on the part of end of the line workers who did not check the parts produced properly). Alternatively, it could be that team operators had taken a corrective action on the dies without clearing up the faulty parts so that, the defect was passed on to the downstream process. Again, they did not follow the procedure for correcting defects which requires going backwards through the lot in order to detect the first non-defective piece, and sending all the faulty parts to repair. Now, in order to perform a diagnosis, we must work backwards: the die maintainer is going to examine the die responsible for the faulty operation. He is going to open the die and check the 'blueprint'. If the blueprint is broken, it means that the problem occurred at the end of the lot and nobody noticed it. Conversely, if the blueprint is in order, that means that a corrective intervention was performed, but without amending the faulty parts.

Before proceeding to the die area, we decide to check the position of that part on an assembled car. Taking the defective dashboard with us, we walk to another area where a sample Panda is on display. We match the part with the car body in order to assess the deviation of the hole and decide how to perform the repair job. Now the chief repairman knows how to repair the defective parts, but we still need to understand what caused the anomaly in the first place. We move to the die area, still taking the component with us. The die maintenance leader and the die operator open up the die that has produced the component in order to check its integrity. The blueprint of the die looks in order. This means that it had been replaced before the target lot was completed. This fact seems to exclude one of the two hypotheses, but at one point the die operator comes up with a third hypothesis, that attributes responsibility to workers at the assembly plant. Basically, there is a possibility that the anomaly was generated in the body welding unit, before reaching the final assembly stage. The group seems satisfied with this new possibility and decides to visit the assembly plant the following day. I go back to the UTE box with the technologist. While the solution is still pending, I ask him to reflect on the episode. As we shall see, the language and the narration style are particularly relevant:

The anomaly was reported yesterday to the chief repairman, who had passed the information to us. The customer had returned five containers of defective parts, 156 in total, because they presented a deformed hole. We took the faulty component from the repair team, it was about 3–3.30 p.m. Together with the UTE leader of the second shift, I had a look at the anomaly. We consulted the maintenance person who was on duty when the lot was being produced. He said he had not done any work on the machines. Then we had a word with the die maintenance leader and with the line conductor of the second shift because they had completed the lot. Basically they had worked for three hours on Monday afternoon—*because the problem occurred on Monday afternoon*—before they changed the dies. At 6 p.m. they performed the die change. I wanted to find out whether they had noticed any problem. They insisted that they had not noticed any problem nor had they performed any intervention work. This was confirmed by a line conductor, who called me about a different problem, at around four o'clock. Meanwhile we had a look at the component, and the anomaly was not there, it did not exist at four. The die change took place at six. I do not know what happened between four and six, but the problem must have occurred within that lapse of time. Yesterday when I took the part and saw the anomaly, the first thing I wanted to establish was who had caused the fault. I wanted to establish whether it was a problem related to the end of the batch, or if an intervention had been performed, without amending the faulty parts. Yesterday I was unable to solve the puzzle. I went home without having solved my problem. This morning I arrived in the office and I saw a sheet reporting the 156 defective pieces. I asked the UTE leader whether any intervention work on the machines had been done on Monday morning. He replied that there hadn't. We decided to investigate the problem further and we did what you have just seen.

Later, a phone call informs the technologist that the puzzle has been solved, revealing yet another possibility that had not been envisaged. The defective parts returned by the assembly plant did not belong to the lot that had just been completed on Monday. Instead they belonged to the previous lot of the same component, produced a few days earlier. The problem had occurred during the second shift and the die change had been brought forward because there was a broken blueprint on one die. The operators had detected the defect on the components, but had not performed the backward check on the containers that presented the anomaly:

They detected the anomaly; so they brought forward the die change and started processing the next component; the next step would have been to clear up the faulty parts in the previous containers. They did not do this because they thought that the problem had only just occurred, without realizing that they had already produced five containers of defective parts. Thus the anomaly concerned a previous lot and the intervention (substitution of the blue print) had been performed on the die.

Now that the problem had been finally resolved what remained of the above episode? Was it an event that ended in its resolution? The 'moral' of the story prompts some interesting considerations about the experience-related nature of learning, the professional identity of middle managers and the division of knowledge among different roles:

A procedure is what we have in this case because such a procedure was already identified and written and therefore we are confident on *our side*.[3] In fact, this is a problem that we have already seen many times, it is not the first: we have deformed holes, damaged ones, missing ones. It is just a matter of understanding that we already have a procedure to tackle the issue, and that has been overlooked. To *them* (the line workers) it means that they have to gain further understanding of the method and consider it useful, because, at the end of the day, the line conductors are those who produce. *We* as technicians or chief of the UTE do not need to experience this problematic event. For *us* it is important to know that this experience is part of a method, it is part of some occurrence we have faced and thus if we had acted according to some written procedure, we would have avoided the problem in the first place.

The failure in applying the procedure points up the organizing practices of the team and the values underlying such practices. In this respect, adherence to a procedure becomes part of a broader compliance with the team's code of conduct.

7.4 Detective stories and the search for blame

The problem-solving activity depicted in the above episode seems to be linked to a distinctive sense-making strategy, whereby human and non-human 'actants' (Latour 1987) are involved in a process of investigation.

---

[3] The procedure in question is one related to quality control. Typically continuous defects are discovered through sampling inspection, performed by the line conductor every hour or every 500 pieces produced. When one is found, the machine is stopped and the problem corrected. One hundred percent inspection is then conducted on parts previously processed to remove the defective items. In addition, a less accurate quality inspection is carried out by the workers at the end of the line on each part processed, before stocking the part in a container. In this case the defect was discovered by one of the workers at the end of the line, before the sampling inspection. The target lot was almost completed so it was sensible to move forward the die change rather than performing a repair intervention on the dies. However, the quality control backwards was not performed.

The problem-solving procedure entails a set of moves aimed at detecting the cause of the problem, performing a diagnosis and agreeing upon corrective actions. More generally, what we see in the episode is a dramatization process characterized by the typical ingredients of a detective story. Investigation is triggered by the occurrence of a breakdown which is treated as a murder case. Problem-solving takes the form of an inquiry where the detective collects clues and seeks to reconstruct the facts. It entails locating the anomaly in space and time, formulating hypotheses and conjectures, and conducting interviews. Even inanimate objects are summoned up as witnesses: dies, blueprints, car parts, and samples. The process of investigation inherent in the detective stories defines a distinctive sense-making activity aimed at constructing a plot out of a disruptive event and proceeding through a series of inferences.

As we saw earlier, breakdowns introduce discordance into the smooth flow of action. In so doing, they trigger a sense-making process whereby actors switch their cognitive gears from habits of mind to active thinking (Luis and Sutton 1991). Detective stories involve a process of *mise-en-intrigue* (emplotment) by which, as Ricoeur put it, 'goals, causes, and chance are brought together within the temporal unity of a whole and complete action' (Ricoeur 1984). The emplotment of an equivocal happening in the form of a detective story provides operators with a meaningful representation of action. 'Intrigues' turn action into narratives, unfolding in a chronological/ sequential manner. Admittedly, the location in space and time and the presence of a subject matter are the typical ingredients of a story. However, what makes a story meaningful is precisely the process of sequencing inherent in the enchainment of facts and events. This latter point is clearly addressed by Karl Weick (1995). According to him, stories involve building a plot for an outcome through a process of sequencing. The plot follows either the sequence beginning–middle–end or the sequence disruption–transformation–solution. But sequence is the source of sense in that it enables organizational actors to impose a formal coherence on equivocal happenings. Correspondingly, sequencing is a powerful heuristic for sense making (Weick 1995: 128–9). Dramatic and temporal units are brought together in the narrative: time becomes human in so far as it is articulated in a narrative fashion. The process of dramatization of action also highlights the emotional quality of breakdowns. As in Greek tragedy, the emotional response of the spectator is built into the drama (Ricoeur 1984). Ultimately, the narrative process and the construction of a plot around a disruptive occurrence is a strategy to absorb discordance. Catharsis, that is, emotional release, is what turns discordance into concordance by bringing consistency back into equivocal action. In this regard, catharsis provides a form of epistemological closure in that it joins cognition, imagination, and emotion.

Detective stories are deeply embedded in the social fabric of the shop floor and in the broader cultural system of the integrated factory, where working together becomes a sort of ethical principle. The narratives of the team members emphasize such values as commitment, dialogue, transparency, being humble and keeping a low profile, collective responsibility, harmony, and mutual respect. These values are part of how the team represents itself. They are reflected in a number of emblematic stories reported by the team members during the fieldwork. Below are some examples:

UTE leader B: 'once a conductor accidentally broke a robot's arm. He immediately came to report the incident, assuming responsibility for it. This spared us the trouble of analysing the causes of the incident and made us save a considerable amount of time.'

Technologist: 'let me tell you about an episode that made me particularly happy. During a visit to the shop floor the director of the plant noticed a container upside down and the pieces inside it scattered on the floor. He called the UTE leader and the technologist to account for the episode. Meanwhile the forklift driver stopped and explained how the incidents had occurred, saying that it was his fault. The director thanked us and went away. At a subsequent meeting the director congratulated us on the atmosphere established in the factory and cited the episode of the forklift driver as emblematic. He was very glad that the forklift conductor had admitted his error.'[4]

UTE leader A: 'Let me tell you a little story. Once I was talking to the head of the operating unit and I was telling him: you say that somebody is good because he comes to you and tells you that he has produced 30,000 pieces. The operator who has produced 28,000 pieces is less good, and the one who has produced only 26,000 is still less good. Then you discover that the one who produced 30,000 has sent everything forward: yes he has made 30,000 pieces, but 4000 of them have gone to repair and 400 have been wasted; he has exceeded the lot size twice on two production lines, he has not performed the die change when it was required and he has placed the burden of changeover operations on the next shift. The worker making 28,000 pieces has performed the die change when it was required, he has done almost everything expected of him, but he has overlooked quality problems. The one making 26,000 has performed the die change according to the schedule; if he detected defects

---

[4] This episode is well known within the factory. The HRM manager reported the same episode during a subsequent conversation.

on the parts he stopped the line and did the repairs. In my opinion he is the one who worked the best among the three. In my opinion a performance evaluation based on sheer measurement of output is not accurate. One should deduct the number of pieces sent for repair and those that were discarded from the total output. Time spent in changeover operations should also be included. If we accounted for those factors we would have a better sense of who is working well and who is not.'

The above narratives highlight a consistent pattern of causal attribution within the team. Specifically, the team seems to reward those behaviours that prevent painful investigations aimed at discovering a culprit. This is consistent with the team spirit and the new values brought by the integrated factory model (e.g. working together, harmony, being part of a family). In this regard, oversights and human errors are tolerated (and indeed are turned into emblematic stories) in so far as they reinforce existing team values. Consider the stories of the line conductor who broke a robot's arm and that of the forklift driver who accidentally hit a container. The two stories contain the following essential ingredients: a disruptive event, a power relationship (line conductor *vis-à-vis* the UTE leader, forklift driver *vis-à-vis* the director of the plant), high emotional involvement, a happy ending and a moral. These ingredients turn the story into a noteworthy experience that can be remembered and which acquires a prescriptive value (guide to conduct). The narrative reinforces the value of taking responsibility for one's own mistakes, which is crucial when working in a collaborative environment. On the other hand, as the case of the Panda's dashboard illustrates, when the system of spontaneous blame attribution fails, the values of the integrated factory seem to break down. Issues of trust, power play, free riding, and opportunistic behaviour, come to the fore. Hiding the truth is a punishable behaviour for at least two reasons: it involves the entire team into time-consuming investigations, it eludes hierarchical control mechanisms and, more generally, it violates the team's overall code of conduct. From a narrative perspective, the closure of the story is disturbed since hiding the truth delays the process of causal attribution.

The pervasive search for blame is a very simple (if not simplistic) type of detective story where a single actor is expected to be found. The narratives triggered by the occurrence of technical breakdowns seemingly contain some implicit questions concerning causal attribution: who caused the problem? who took the blame? who hid the truth? To be sure, when the team 'solves' a problem it is only a solution in terms of the narrative structure (or knowledge template) that they employ.

They solve it by finding a culprit because their narrative structure for the detective story is of that form. But, interestingly enough, the team members have another, parallel narrative structure of teamwork and the integrated factory which could also be used to solve such problems. A teamwork version of the story would have a solution in which some breakdown in the 'team' was the cause, not an individual. The team breakdown narrative would be a systemic solution in which the training procedures, the climate created by the management, the design of the product, or any number of other systemic factors are identified as the culprit. If they really had an integrated factory mindset they would have an integrated factory detective genre. What is interesting is that the team seems to follow a person blame (finding a 'bad guy') rather than system blame attribution model (Guimond et al. 1989). This model emphasizes human over non-human errors and the responsibility of the individual over collective actors.

In sum, detective stories highlight a distinctive model of factory socialization in which causal attribution is the result of the team members taking on the social perspective appropriate to the team culture. Blaming a person is a matter of drawing a logical conclusion from the commonly accepted system of representations (Moscovici 1982). This model is consistent with socio-cultural explanations of causal attribution according to which the ideology of the social group exerts normative pressure on the individual's cognitive processes (Guimond *et al.* 1989). As individuals undergo socialization they learn to see the world according to the beliefs and values of the social group. To the extent that cognitive processes such as causal attributions are affected, the socialization process can be regarded as prescribing a 'code of cognitive conduct'.

7.5 Detective stories as knowledge templates

The nature of the production process in a pressing plant is such that people are continuously confronted with interruptions, breakdowns, and perturbations in the work process. Lines stop rather frequently, because of both discretionary decisions and unexpected events. Machinery requires constant maintenance work, workforce must be re-allocated whenever the line is idle, changeover operations take place almost every day, and fluctuations in the customer's demands are very likely. All these interruptions and unexpected events require a continuous activity of variance absorption. Production schedules are constantly adjusted. Production voids are envisaged in order to allow for different types of intervention. Teamwork is a fundamental absorption mechanism because it helps to keep the emotional content of breakdowns under control. Moreover, the need constantly to make decisions-making reinforces the group culture.

Taking into account the constraints imposed by the production system, the study has attempted to draw upon the narratives reported by relevant actors on the shop floor in order to investigate those sense-making dynamics that lead to the development of organizational knowledge. The model in Figure 7.3 displays a pattern of knowledge creation and institutionalization based on the resolution of critical incidents.

As it can be seen, sense making is triggered by disruptive events (breakdowns, interruptions, and technological perturbations) occurring at the interface between the 'business as usual' of routine situations and conscious awareness of problem-solving activities. While solutions are still 'pending', operators are confronted by the equivocality of the 'happening'; time becomes a matter of concern and emotions play an important role. The situation is socially constructed through a network of conversations among the members of the team, and through the piecing together of different sources of information.

Diagnosis occurs as a narrative process, in which problems are dramatized and made visible. More specifically, it involves turning equivocal happenings into meaningful stories, characterized by a distinctive plot. The enchainment of events and the representation of action, inherent in the diagnostic process, take the form of a detective story. Detective stories turn disruptive occurrences into cases and, in so doing, they provide

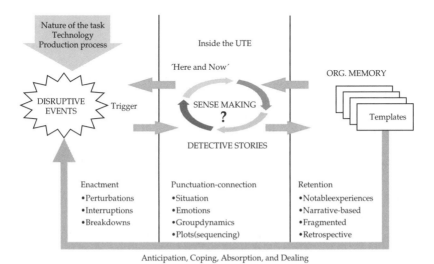

Figure 7.3 *Sense making on the shop floor*

narrative resolutions to technical problems. The conceptualization of these resolutions as 'emblematic stories' is the core of a learning process that promotes the internalization of such stories as part of the stock of knowledge acquired in the workplace. Emblematic stories serve as narrative maps or 'guides to conduct' (Weick 1995). They are stored in the organizational memory and at the same time act as templates for the resolution of future problems.

Under these circumstances, knowledge-making dynamics on the shop floor, seem to be closely associated with memory and the activity of collective remembering (Middleton and Edwards 1990; Walsh and Ungson 1991). In fact, the detective's strategy not only requires solving puzzling problems, but also remembering key resolutions. More importantly, it involves identifying common patterns among cases in order to reconnect present occurrences to past events (as in diagnostic activities) or to make predictions about future occurrences. The above considerations can be rephrased as follows: emplotment as a distinctive sense-making activity carried out by shop floor operators is a necessary, but not sufficient condition for remembering. An important issue in understanding the process of knowledge acquisition, then, is to determine which cases will become part of the knowledge repertoire of the middle managers, which experiences will be retained, which occurrences will be remembered and therefore acquire the status of templates. At Mirafiori, the selection of noteworthy experiences seem to be highly contingent upon the impact of a particular story on the cosmology of the team (values, code of conduct, etc.). In particular, the processes of causal attribution and search for blame inherent in the detective stories on the shop floor influence the extent to which disruptive episodes are turned into myths and sagas that reinforce the core values of the team. Moreover, the degree of emotional content associated with these events is probably crucial in establishing their relevance and accordingly causing the most emblematic episodes to be memorized.

The nature of the template identified at Mirafiori underlines some key features of knowledge-making dynamics in highly institutionalized contexts. Detective stories are ways of ordering experience. They point to a theory of method, which is at the same time a theory of knowledge. Carlo Ginzburg (1990) has conceptualized the detective's strategy of investigation as an emergent epistemological model which he labels 'evidential paradigm'. The essence of the paradigm lies in the formation of conjectures based on the collection of evidence in the form of clues. It stresses the importance of guesses, the systematic gathering of 'small insights', and attention to detail in the process of knowing and discovering reality.

Like the D/A routine in Melfi, detective stories provide an archetypical practice underlying the operations of the team members on the shop floor. Through templates knowledge is stored in the organizational memory, imitated, and replicated. The archetypical nature of templates points to the institutional dimension of knowledge. However, a comparison between the D/A routine in Melfi and the detective stories in Mirafiori highlight different modes of anchoring human knowledge, different strategies for achieving replication of knowledge, and, ultimately different ways of institutionalizing knowledge. Through routines, knowledge is abstracted, delegated to impersonal organizational mechanisms, and replicated through repetitive applications of standard procedures to emerging problems. In this regard, the D/A template provides a sort of 'skill without a place' that can be applied to almost any problem arising on the shop floor. The detective story's template, on the other hand, incarnates a way of capturing knowledge in a narrative form, stressing the role of the human element and of experience. In particular, detective stories point to a structural repertoire that has been developed through selective processes of remembering and forgetting. Through them, knowledge is replicated in the form of cases, sagas, and emblematic stories. This type of knowledge does not seem to reside in standard procedures or written norms; rather, it has been institutionalized as common sense. Indeed, a distinctive feature of the detective's approach is its commonsensical nature. Following Weick (1995), it is possible to argue that common sense is the outcome of inductive generalizations grounded on narratives (rules of thumbs, anecdotes, and war stories).

The tacit nature of common-sense knowledge highlights an interesting paradox related to the question of what it means to be a professional. Common sense is the distinctive feature of middle managers' competence. It is professional knowledge that has been developed through experience by seeing the same problem many times. Because commonsensical knowledge is tacit, it cannot be articulated and therefore transferred to generic workers or to newcomers. On the other hand, if common sense was made explicit it would be transformed into procedural knowledge and probably lose its effectiveness. Once again, Ginzburg's insights into the nature of conjectural knowledge and the impossibility of formalizing it are particularly illuminating:

Knowledge of this sort in each instance was richer than written codification; it was learned not from books but from the living voice, from gestures and glances; it was based on subtleties impossible to formalise, which often could not even be translated into words . . . These insights were bound by a subtle relationship: they had all originated in concrete experience. The force behind this knowledge resided in its concreteness, but so did its limitation—the inability to make use of the powerful and terrible weapon of abstraction. (Ginzburg 1990: 114–5)

7.6   Concluding remarks

The study described above documents the complex interplay between the organizational context, the technology and the practices of a best performing team, showing how the interaction between these three elements affects the processes of creation and institutionalization of organizational knowledge. Specifically, we have argued that operations on the shop floor are governed by a stock of highly idiosyncratic knowledge which is enacted and constructed by means of narratives.

A main finding of the study is that the narratives on the shop floor identify a distinctive strategy of investigation which can be conceptualized as a detective story because of its analogy with the literary genre. Detective stories seem to possess a double edge. From a cognitive standpoint they provide an information processing device through which the complexity of a problem is tamed and the equivocality of action is absorbed. In this respect, the narrative structure of the detective story supports instances of problem-solving by providing a template for making sense of disruptions. On the other hand, the same narrative structure involves achieving epistemological closure through processes of attribution, whereby action is ascribed to an actor (i.e. finding a culprit). This second aspect highlights the issue of blame management and the influence of the social context in which detective stories are embedded.

The dynamics observed over the Mirafiori shop floor emphasize the role of humans in their everyday endeavour to articulate tacit knowledge in a narrative form. Admittedly, stories analysed in the above case engage with the technology in that they tell about workers confronting troubled machines. However, the punch line of the stories collected on the Mirafiori shop floor seem to point to social relations (e.g. transgressing hierarchical boundaries), team working and collective labour. Narratives support the flow of information between people rather than machines. The detective metaphor underlying the daily talks about machines is actually about the unknowability of people, it is about human behaviour and moral conduct (i.e. who is the culprit?). Likewise, common sense as a cultural system is about behaviours, boundaries and censorship. It points to cultural rather than technical knowledge. Under these circumstances, organizational routines seem to have been replaced by narratives as the main carriers of organizational (tacit) knowledge. Common sense, encompassing both the team's values and the distinctive capabilities underlying the execution of factory operations, stands out as a cultural system (Geertz 1983). Within such a type of cosmology, organization as a machine governed by a set of plans seems to recede into the background, its presence confined to the daily talk of the team members.

Part Three

Building a Theory of Knowledge in Organizations

8

Action, Context, and Time:
A Processual Model of Knowing
and Organizing

8.1 Introduction

The inquiry conducted so far has focused on the genesis, evolution, and institutionalization of organizational knowledge systems. In particular we have looked at knowledge making as a process whereby a structure, a code, a practice, or a behavioural pattern, emerges, becomes gradually accepted within a working community and acquires stability over time. The purpose of this chapter is to build generalizations from the main empirical findings of the case studies presented earlier. In order to achieve this purpose, a classificatory system is needed, providing a vocabulary for knowledge-related phenomena as well as explaining how those phenomena develop in organizations. This serves as an interpretative framework that can eventually be applied to the case studies considered in this research. At the same time, the classificatory system ought to be anchored to a conceptual definition of organization and the phenomenon of organizing, here referred to as the ontological argument. In fact, the knowledge-related dynamics described in this study originate from distinctive organizational activity systems that point to the nature (way of being) of organization. The interpretive framework presented in this chapter portrays organizational day-to-day activities as recursive processes of knowledge creation, utilization, and institutionalization. These processes identify the typical knowledge cycle by which organizations produce generic knowledge outcomes. The framework refers to such generic outcomes as organizational black boxes in order to stress both the tangible and the intangible aspects of knowledge in organizations.

The second part of the chapter applies the notion of knowledge cycle to the main empirical findings of the study in order to emphasize the linkages between process and content of knowledge development in each case study. Accordingly, I move from abstract knowledge contents, generically defined as organizational black boxes, to specific ones. I label the principal knowledge contents identified in the study *blueprints, routines,* and *common sense*. In addition, the combination of knowledge processes and contents highlights specific knowledge types. Three main knowledge types are identified in relation to the transformations that knowledge undergoes over time: *foundational knowledge* is connected to the design of the organization; *procedural knowledge* refers to the routinized character of organizational action in consolidated work settings; *experiential knowledge* relates to more mature stages in the evolutionary trajectory of knowledge and organization. Finally, by juxtaposing the three case studies in a sort of 'photo-montage', I try to identify knowledge trajectories within organizations and speculate on some possible evolutionary trends in knowledge-making processes.

The chapter is organized as follows. Section 8.2 defines a main ontological argument underlying the mode of existence of organization. Based on a phenomenological description of the dynamics of organizing, the ontological argument relies on the categories of being and becoming as main determinants of organizational behaviour. Section 8.3 develops a classificatory model of knowledge linking the three dimensions of process, content, and context in a coherent whole. The model, to which I refer as the 'knowledge cycle', constitutes the essence of the epistemological argument of the study. Section 8.4 applies the above interpretative framework to the case studies developed in this research. Section 8.5 generalizes from the findings of the study and develops a co-evolutionary model of knowing and organizing. Section 8.6 stresses the heuristic nature of the above model in so far as it is built on ideal types of knowledge. This is exemplified by showing elements of continuity across the cases and identifying possible overlapping regions between different knowledge types within the same setting.

8.2   Being and becoming: the ontology of organizations

A linking theme of this study is that a dynamic theory of knowledge in organizations should be grounded on a conceptual definition of organization and the phenomenon of organizing. In contrast to functionalist views of organizations (e.g. Parsons 1951; Selznick 1957; Blau 1964), which privilege unity and instrumental order, my main ontological argument is that organizations are characterized by an intrinsic condition of ambiguity and disorder (Cooper 1990). Under these circumstances, the mutuality of the organization–disorganization opposition becomes a central issue in the analysis of social organization and social action (Cooper 1990: 172). Following the above line of argument, Cooper and Law (1995) have attempted to move from a view of organization as a *fait accompli* to the process of organizing, in order to capture the *in fieri*, emergent character of organizational phenomena. Accordingly, organizing rests upon the dynamic interactions between order and disorder, routines and breakdowns, and steady states and controversies. These interactions can be described by referring to the ontological categories of *being* and *becoming*, to which Cooper and Law allude as distal and proximal modes of thinking in organizational analysis. The two modes are somewhat complementary. Distal thinking emphasizes outcomes and ready-made aspects of organizations. Proximal thinking focuses on processes and looks at organizations as ongoing accomplishments. The shift from the proximal to the distal occurs through a process of translation whereby equivocal actions are transformed into stable structures and effects. This process becomes apparent when we consider the authors' phenomenological description of action:

In its most callow sense action is a *happening*; before anything else—before meaning, significance, before it's fitted into any schema—*it simply happens*... The happening is 'nothing'—or rather no thing, no object, no form—because it doesn't possess any meaning, it is equivocal and symmetrical; it's not yet properly articulated, ordered, organized, not yet been converted into a product or effect. In other words, the happening is a heterogeneous process that has no before or after, no start or finish, no cause or effect: it always remains 'unfinished'. Only when it takes its place in the network of what has *already* happened does it become ordered and organized, translated into an effect. (Cooper and Law 1995: 241–2)

In the pursuit of knowledge, the distinction between the proximal and the distal underlines the way organizations seek to make sense of the flows and processes which characterize their activity. It highlights the importance of the kind of sense-making processes which have been most carefully dissected in the work of Karl Weick (1979, 1995). According to Weick, action is a continual flow which shapes and is shaped by the unfolding of time. Following the philosophical ideas of phenomenologists like Schutz, Weick observes that time exists in two different forms, as pure duration (happening) and as discrete segments. Pure duration is a 'coming-to-be and passing-away that has no contours, no boundaries, and no differentiation' (Schutz 1967: 47). Pure duration makes sense making somewhat transparent, as it renders actors unaware of the activity in which they are engaged. In pure duration, action is experienced as a *continuum* characterized by symmetry and equivocality. In other words, action is 'raw material' that needs to be put into some frame of reference in order to become meaningful. Retrospection is crucial to sense making. As Weick puts it, 'people are always in the middle of things (projects), which become things only when those same people focus on the past from some point beyond it.'

The phenomenological description of action suggests that making sense of equivocal and symmetrical occurrences is closely connected to the experience of time. Anticipation and retrospection act as temporal devices whereby 'happenings' are harnessed into structures of signification, and action is rendered meaningful. Anticipation and retrospection can be related to the design of organizations. As Akrich (1993) has pointed out with respect to the design of objects:

Designers define actors with specific tastes, competencies, motives, aspirations, political prejudices, and the rest, and they assume that morality, technology, science and economy will evolve in particular ways. A large part of the work of innovators is that of *inscribing* this vision of (or prediction about) the world in the technical content of the new object. I will call the end product of this work a 'script' or 'scenario'.

Likewise, organizations are designed to anticipate action in space and time, and to direct and prescribe the behaviour of organizational actors according to a particular vision of the social reality. The script refers to a pre-understanding of reality, a pre-interpreted world that provides the background knowledge underlying organizational performance.

However, this pre-understanding is grounded on retrospection, that is, on the possibility to focus on the past from some point beyond it and consequently to foresee certain outcomes: 'the problem of what will come next is perhaps the fundamental problem of ordering and organizing' (Cooper and Law 1995: 242). Hence, organization can be seen as the ex-post rationalization of action, a mechanism that continuously swings between anticipation and retrospection. The latter is considered by Cooper and Law as a real *engineering* of time: 'without retrospection there is no anticipation, no ordering, no organization . . . it is a matter of constructing the future so that it looks like it's always been there' (Cooper and Law 1995: 242).

As stated above, anticipation and retrospection highlight the importance of the factors of time and tense and their influence on the way organizations seek to make sense of their activities. More specifically, they point to the difficulty, within organizations, of dealing with the unknown, of living the present as 'here and now', of perceiving action as a happening, as an equivocal and symmetrical experiencing. In order to overcome this difficulty, a third mechanism, which provides a perspective on the present *from* the present, needs to be introduced. Here is where repetition comes into play. Repetition transforms novel experiences into ordinary events. Once again the work of Cooper and Law provides a useful insight: 'an obvious (but neglected) feature of organization is that it has to repeat itself in time, to renew actions every working day'. Repetition, in the form of routinized activities, allows organization to cope with everydayness by turning the 'happening' of action into a familiar sequence of events. Routines represent the liturgy of organization, the effort to frame the equivocality of action through rituality. Action is thus encapsulated into stable patterns, entangled into standard plots. Anticipation, retrospection, and repetition make the circularity of time a permanent feature of organization. Anticipation casts a glance on the future from some point behind it; retrospection focuses on the past from some point beyond it; repetition attempts to harness the present into some stable, recognizable pattern. In this way, organization is turned into a sort of clockwork, whose functioning depends on the possibility of rendering time transparent. The above activities—and the related processes of planning, ordering and sequencing—embody the strategies whereby organizations manipulate action in an attempt to appropriate order from disorder.

To sum up, the division of labour, the production system, the design of standard operating procedures and interlocking routines can be viewed as an attempt to anticipate action in space and time. These devices do so by providing sense-making mechanisms and pre-determining resolutions to problematic situations. As with any object, organizations are designed on the basis of a pre-understanding of reality (Winograd and Flores 1986). At the same time, the above devices point to what organizations take for granted, thus making them more transparent. Put differently, sense making in organizations relies on the presence of black boxes which can be seen as embodiments of organizational knowledge and constitute a pre-condition for the utilization of that knowledge.

8.3 Building a classificatory system of knowledge: the epistemological argument

As stated in the introduction, a theory of knowledge cannot be divorced from the conditions underlying the way of being of organization.

Accordingly, the epistemological argument underpinning this study should spell out the processes by which knowledge is progressively inscribed into the organization. The epistemological argument is based on the assumption that knowing is an action-based process unfolding in a controversial manner. Action is equivocal, it generates problems of interpretation and sense making. Action is an open work whose meaning is in suspense (Ricoeur 1981). Accordingly, a main issue that needs to be addressed is the problem of epistemological closure; that is how controversial processes are turned into stable and durable outcomes. The translation from controversies to agreed facts and the description of the processes through which meaning is institutionalized are critical to the construction of a theory of knowledge.

In order to address the above issues I propose a model that combines functionalist and social constructionist arguments. The model can be seen as a phenomenology of performance describing the unfolding of knowledge-making dynamics in a given organizational setting. In particular, I contend that organizational knowledge springs from the processes through which organizations appropriate order from disorder. Knowledge arises through controversies and is subsequently crystallized into stable structures of signification by processes of inscription and delegation of human agency to organizational devices.

Finally, a classificatory system of knowledge in organizations ought to be able to capture the changing forms that knowledge assumes over time by dynamically deriving knowledge outcomes from knowledge processes. This section seeks to construct such a system.

8.3.1 *Organizational black boxes*

In analysing the nature of knowledge in organizations, two arguments seem to collide. On the one hand, knowledge can be regarded as a 'presence', as a 'ready-made' product, which can be manipulated and used instrumentally with respect to the goals of a firm. As a consequence, knowledge is considered a strategic factor of production and causally linked to organizational performance. This functionalist argument is consistent with the definition of organization as a steady state and resonates with the strategy literature on knowledge analysed in Chapter 2. On the other hand, there is the constructionist argument privileging the notion of becoming, and for which knowledge creation is about resolving controversies. Accordingly, the constructionist approach focuses on the translation of controversial knowledge into hard facts and products. This process of social construction and utilization of knowledge is supposed to explain how organizational actors make sense of the everyday practice in which they engage.

Despite the sharp contrast in the assumptions informing them, the two arguments seem to have at least one point in common: the presence at some point along the path of knowledge creation of a durable outcome. In order to capture the nature of knowledge outcomes in organizations I introduce the notion of black box. The term 'black box' contains a fundamental semantic duality. On the one hand, it evokes the idea of durability (a physical object) and therefore points to a commodified view of knowledge. The black box has clear boundaries and shape, it can be seen, touched and manipulated. At the same time, the box is black and therefore opaque to the user. But what is invisible in the black box? To answer that question, let us consider a concrete example. What is invisible in a personal computer, a television (TV) or a video casette recorder (VCR)? For the end user, it is certainly not the physical piece of equipment, but its inner workings. However, the mechanism that makes the black box work is not simply the array of electronic and mechanical sub-components that we could see if we only had the patience to unscrew the box that contains them. Rather, that particular configuration of sub-components is the result of a controversial process of knowledge creation that at some point has been settled and concealed in the box. The box is black also in another sense. It is an obvious, unproblematic entity that can be taken for granted by the user. A computer, a TV or a VCR only needs to be switched on in order to function, without requiring any knowledge of its technicalities. Therefore, black boxing is a pre-condition for use. The user does not care about what is inside the black box, but only about its instrumental character, that is, what the black box *does*. The black box allows the user to make sense of the functioning of a computer, a TV or a VCR without questioning the artefact.

The above example demonstrates that the notion of the black box acts as a watershed between the two arguments considered above. For this reason, I believe that the two approaches are to a certain extent complementary, although the different purposes underlying them produce different methods of inquiry into knowledge. For the functionalists, the black box is a point of departure. They need to solve a fundamental problem related to the fact that, unlike other strategic factors of production, knowledge is 'intangible'. For this reason, they take for granted the facticity of knowledge and treat it as a 'ready-made' product. The commodification of knowledge makes it visible, transferable, and even measurable. This operation is instrumental in defining knowledge as a source of competitive advantage. In different versions within the same paradigm, knowledge is conceptualized as intellectual capital, competence, capabilities, and core capabilities—all terms that clearly contain a prescriptive value and point to a causal/ functional link with organizational performance. For the construction-ists, the black box is a point of arrival. They are interested in the process of materialization of knowledge which culminates in the epistemological closure of the black box. Their method is to follow the agents of know-ledge creation while they are busy at work, present the different factions involved in the process and make explicit the controversies characteriz-ing the contest. But this controversial process can be reconstructed only after the fact, only in the presence of a black box that can be reopened. One approach stops exactly where the other begins. In the next section I present a theoretical model that builds on the complementarity of the two approaches outlined above in order to bridge the gap between them and hopefully provide a more holistic picture of knowledge-related phenom-ena in organizations. Specifically, the model describes the fundamental processes leading to the production of organizational black boxes (or knowledge contents). In metaphorical terms, the model is concerned with explaining *why* the box becomes black.

8.3.2   *The knowledge cycle*[1]

Transforming knowledge into black boxes is a fundamental requirement for the use of that knowledge. However, in order to be turned into a black box, knowledge has to be recognized as valid: the closure of the black box implies an act of social acceptance and legitimization. Therefore, in order to understand the transformations occurring along the value chain we need to explain the process whereby knowledge comes into existence, becomes socially accepted, and is eventually embodied in durable out-comes. This section seeks to provide a description of the dynamic cycle that leads to the production of generic knowledge contents, herein referred to as organizational black boxes. This cycle can be articulated in

[1] The knowledge cycle resonates with existing models in the literature. For example, Choo (1997) has elaborated a 'knowing cycle' dealing with the ways in which organizations use information strategically in order to construct meaning, create knowledge and make decisions. Likewise Kolb's (1979) idea of a 'learning cycle' links knowledge dynamics to agency theories and problem-solving. Beyond the commonalities in labels, however, the knowledge cycle is substantially distant from the above models. In fact, here emphasis is placed on the interplay between knowledge creation and institutionalization rather than on the information-based and experience-based processes leading to cognitive growth.

three main processes: creation, utilization, and institutionalization. Figure 8.1 provides a diagrammatic representation of organizational knowledge processes.

Knowledge creation. Creation belongs to the domain of arts. It is the act of making, inventing or producing knowledge. In the classic work of Nonaka and Takeuchi (1995: 3), knowledge creation is defined as 'the capability of a company as a whole to create new knowledge, disseminate it throughout the organization, and embody it in products, services and systems'. This definition portrays knowledge creation as a self-contained process, with a beginning, a middle and an end. In this study, however, I place knowledge creation within a broader knowledge cycle. In this regard, creation is an incipient, generative process, identifying the sources and agents involved in the production of knowledge-related phenomena. At the outset, the knowing cycle is a set of tensions between opposites: organization and disorganization, being and becoming, order and disorder, permanence and change, routines and breakdowns, and so on. Knowledge is subsequently crystallized into stable structures of signification through processes of inscription and delegation of human agency to organizational devices. Creation is about knowledge that is contested, controversial, and provisional and therefore cannot be used in a systematic fashion. In particular, the contested nature of knowledge-creation processes can be connected to the equivocal character of social action. Action generates controversies; it is an open work in search of a closure. As such, action-based knowing is subject to conflict of interpretations that can be resolved only by a process of argumentation and debate. In this regard, knowledge creation is the start of a recursive process that goes from controversies to closures. Such a process unfolds along intermediary pathways and

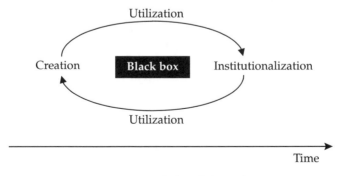

Figure 8.1 *The knowledge cycle*

transient constructs which are punctuated by uncertainty and ambiguity. In its hypothetical connotation, knowledge creation represents a potential for the production of durable contents.

Utilization. Utilization refers to the application of a particular stock of knowledge in concrete situations and therefore identifies a distinctive 'modus operandi' of a firm. More specifically, it points to the manipulation of knowledge exercised by the users in their day-to-day practices. Utilization conveys a vision of knowledge 'in flux', defining trajectories that unfold from the controversies of knowledge creation to the institutionalization of organizational black boxes. In this respect, the dynamics of knowledge utilization depict a model of knowledge evolving through cycles of production and consumption. This process occurs along a value chain that comprises 'makers' producing certain goods, and 'users' taking up (black boxing) the work performed in the previous stage and transforming those goods. On the other hand, the distinction between the user and the maker is not a neat one. As de Certeau (1984) has pointed out, the consumption of a product can be seen as a form of secondary production that is hidden in the process of its utilization. Through the process of consumption, the users enrich the materials at hand with new meanings and continuously reinvent them. Likewise, Latour (1987) has argued that the fate of a fact or machine is in the hands of its latest users. Accordingly, the notions of final product or end user are relative to the stage of knowledge creation that is being considered. The above considerations characterize knowledge creation as a circular, recursive process. In other words, through the dynamics of utilization institutionalized knowledge is constantly manipulated and transformed, leading to further processes of knowledge creation. As a consequence, knowledge utilization accounts for the dynamic character of knowledge in organizations, stressing processes of change and transformation. In mediating the interaction between knowledge creation and institutionalization, the process of utilization maintains the tension between being/becoming, order/disorder, opening/closure, from which knowledge springs.

Institutionalization. To be sure, as the management literature has pointed out, the ability of a firm to create new knowledge is a major source of competitive advantage. However, in order to capitalize knowledge and make it usable firms need to incorporate such knowledge in stable organizational devices such as structures, routines, procedures, cognitive maps, artefacts, and so on. Institutionalization is the process by which human agency and knowledge are progressively delegated to the organization and inscribed into stable structures of signification. In this regard, institutionalization produces epistemological closure. By sealing emergent stocks of controversial knowledge, institutionalization produces a stable configuration of background and foreground. But this configuration susceptible to revision, for example during major episodes of technical breakdown, industrial conflict, or radical change. Current organizational structure or procedure only gives a temporary closure and a 'fixing' to a never-ending, ever evolving process of the reshuffling and restructuring of knowledge (Lanzara and Patriotta 2001). Institutionalization adds two important aspects to the process of knowledge creation. First, it implies an act of social acceptance whereby certain codes, patterns, structures, and practices become progressively taken for granted within a given community. The legitimization of organizational knowledge points to the importance of reaching a consensus around what is 'valid' knowledge, whilst highlighting a problem of conformity with existing organizational standards. Second, once it has been created and recognized as valid, knowledge needs to be represented and formalized in order to be transferred and diffused at a corporate level. For instance, organizational charts display a formal definition of the division of labour within a certain company which has been socially accepted and legitimized by its members. However, the controversial process that has led to that particular division of labour has become draped or hidden in apparently established organizational artefacts and settings. The organizational chart has been turned into a black box, into an unquestioned artefact. In order to trace back the process of social construction, we would need to reopen the black box following the strategies outlined in Chapter 3.

Through articulation, knowledge is represented and made visible. In fact, articulation can be defined as the act of making knowledge manifest. Controversies recede into the background and legitimate knowledge is 'sealed' into organizational black boxes: organizations create knowledge that can be fitted into purposeful devices. The organization is formally represented and reduced to an abstraction. Only now can we see knowledge as a product or a commodity. The commodification of knowledge lies precisely in this apparent paradox of making manifest while hiding (see the duality of black boxes discussed above). As a result of institutionalization, knowledge is inscribed into a system of norms, practices and conventions, and incorporated into stable structures. Knowledge becomes canonical, factual, definite and certain. Institutionalization implies a process of epistemological closure similar to the creation of a black box. This process responds to the need of organizations to secure and protect the patrimony of knowledge they create. Finally, institutionalization entails a process of infusion with values (Selznick 1957) pointing to the philosophical definition of knowledge as 'justified true belief'. In that sense, institutionalized knowledge can be seen as a source of 'difference'; that is, it stands as the factor that makes a firm what it is. Institutionalized knowledge is not related to organizational performance, but rather to the distinctive identity of a firm expressed in such concepts as reputation, accountability, prestige, fame, and distinction.

8.4   Making theoretical interpretations of the case studies

Having defined a classificatory system of knowledge processes, this section applies the model described above to the three case studies. The three cases represent variations in context, and accordingly provide alternative backgrounds against which the knowledge cycle unfolds. The analysis of the case studies highlights three main generic outcomes—here categorized as blueprints, routines, and common sense—resulting from the transformations that knowledge undergoes over time.

8.4.1   *Blueprints: the mark of organization*

Case one depicts a situated learning process related to the coming into existence of a new factory. The essence of the case lies in the description of the successive transformations whereby a blueprint—expressed in the design concept of a new avant-garde factory—is turned into a complex hard product (the physical factory). The translation from the blueprint to the factory is not straightforward. Rather, it occurs through intermediary pathways that need to be carefully described. In this case study, I attempted to identify a number of phases by following the chain of transformations that knowledge undergoes over time. In its connotation of 'in between', the 'construction work' stands at the core of this process of knowledge transformation. It embodies precisely the gap (in this case a radical discontinuity) that separates the blueprint from the coming into existence of a real organization, and in this respect stands as a metaphor of knowledge construction.[2]

---

[2] The involvement of the future workforce in the construction work makes matters more complicated. Not only is the distinction between physical and social construction blurred, but so too is the one between producers and users.

The longitudinal analysis of the phases from the design of the factory to its official opening made it possible to follow a process of knowledge construction in a very detailed way. The analysis highlighted the role of the actors involved, the structural constraints and opportunities offered by the greenfield site, and the learning processes and knowledge outcomes resulting from the construction of the factory.

The case portrays two interconnected processes of knowledge creation-institutionalization. The first, related to the decision-making process upstream of the design concept, involves the top management of the company and revolves around a controversial process of change and innovation. The second concerns the implementation of the design concept. It involves a larger number of organizational actors and is centred around the construction work that leads to the opening of the new factory.

Knowledge creation is initially triggered by some kind of discordance: environmental perturbations in the automotive sector call the current performance of the company into question and emphasize an urgent need for innovation. The latter will eventually take the form of a radical paradigm shift. In fact, the decision-making process following the onset of the crisis situation revolves around the question of how to handle the transition towards a new organizational model, one that is alternative to the Fordist production system. The initial controversy faced by the management of the company relates to the content and the scope of the innovation process and involves a strong debate between innovators and defenders of the old organizational model. The debate leads to the definition of a project for the construction of an avant-garde factory which will incorporate in its design principles the main assumptions of the new production paradigm known as the 'integrated factory'. The project is grafted on to substantial benchmarking activities (a knowledge-creation process in itself) and the contributions of the task force endorsing the project. Interestingly, the company's board acts as a sort of tribunal set up to settle controversies, assess and select proposals. Furthermore, the board is a legislatory body legitimating propositions and translating them into normative criteria for the definition of the project. At the end of this controversial process of legitimization and articulation of the main guidelines of the Melfi project, we find a charter stating a mission and the main objectives of the project, and providing a blueprint for the design and implementation of the new factory. The blueprint is the result of a collective decision-making process highlighting the gap existing between knowledge creation and institutionalization. It contains strategic choices selected from a variety of options available and recognized as valid through a process of legitimization. Secondly, the blueprint articulates organizational knowledge around a specific vocabulary (the integrated factory, lean production, JIT, and TQM), outlines the rationale for the above choices, and defines in detail the guidelines and operational steps for the implementation of the project. Finally, the blueprint incorporates new company values related to the process of innovation. In this respect, the epistemological closure embodied by the written project is achieved through a process of infusion with values. Knowledge is sealed into normative principles which make it possible to put it to use, and acquires a prescriptive value for the organizational actors.

The blueprint contained in the written project can be seen as a black box, a temporary stable outcome of knowledge creation which marks the coming into existence of a core nucleus of organizational knowledge embodied in the design of a new factory. At the same time, the design concept of a new avant-garde factory like Melfi is the expression of controversial knowledge in so far as it contains hypotheses about the future functioning of organization, which need to be tested and put to work. In other words, the translation of a blueprint into a real work setting does not necessarily occur as a smooth, unproblematic process. Another way to express the contested nature of knowledge embodied in the blueprint is to view it as the espoused theory of innovation formulated by the company (Argyris and Schön 1978). In this respect, the blueprint is the carrier of a gap between hypotheses and reality. It bears a number of open questions exhibiting the uncertainty of the outcomes of the project (e.g. Will the project fulfil the company's expectations? Will the green workforce be suitable for the job?). On the other hand, the greenfield site stands as the empirical counterpart of the project written on paper, and in this respect sets the stage for a subsequent knowledge-creation process.

As explained earlier, the greenfield site and the contingencies surrounding the design of the Melfi factory represent a very peculiar situation characterized by low levels of knowledge institutionalization. Clearly, organizations are never constructed *ex nihilo*. Like laboratories, they rely on the indefinite sedimentation of languages, equipment, institutions, practices, and conventions (see Latour 1995). The latter define the accumulation of successive layers of knowledge. In this respect, Melfi's greenfield rests upon the highly institutionalized stock of knowledge stemming from the history of the company and, more generally, the historical evolution of car manufacturing. Yet, as the literature has pointed out (see Chapter 5), the greenfield situation seems to impose fewer constraints for the construction of knowledge. Its character as a *tabula rasa*, as *terra incognita*—not to mention the 'virgin' workforce—make the Melfi greenfield almost an exotic place. To a certain extent, here it is possible to see the phenomenon of organizing making its debut.

On the greenfield, we witness a process of organizational becoming; one that moves from an embryonic form of knowledge embodied in the design concept to a more sophisticated one (the operational factory). The construction work that leads to the opening of the factory exemplifies a process of knowledge creation based on the appropriation of order from disorder, and stemming from increasingly complex interactions within a heterogeneous network of human and non-human actants. The network includes the design concept, the top management of the company, the greenfield, the newly recruited workforce, the variety of actors involved in the construction work, the trade unions, and the local authorities. The construction work entails the progressive transformation of 'raw material', in the form of heterogeneous knowledge sources, into stable outcomes.

The main knowledge outcome is epitomized by the factory itself. The factory represents a steady state, a state of order born out of disorder, a clockwork mechanism whose functioning is based on the presence of stable organizing principles. Routines are the emblem of the knowledge institutionalization process related to the 'formal' opening of the factory and defining both the technical and epistemological closure of a black box. The blueprint is now instanced by and articulated in the concrete functioning of the factory embedded in organizational routines. Routines have now gained the front stage, but this does not mean that the stock of knowledge embodied in the blueprint has disappeared. Rather, by receding in the background it has become invisible, undisputed and taken for granted. However, as we will see in the next section, the analysis of breakdowns on the shop floor has brought to the surface some elements of continuity between the original blueprint and organizational routines, stressing the pervasive analogy between the design concept and the current factory operations.

8.4.2 *Routines: organizations as clockwork*

The black boxing of technical knowledge described above is a process of institutionalization. In fact, once knowledge has been created and accepted as valid, organizations need to devise mechanisms to secure knowledge and make it durable. Case two addresses this

Organizational Knowledge in the Making

issue. In other words, the case asks: how is knowledge put to work and made durable? what are the distinctive learning and knowledge-acquisition processes related to the dynamics of institutionalization? In order to tackle these questions, we need to look at the further transformations and translations that knowledge undergoes over time.

The description of the Melfi plant, once it has become operational, points to the ways in which knowledge is proceduralized and articulated in a variety of organizational devices, and highlights the presence of the defining elements of organization. The dynamics observed on the shop floor bring to the fore a network of human and non-human actants carrying out concrete activities. However, in order to become meaningful, organizational actors and activities need to be inscribed into organizational devices and translated into specific plots. Actors are turned into roles and stylized into organizational charts portraying the division of labour; tasks are delegated to the technology and organized around a production system; machines are ordered into a particular layout; activities are enchained according to a workflow; time becomes measurable and punctuates the duration of the working day through the creation of shifts; the rhythm of machines is ruled by working cycles; the future is arranged into production plans and deadlines. What characterizes organizations is precisely this formal translation of a material network of actors and activities into a more abstract entity, of the proximal into the distal.

By putting boundaries around organizational actors and activities, knowledge is harnessed into stable structures of signification or organizational black boxes. The latter provide sense-making devices and set the contours of action. As explained earlier, the commodification of knowledge through organizational black boxing entails a deliberate manipulation of time. Anticipation, retrospection and repetition—and the related processes of planning, ordering and sequencing—are the mechanisms which make it possible to relate present occurrences, or equivocal happenings, to the network of what has already happened. Furthermore, the notion of a black box conveys a dual emphasis: on the one hand it refers to the presence of boundary objects; on the other hand, it points to the fact that those 'objects' can be taken for granted and are transparent to the user. As stated earlier, the transparency of black boxes is a pre-condition for the effective execution of work practices and routines.

The above description seems to depict organization as a clockwork mechanism where, to use Mary Douglas' felicitous expression, 'individual thought has been turned over to an automatic pilot' (Douglas

1986: 63). On the other hand, the perspective taken in the study points to a definition of knowledge as situated performance (Pentland 1992), stressing the conceptualization of work as practice. In fact, practices can be seen as the empirical counterpart of the clockwork. Case two portrays a further process of knowledge creation and institutionalization centred around work practices, and related to the utilization (consumption) of the existing stock of knowledge.

The transformation of the factory into a clockwork mechanism, where knowledge has been proceduralized and embedded in organizational routines, renders knowledge somewhat transparent. In order to enter this new level of complexity we need a different lens, a technique which allows for the displacement of tacit knowledge. In this situation of relatively advanced institutionalization, breakdowns have provided a valuable entry point. As explained in Chapter 3, the rationale behind the methodological tool is counter-intuitive: if organizational knowledge has become institutionalized—and therefore transparent—as a result of a routinization process, the solution is to look at what happens when routines are disrupted or called into question. Accordingly, breakdowns offer an alternative method to open organizational black boxes. They provide a cleavage between organization–disorganization and thereby point to the dynamics whereby organization appropriates order from disorder. In the process of knowledge creation, disruptive events can be seen as a source of controversy, since the lapse of time separating the occurrence of a disruption to its solution is intrinsically characterized by ambiguity and uncertainty. In other words, breakdowns stand as a challenge to the 'business as usual' of routine situations because they trigger the application of existing knowledge in a deliberate way or the creation of new knowledge. In this respect, breakdowns can be seen as 'moments of truth', providing access to the stock of tacit knowledge which governs the execution of routines and revealing their *raison d'être*.

The observation of the dynamics of knowledge utilization in day-to-day activities on the Melfi shop floor highlights processes of knowledge production and re-production occurring in the here and now. The D/A routine, applied by shop floor operators in response to disruptive events along the assembly line, provides a basis of certainty, a structural framework for problem-solving. My analysis has shown that the D/A routine is grounded on a deep-seated stock of background knowledge presiding over the execution of factory operations and characterized by situatedness, concreteness and pervasiveness. A main finding of the case study is that this stock of knowledge seems to be grounded on a 'founding analogy' (Douglas 1986) born on the greenfield and institutionalized in a subtle way once the factory reached the full production stage. What I called the D/A analogy is in fact mirrored and articulated in a variety of organizational devices underlying the functioning of the plant and relating work practices to organizational routines, core capabilities and the formative context of the factory. The presence of a founding analogy also connects the process of knowledge institutionalization to theories of imprinting (Stinchombe 1965). The linkage between blueprint and organizational routines—embodied by the D/A template—highlights elements of continuity between the greenfield and the operational factory, and thus provides a valuable insight into the genesis of organizational routines. The importance of routines in organizations has been widely recognized in the literature. Nelson and Winter (1982) offer the most powerful conceptualization of routines within the field of organization studies. They view routines as the genetic code of organizations, hinting at the primacy of structural elements over human ones and ultimately pointing to a definition of organization as a clockwork mechanism which evolves in a random fashion. A major omission of the above theory, however, is the issue of the origin of routines.

The present study has attempted to relate routines, as we observe them in the everyday life of organizations, to organizational design as articulated in a blueprint. The D/A template clearly relates the current routines and practices observed on the shop floor to the design of the factory and, more generally, to the archetype of the assembly line. More importantly, the template highlights the isomorphism between organizational design and organizational practices. In this respect, it stands at the core of a knowledge institutionalization process, pointing to some kind of organizational 'cosmology' (Weick 1993) and emphasizing the cognitive imageries and institutional arrangements that operators take for granted in their everyday coping with both routine and breakdown situations (Ciborra and Lanzara 1994).

The isomorphism among the task, the technology, the organizational artefacts, and the cognitive structures governing the execution of routines bears important implications for the institutionalization of organizational knowledge. Institutionalization is evidenced in the pervasiveness of certain organizational patterns, images, and so on; that is, in the equivalence of certain organizational forms. Knowledge is formalized and articulated, mirrored, represented and reproduced in a variety of organizational devices. In analysing the dynamics of institutionalization, Di Maggio and Powell (1983) have defined institutional isomorphism as the engine of rationalization and bureaucratization. Put another way, isomorphism is the essence of institutionalization in that it allows knowledge to be formalized, secured, and articulated in organizational artefacts. Isomorphism defines the consistency between a set of institutional arrangements and the cognitive imageries characterizing a specific work setting. In this respect, organizational isomorphism is a pre-condition for rendering knowledge durable and usable.[3]

The relevance of institutional isomorphism is apparent in the learning dynamics underlying problem-solving activities on the shop floor. The D/A template possesses a normative value in that it sets a path for learning and pre-determines a repertoire of moves to be enacted in the face of disruptive events. But what makes the template work? In order to address this question we need to look at cognitive systems as inferential structures governed by dominant analogies. An analogy is an efficient cognitive tool in that it helps people to make sense of complex situations by providing short cuts in the execution of everyday practices. In every cognitive system it is possible to distinguish between an analogical system (as-if) and an inferential one (if-then). The as-if of the analogical structure rules the system of inferences. In other words, the analogy of 'disassembling', based on an as-if syntax, enacts a specific problem-solving procedure. In this regard, the efficiency of the cognitive structure is based precisely on the isomorphism of the analogical and the inferential structures.

8.4.3 *Common sense: organizations as human artefacts*

Although there is no historical continuity between this case study and the previous ones, the institutional characteristic of the Mirafiori Pressing plant seems to offer a fertile ground for speculating about a further transformation of knowledge occurring over time.

Case three is the emblem of a mature stage of knowledge creation and institutionalization. With Mirafiori we move to a brownfield, that is, a setting characterized by an experienced workforce and stickiness of organizational knowledge (Szulanski 1996). Experience adds a heavy

---

[3] In the context of institutional theories, the notion of isomorphism is typically applied in order to describe the interplay between organization and environment. Within this view, organizations plastically adapt their structures, forms and procedures in order to comply with the dominant or diffused social values and norms of the technical and institutional environment (industry sector, national context, legal frameworks, etc.) (DiMaggio and Powell 1983). The knowledge implications of isomorphism, on the other hand, refer to the *internal* consistency and morphological convergence of the elements that compose an organizational activity system.

layer to the sedimentation of organizational knowledge, making it difficult to articulate. After so many years of operation, automatisms have become so deep-seated that it is hard for the observer to grasp the purpose of organizational actions. Indeed, the contention that 'all that is planned is organization', expressed by one team member in Mirafiori, seems to capture a further transformation of knowledge. More specifically, the maxim reveals the presence of a distinctive stock of knowledge which is enacted against the background of organizational mechanisms. In other words, planning may well constitute the essence of organizing. However, in order to cope with the everyday micro-disruptions occurring on the shop floor, a different type of knowledge needs to be mobilized, one that is experience-related and characterized by a human component. Improvisation and common sense are the outcome of a deep-seated learning process whereby knowledge is progressively stocked in a repertoire of noteworthy experiences and becomes part of the organizational memory.

Common sense provides a further perspective on knowledge creation and institutionalization. What is common sense and how can we open this third organizational black box? Common sense is difficult to capture in a straightforward definition. Clifford Geertz (1983) has attempted to conceptualize it in a well-known essay on local knowledge. According to the prominent American anthropologist, common sense can be defined as a cultural system, equivalent to religion, art and the like. Accordingly, its prescriptive value is very strong, as common sense points to 'what everybody knows'. Common sense draws its authority from an unspoken premise and therefore points to a stock of tacit knowledge which the members of a collective enact in their everyday coping with the world. This knowledge possesses a practical connotation; that is, 'its tenets are the immediate deliverances of experience' and 'it can be defined as a sound working knowledge' (Geertz 1983: 76). Unfortunately, the English term does not convey the important distinction between 'common sense' and 'good sense'. While the former emphasizes the notion of conventional wisdom (what everybody knows), the latter refers to the performative character of common sense (effectiveness of commonsensical solutions). As Geertz points out, common sense is prompted by the occurrence of disruptive events, which provide a typical domain of application: 'common sense is enacted in coping with everyday problems in an everyday way with some effectiveness'.

Although Geertz does not explicitly distinguish between 'common sense' and 'good sense', he actually refers to common sense as a network of practical and moral conceptions (Geertz 1983: 81). The dual emphasis on the practical (the immediate deliverances of experience) and the moral (the stable configuration of values or cultural system) is probably one of the key features of the concept. This duality is apparent in the findings of the case study, namely in the distinctive character of detective stories. On the one hand, detective stories stress the empirical character of knowledge applied in problematic situations; that is, they refer to a repertoire of past solutions which have been proven to work in practice. On the other hand, the sedimentation of narratives relies on the presence of recognizable patterns in their plots which turn ordinary stories into noteworthy experiences. Detective stories are grounded in the distinctive values and identity of the team members. They refer to a particular organizational cosmology (Weick 1993) or 'common sense view of the world'. Put another way, common sense points to 'the obviousness of the obvious'. In commenting on the introduction of a TPM (total productive maintenance) activity following the Japanese principles of lean production, one team member remarked: 'there is nothing new in it, we've always done it like that; it's just common sense; this is something we were taught twenty years ago at the company's training school'.

When compared to procedural, methodical ways of operating, the contrast is quite striking. In its practical connotation, common sense focuses on performance. It implies searching for quick solutions, choosing short cuts in order to get straight to the heart of the problem, rather than following a decision tree. Most of the time, the distance between thought and action is reduced to the point where certain solutions seem almost obvious. Of course, in striving to get around procedures, common sense knowledge is more exposed to fallacies and human error, as detective stories illustrate.

Common sense provides a general background against which notions of natural causations are developed (Geertz 1983: 77). In this respect, it acts as an interpretative system focusing on the immediacies of experiences and directing human behaviour in accordance with a shared set of values and visions. However, unlike scientific theories, common sense is unarticulated and deeply tacit. For this reason, commonsensical knowledge is difficult to grasp. Unlike routines and standard operating procedures, common sense is not inscribed (and therefore visible) in organizational artefacts or any other type of sensible structure. Here is where narratives come into play. While common sense is based on unspoken premises, common sense wisdom is enacted in organizational discourse: narratives, anecdotes, jokes, and war stories. Narratives (articulated as plots) are the carriers of such a deep-seated, sticky, commonsensical stock of knowledge. The deconstruction of organizational narratives should then allow the analyst to penetrate a knowledge system that has become deeply tacit and institutionalized.

Through narratives, collective knowledge is to a certain extent articulated and translated into a text on which both the actors and the observer can reflect. The task of the researcher, then, consists in making sense of this text, indeed a second order interpretation in itself. The problem of interpretation lies precisely in dealing with 'interpretations of interpretations', that is, how certain organizational actors make sense of sense making.

In Mirafiori we looked at how organizational actors weave webs of signification (Geertz 1973) by means of narratives. The knowledge-creation process in Mirafiori is triggered by the occurrence of disruptive events resulting either from technological perturbations (e.g. die changes) or technical breakdowns. As noted earlier, breakdowns are a source of controversy since they temporarily question the effectiveness of the existing stock of knowledge governing the execution of factory operations. The case highlights a distinctive process of investigation and interpretation of disruptive occurrences which I have characterized using the metaphor of the detective story. The latter points to a distinctive mode of knowledge utilization, grounded on conjectural, evidential strategies and stressing the narrative dimension of knowledge. Interestingly, detective stories seem to draw on a repertoire of existing solutions which have sedimented over time. Success stories of the past provide operators with effective templates for the solution of present occurrences. To be sure, narratives stress the importance of the time dimension in relation to knowledge and sense making. For example, the construction of plots and narratives implies locating organizational occurrences in space and time and accordingly translating equivocal happenings into meaningful events. In fact, the strength of narratives as interpretative devices (guides to conduct) stems precisely from their ability to link the present to the past and the future, anticipation to retrospection and repetition. Finally, narratives emphasize the role of collective remembering and organizational memory.

On the other hand, the normative value of success stories points to the dynamics of knowledge institutionalization within the factory. The case study has attempted to describe the process whereby success stories become infused with value and thereby direct and prescribe human behaviour. More specifically, I have identified a set of crucial ingredients which turn ordinary disruptive occurrences into noteworthy experiences. Those ingredients point to the specific cosmology—what everyone takes to be part of the way in which the world is arranged—of work teams on the shop floor. They include, for example, the appearance of a technical disruption (disorder), the presence of a power relationship, a happy ending. From an epistemological perspective, the solution of the riddle contained in the story can be seen as a way of appropriating order from disorder and therefore can be connected to dynamics of knowledge creation and institutionalization. Organizational memory, in the form of story templates, points to the factory's patrimony of knowledge which has become institutionalized over time and ingrained in collective common sense.

8.5   Linking knowledge to organizational becoming

The empirical findings of the case studies highlight distinctive knowledge outcomes that unfold according to the processual model described in Section 8.2. I categorized the above outcomes, respectively, as *blueprint, routines* and *common sense*. In this regard, the greenfield, the D/A template and the knowledge templates underlying detective stories can be seen as descriptive as well as prescriptive analogies epitomizing the main knowledge patterns which emerged in the three case studies (see Figure 8.2).

At the same time, the above knowledge outcomes incorporate a meta-level temporal dimension, as they refer to processes of knowledge

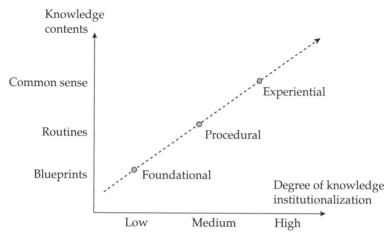

Figure 8.2   *A classificatory system of knowledge in organizations*

institutionalization occurring over time. As specified in the research design, the selection of the three cases reproduces 'artificially' different phases of the knowledge-creation and institutionalization process. In this regard, the three cases represent variations in context. By juxtaposing the three cases, we describe the transformations that knowledge undergoes over time. More specifically, we move from visible forms of knowledge to more 'sticky' ones. The presence of a temporal dimension in the research design allows the researcher to speculate about tentative evolutionary paths of organizational knowledge. Specifically, by following the transformations of knowledge over time, one could link those transformations to the dynamics of organizational becoming. Figure 8.3 exemplifies the above considerations.

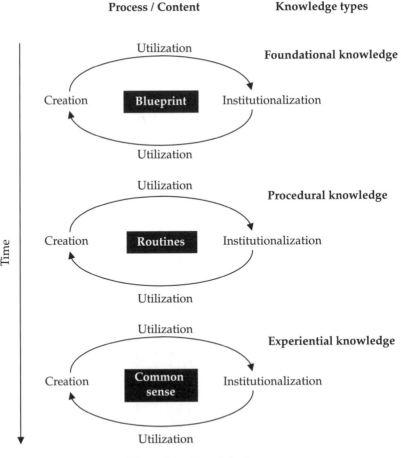

Figure 8.3 *Knowledge types*

At the diachronic level, the combination of knowledge processes and contents at different stages of organizational evolution identifies three main knowledge types, which I label *foundational, procedural,* and *experiential* knowledge. The three types/contents of knowledge identified in the case studies have different implications in relation to the phenomenon of organizing. Foundational knowledge points to the definition of epistemology as the foundations upon which human knowledge stands. Specifically, it relates the nature of organizational knowledge to the origin of that knowledge as reflected in organizational design. Procedural knowledge stresses a teleological definition of organization as a goal oriented-mechanism. Finally, experiential knowledge embodies a conceptualization of organization as a human artefact which cannot be entirely kept under control by means of mechanical devices. The above findings describe a path-dependency of knowledge-related phenomena with knowledge trajectories following organizational trajectories.

Admittedly, what appears to be a coherent account of an evolutionary process is the result of a 'photo-montage' (Latour 1995), once again a narrative construction devised by the author. In this respect, what is captured by the three case studies is a series of transformation states (i.e. knowledge outcomes) rather than an evolutionary transformation process. Furthermore, rather than distinct types/outcomes of knowledge creation, the three stages identified above have to be seen as ideal types existing at the same time in any organization. In this respect, the evolutionary path identified above has a heuristic value and needs further research to be validated (see Chapter 9).

8.6   Conclusion

In this chapter I have revisited the empirical findings of the case studies in order to make theoretical interpretations as well as identifying empirical patterns within and across the cases. This chapter has addressed a number of important questions: what are the specific knowledge outcomes emerging in each case? How do knowledge outcomes come into existence and are eventually crystallized into stable structures of signification? To what knowledge types can knowledge outcomes be connected? These questions have led to the elaboration of a classificatory system of knowledge conceptualized as the 'knowledge cycle' able to link in a systematic way knowledge content, process and context emerging from the findings of the study. The classificatory system has also provided a vocabulary for the dynamics of knowledge in organizations.

In attempting to label the specific knowledge outcomes emerging in each case, I have referred to the notion of the black box as a generic knowledge content. As we have seen in Chapter 2, the metaphor of the black box can have insidious empirical consequences because it glosses over the transformation process leading to specific knowledge outcomes. The model presented in this study initially black boxes the outcomes of knowledge creation. However, this operation is done on purpose, and only temporarily. By black boxing the outcomes, we problematize the content of knowledge creation while searching for a solution. The contents/types of knowledge creation are only thereafter labelled—following the empirical findings emerging from the study—and categorized as a classificatory system. Furthermore, the transformation process that led to the creation and institutionalization of those outcomes is analytically defined.

The analysis has highlighted three main knowledge contents—blueprints, routines, and common sense—corresponding to three main knowledge types identified in relation to the transformations that knowledge undergoes over time: *foundational knowledge* is related to the design of organization; *procedural knowledge* refers to the routinized character of organizational action in consolidated work settings; *experiential knowledge* points to more mature stages in the evolutionary trajectory of knowledge and organization.

As explained in the introduction, the model has a heuristic value. Accordingly, the linearity of the model does not mean that one should take symmetry for granted. Blueprints, routines, and common sense do not evolve separately. Rather, they have to be seen as ideal types existing at the same time in different evolutionary phases. In any firm we find overlapping regions between different knowledge types. Although, for analytic purposes we have not explored in depth those regions in the above case studies, it is nonetheless possible to exemplify the idea.

Foundational knowledge in Mirafiori is related to the design of the plant back in the 1950s. The latter took place under specific historical and socio-economic contingencies that have been described in some detail in Chapter 4 (e.g. immigration, booming of the Italian economy, the car as an emergent product, and the pervasive presence of conflict). Additional contextual elements included state-of-the-art knowledge in the car industry (e.g. Fordism and mass production) and the specific know-how of the company. These contingent factors were all encoded in the imprinting of the factory and still affect its functioning. In the case study on Mirafiori I stressed, for example, the traditional values of hierarchy and seniority as an integral part of the team's cosmology. Likewise, procedural knowledge is present in a variety of organizational aspects and chiefly in production plans.

In the first case study on Melfi, the overlap is apparent in the dual connotation of the greenfield site. The greenfield can be seen as a 'spring board' enabling the company to build a factory from scratch; at the same time the design of the avant-garde plant is constrained by the existing company know-how and the industry recipes available in a mature business sector like car manufacturing. As for Mirafiori, the design concept necessarily takes for granted the knowledge available on 'how to make cars' as well as the company's distinctive know-how. The latter clearly emphasizes the role of experiential knowledge in organizational design.

In the second case study on Melfi, I stressed elements of continuity between the greenfield and the fully operational factory, thus relating procedural knowledge embedded in routines to foundational knowledge. The so-called D/A template epitomizes this continuity. Interestingly enough, the presence of experiential knowledge at Melfi is just emerging and will become more conspicuous with the passing of time. However, common sense is apparent in a number of organizational dilemmas and trade-offs which the factory is currently facing. Those dilemmas are related to the strong emphasis that the company has given to the human element from the beginning and which is increasingly shaping the functioning of the plant. They are visible, for example, in the trade-off between trouble-shooting (reaching solutions quickly by deliberately violating the existing procedures) and problem-solving (fixing a problem by relying on method, analysis, and deductive reasoning), between the imperatives of production (keeping up with the output targets) and maintenance (preserving machinery from wear and tear), and, ultimately, between immediate deliverances and long-term commitments. The above organizational dilemmas emphasize the need for improvised practices, albeit grafted on to procedural knowledge. In addition, craftsmanship at Melfi provides a fertile ground for the use of experiential knowledge.

9

Re-thinking Knowledge in Organizations

9.1 Introduction

In this book I have attempted to lay the foundations of a phenomeno-logical perspective on knowing and organizing. The concern through-out has been with the nature, origins, and limits of organizational knowledge. The formulation presented in this book is not intended to be an exhaustive description of knowledge-oriented phenomena in organizations; it is best thought of as a preliminary effort to develop an epistemology of knowing and organizing.

In the quest built around the concept of organizational knowledge we moved from the age of silence to the age of noise, from the city of Prague at the beginning of the century to the shop floor of a modern factory. In both settings we were confronted with pre-interpreted worlds in which the knowing activity of the participants was hidden in the structure of everyday life. The assembly plant built from the green-field at Melfi and the Mirafiori shop floor constitute distinctive organ-izational cosmologies characterized by a particular configuration of routines, procedures, equipment, conventions, and institutions. Within these settings we followed the day-to-day activities of different com-munities of practice: the pioneers and constructors at Melfi while they were involved in the assembly of an avant-garde factory from the green-field; a few years later, the same operators in the Melfi assembly plant while they were engaged in making sense of breakdowns and bottle-necks along the assembly line; and finally, the detectives on the Mirafiori shop floor while they were busy with complex processes of investigation into production breakdowns. At the end of this journey around the con-cept of organizational knowledge we are in the position to spell out the main contributions of the book and to outline its implications for research and practice.

A first conclusion that can be derived from the inquiry conducted throughout the book is that we are left without a clear definition of *what* organizational knowledge is. Looking at the literature, it seems that the essence of knowing and organizing can only be captured through metaphors and analogies. Indeed, the literature has offered different images of knowledge (see Blackler 1995), which are grounded on a distinctive set of assumptions. The metaphors and key concepts underlying the four perspectives on knowledge reviewed in this book include mind and representation, commodity and performance, community and situation, and laboratory and fabrication.

Second, the theoretical perspectives present in the literature together with the empirical evidence derived from the case studies in the book have provided a sketch of *where* organizational knowledge resides. Knowledge is situated in plans and cognitive maps, resources and competencies, routines and procedures, practices and narratives, and organizational artefacts and technological implements. Under these circumstances, organization is an embodiment of a particular way of seeing the world, an inscription of human knowledge and agency, an assemblage of heterogeneous materials. I have argued that knowing and organizing are mutually constituted. Collective performance rests upon the presence of organized backgrounds or cosmologies that provide ready-made categories for understanding the world on a day-to-day basis. At the same time, knowing and thinking activities result in the progressive formation of a coherent universe thought of as an ordered and integrated whole. In this respect, what we normally define as organizational knowledge has been referred to as how organizations know about themselves, how they make sense of performance, and what they do on the basis of that understanding.

Third, the concern throughout the book has been with what knowledge *does* rather than what knowledge *is*. Indeed, the focus has been on processes and on the ways in which knowledge making unfolds. In our journey around the concept of organizational knowledge, we have progressively moved away from a static, commodified definition of knowledge and focused on those phenomena that constitute the essence of knowledge in the making, namely action, context, and time. The analysis performed in the case studies was aimed at deconstructing organizational knowledge as something that is never a perfected reality but is always 'in the making'. In particular, knowledge in the making stresses the idea of 'becoming' while pointing to the controversial, ephemeral, and experimental character of both cognitive and practical activities underlying the transformation of organizational knowledge systems. In this endeavour we have been comforted by a good deal of organizational literature that has attempted to explore the dynamics surrounding the construction of knowledge in organizations and to look for ways to make knowledge empirically observable.

9.2 A new vocabulary for knowledge

As always happens, the formulation of a new perspective requires first of all the adoption of a new vocabulary. Below I suggest the essential terminology informing a phenomenological perspective on knowing and organizing.

From abstract knowledge to action-based knowing
As was shown in Chapter 2, most of the existing theories of knowledge have focused on the content (e.g. knowledge as a commodity) rather than the process of knowledge creation. The lack of explanation of the transformation process leading to the production of knowledge assets was a major omission of those theories. This study has looked at organizational knowledge 'in action' in order to emphasize the fact that knowledge, or better the activity of knowing, can only be understood through its practice and not as an abstract phenomenon. Admittedly, the focus on what knowledge does rather than what knowledge is has made clear that knowing in organizations is inextricably intertwined with action. In different versions, the link with action is apparent in all the four perspectives considered in this book: organizational action has a cognitive basis; knowledge is a main determinant of firm performance; knowledge provides an activity context for thinking and acting; knowledge endows human and non-human entities with the ability to act. Accordingly, both the ontological and epistemological arguments of this study are grounded on a phenomenology of action, emphasizing processes of sense making and social becoming (Sztompka 1991). In this regard, the study of knowledge-oriented phenomena in organizations requires the adoption of a processual vocabulary emphasizing action over structures, flows over stocks, and processes over contents. In this book knowledge making has been defined as an action-based process that unfolds in a controversial manner. Action is equivocal, it generates problems of sense making and the institutionalization of meaning. The problem we addressed in the case studies was how organizations achieve epistemological closure; that is, how controversies are settled, how the equivocality of action is harnessed, how meaning is institutionalized, how knowledge is encoded and crystallized in stable structures of signification. The three case studies illustrate

the above problem in different manners. At Melfi, we followed the knowledge-making dynamics leading from the greenfield to the technical black boxing of the factory. Epistemological closure was achieved through the delegation of human agency and knowledge to impersonal mechanisms such as routines, procedures, technological implements, organizational artefacts, and so on. In the second case study I showed how a knowledge template based on the idea of assembling provides closure by offering a generalized method for the resolution of breakdowns and bottlenecks along the assembly line. In particular, I connected that knowledge template to the learning processes observed on the greenfield and the construction site. In this respect, the idea of assembling was a source of both historical and systemic understanding of the factory for the shop floor operators. At Mirafiori, I showed a pervasive mechanism of epistemological closure by shadowing a best performing team in the resolution of disruptive occurrences on the shop floor. Problem-solving was based on a distinctive strategy of investigation which unfolded as a detective story. As in a detective story closure is achieved by invoking blame and finding a culprit. In this case I analysed the knowledge implications of such a method and identified an emerging epistemological archetype which I labelled the evidential paradigm because of its conjectural and commonsensical nature.

The problem of epistemological closure is crucial for understanding the interplay between knowing and organizing in a given setting. It amounts to understanding how knowledge is made durable by being translated and inscribed into organization. On the other hand, the problem of epistemological closure raises the issue of the relationship between agency and structure. The findings of the study provide an explanation of the agency problem which differs from both classic institutional theories and structuration theories. As well known, institutional theories (e.g. Selznick 1957) have stressed the symbolic contours of collective action as instantiated by norms, values, and representations, thus neglecting the material substratum underlying organizational performance (artefacts, technology, equipment, and so on). Structuration theories (Giddens 1984; Barley and Tolbert 1997), on the other hand, have suggested that agency and structure are not independent from each other but instead mutually interact and shape each other (see duality of structure). Emphasis is placed on the modes of production and reproduction of knowledge structures in organizational practices. In this regard, context and structure are not treated as independent variables, but are subsumed within action. They are viewed as enacted (Weick 1977; Smirchich and Stubbart 1985) in the content of what people do and how they do it. The phenomenological approach developed in this book goes a step further. Specifically, it tells us that the study of knowledge-making processes should consider both human and non-human agencies (Latour 1999b). Accordingly, the relationship between agency and structure is redefined as a problem of translation, inscription and delegation of human knowledge into organizational devices. Under these circumstances, material artefacts, equipment, physical objects, practices, and routines become more salient than symbols, values, and norms in shaping organizational action.

From being to becoming
The findings of the study support a view of knowledge which is substantially distant from the reductionist argument propounded by the mainstream literature. Knowledge is not seen as a discrete commodity; instead it is conceptualized as an 'assemblage' subject to continuous transformations and reconfigurations. Emphasis is placed on transient constructs rather than final outcomes. As Cooper (1998) has pointed out, 'assemblage' derives from the Greek word *sumbolon*, the act of bringing together separate parts. Assemblage is defined by the dialectic of separation and joining, dispersions and collection, disorder and order. In other words, the concept of assemblage goes back to ontological categories of being and becoming and to the definition of knowledge creation as the appropriation of order from disorder. Assemblage stresses the dynamic character of knowledge systems: '(Assemblage) is the continuous movement of parts in a restless flux in which the separate identities of the parts give way to a mutual coming *and* going, uniting *and* separating' (Cooper 1998: 110). An assemblage is neither a unity nor a totality, but a multiplicity, a collection of heterogeneous materials which are mutually interrelated. In other words, assemblage stresses the importance of relations over the elementary parts; that is, what goes on 'between' the parts (Cooper 1998: 112). In this regard, what makes knowledge distinctive is not the discrete collection of commodities, but the nature of the assemblage. In sum, the notion of assemblage emphasizes the pasted-up and dynamic nature of knowledge systems, and reinforces the definition of knowledge as a phenomenon in the making.

The study has developed a classificatory system of knowledge linking in a systematic fashion organizational knowledge content, process, and context. In so doing, this study has offered a theory of organizational becoming able to explain the transformations that knowledge undergoes over time. The knowledge cycle presented in Chapter 8 captures a fundamental transformation process unfolding in a recursive

fashion and progressively leading to the creation and institutionalization of durable knowledge outcomes. Knowledge cycles emphasize
processes of construction and evolution rather than conversion.
Through them organizations deal with the equivocality of the happening
and accordingly appropriate order from disorder. In this respect, knowledge systems provide fundamental organizing principles. They are
embodiments of organization. They point to the tacit features of organizations which have sedimented over time as a result of institutionalization processes. The study has identified three main systemic forms, which
were labelled blueprints, routines, and common sense. While these forms
can be traced in any organization, their nature and content varies according to the context. In the case studies, for example, the greenfield, the D/A
template and the detective stories underlying the resolution of problematic situations qualify existing knowledge systems according to specific contingencies and historical evolution. In this respect, knowledge
systems are subject to local adaptation within specific organizational
contexts. Furthermore, by being context-dependent, knowledge systems are also time-related. Knowledge cycles and the corresponding
knowledge systems contain a temporal dimension which points to the
transformation of knowledge in organizations as a result of increasing
levels of institutionalization. The findings of the study portray a parallel
transformation process of knowledge and organizations which occurs
over time. Although, this result is obtained through an artificial manipulation of time, its potential implications are particularly relevant in so far
as they open up the possibility of relating the evolution of organizations
to the knowledge systems underlying their functioning.

From tacit/explicit to background/foreground

The distinction between tacit and explicit knowledge is one of the cornerstones of current knowledge-based theories. The distinction aims to
identify distinctive properties of knowledge. A number of implications
are derived from this distinction. Knowledge management involves
making knowledge available throughout the firm by turning tacit into
explicit knowledge. This entails codifying and bringing to the surface
tacit stocks of knowledge (e.g. translating knowledge into information
and storing it in databases). Knowledge creation occurs through conversion processes of tacit and explicit knowledge that start from the
individual and are eventually amplified at the organizational level
(Nonaka and Takeuchi 1995). Tacit knowledge is embodied in organizational routines that account for a firm's evolutionary processes
(Nelson and Winter 1982).

In this book I have suggested that the dichotomy between tacit and explicit knowledge be replaced by the distinction between background and foreground knowledge. Background and foreground can be seen as ontological categories explaining how individuals and organizations make sense of their worlds on a day-to-day basis. Understanding the particular configuration of background and foreground provides a wealth of information about the inner workings of a given organizational setting: how organizational actors make sense of everyday practice; what they take for granted; what they deem as necessary, obvious, natural, and inevitable. The ontological categories of background and foreground are related to the concept of pre-interpretation. Pre-interpretation deals with how individuals in organizations construct reality on a day-to-day basis and how such construction affects organizational behaviour; why organizations face knowledge dilemmas, rigidities, and paradoxes; and how this may lead to inertia and poor performance. At the diagnostic level the analysis involves understanding whether a particular configuration of background and foreground is functional or dysfunctional to organizational performance; that is, whether the idiosyncratic stock of knowledge possessed by a firm supports its capacity to compete or, conversely, is an obstacle to the accomplishment of desired goals. Only then is it possible to analyse learning and change requirements, and accordingly devise courses of action aimed at improving the firm's level of performance.

The particular configuration of background and foreground provides knowledge templates which govern the sense making endeavours of organizational actors. At Melfi, we followed the construction and evolution of a particular configuration of background and foreground knowledge. As the novice workforce moved from the construction of the factory to the construction of the car we witnessed a silent transition among different contexts: the greenfield, the construction site, and the shop floor. As a result of such transition the factory progressively receded into the background, it became an inscribed world supporting the execution of distinctive organizational practices. Today, the idea of (dis)assembling–informing both the construction of the factory from the greenfield and the execution of shop floor operations stands quietly in the background and provides a critical sense-making device in the face of both routine and breakdown events. At Mirafiori, we found a different configuration of background and foreground. The reliance on visible organizational structures and routines was minimal, while knowledge was mobilized in the form of conjectures and common sense. As a result, coping with everyday problems on the shop floor was driven by the use of detective stories as a strategy of investigation, as well as by narrative devices to reinforce the team's code of conduct.

From commodities to controversies
A main contribution of the case studies is the recognition of the contested and provisional nature of knowledge making. As in science, knowledge is treated as an empirical phenomenon which is subject to conflicts of interpretation and controversies. In particular, the importance of controversies in studying knowledge-making dynamics is at least two-fold. First, controversies provide a rule of method to study the inner workings of knowledge and thereby make knowledge-oriented phenomena empirically observable. They allow the researcher to document the unfolding of knowledge-making dynamics by following the characters while they are 'busy at work'. Second, and perhaps more importantly, the findings of the study suggest a shift in knowledge-management issues from knowledge as commodity to knowing as a controversy-based process (Lanzara and Patriotta 2001; Patriotta 2003). In fact, equivocal happenings, multiple representations, conflicting interests and stances that must be resolved by inquiry and political process are an integral part of knowledge making in the everyday life of organizations. In any work setting, controversies constitute a *substratum* or a set of accessory conditions informing organizational practice. More often than not, however, controversies may not be overt, or explicitly visible, but draped in organizational structures, procedures, processes, or social relationships. In this regard, current organizational structure or procedure only gives a temporary closure and a 'fixing' to a never-ending, ever evolving process of reshuffling and restructuring of knowledge. Controversies provide the engine for knowledge creation and organizational change by challenging established organizational arrangements and engaging organizational actors in processes of collective inquiry about the world they live in. Thus, organizational knowledge results from dialectics among divergent perspectives. It is a negotiated outcome that needs to be stipulated over and over again (Lanzara 1990; Olafson 1979). It can be appreciated in the 'becoming' rather than in the 'being' of the organization.

More generally, managing knowledge is handling and settling controversies and debates, particularly in situations of ambiguity and in processes of innovation and change in which new knowledge needs to be created and tested, or the pre-existing body of knowledge needs to be updated, and where actors hold multiple perspectives and criteria about how it should be done (i.e. what is valuable, or feasible, etc.).

Rather than neat conversion processes, we have multiple transactions and trade-offs through which actors try to reconcile divergent views and interests into a shared body of legitimate knowledge. Accordingly, knowledge management practices can be better pictured as social processes that at times entail building consensus and cognitive alignment and at other times entail provoking dissent and deviation from standard knowledge, but for sure not simply storing knowledge in organizational databases.

From creation to institutionalization

Knowledge creation cannot be divorced from the corresponding process of institutionalization through which organizations consolidate durable outcomes and achieve epistemological closure. Within this perspective, the stability, resilience, and legitimacy of organizations are connected to their ability to institutionalize particular modes of knowing, that is, to reproduce distinctive patterns of interaction in self-sustaining and self-activating structures. In this respect, knowledge making involves the emergence of structures, codes, and patterns which become progressively accepted and taken for granted within a given community.

Institutionalization is inextricably associated with epistemological closure. Firstly, at the systemic level, institutionalization confers internal consistency on a knowledge assemblage and accordingly provides the basis for the co-ordination of individual behaviours within a community of practice. Specifically, co-ordination is achieved through the institutionalization of meaning. In this respect, knowledge systems act as formative contexts (Unger 1987; Blackler 1992; Ciborra and Lanzara 1994). They provide a set of institutional and cognitive assumptions presiding over the behaviours of the participants in a social system. Secondly, institutionalization is a function of time. Through institutionalization, knowledge becomes habitualized; it can be repeated, represented, and reproduced in day-to-day activities. Put another way, the institutionalized nature of knowledge systems points to a set of dispositions and habits of thinking that have been acquired by the members of a community through past socializations and that are enacted in particular situations of action. Like Bourdieu's (1990) concept of *habitus*, knowledge systems mediate between structures and practices in the conduct of everyday life. Furthermore, the habitual, taken for granted character of knowledge explains why knowledge systems are highly idiosyncratic and characterized by stickiness. Finally, the concept of *habitus* as instanced by a particular *modus operandi* resonates with the notion of structural repertoires (Whipp and Clark 1986). Like the *habitus*, structural repertoires refer to a historically formed habit of thinking through which individuals in organizations deal with a particular set of problems.

The construction of the Melfi factory emphasizes endogenous forces of institutionalization that involve the progressive alignment of technology, sense making, and identity within a relational whole. In particular, the technical operations underlying the construction of the Melfi factory are to be understood as acts of institution building (Patriotta and Lanzara 2001) by which significant components of human agency are progressively encoded into stable organizational structures, procedures and other artefacts. Subsequently, the D/A concept provides a knowledge template governing the way operators on the shop floor make sense of routine and breakdown events. At Mirafiori, I showed how noteworthy experiences were institutionalized as knowledge templates that became part of organizational memory and reinforced the team's identity. The knowledge template based on the detective method is the main outcome of a process of institutionalization of commonsensical and conjectural modes of knowing. Such knowledge template possesses a double edge. On the one hand, it functions as a cognitive resource promoting the resolution of ordinary breakdowns; on the other hand, such resolutions are constrained by a particular genre. In this respect, institutionalized knowledge can lead to dysfunction and rigidities (e.g. finding a culprit).

9.3 Methodological contributions

The main methodological challenge taken up by this book has been the possibility of documenting empirically the processes of creation, accumulation and maintenance of knowledge in organizations. In fact, there is a sort of ontological blindness related to the difficulty of making sense of experiences that are deeply entrenched in routine contexts, taken-for-granted backgrounds, and pre-interpreted worlds. The book has developed a compact framework dealing with the epistemological, methodological, and operational assumptions underlying an inquiry into organizational knowledge. This framework includes phenomenology as the overarching intellectual perspective, anthropology as a strategy of investigation, and a set of methodological lenses as operational tools to gain access into knowledge-based processes.

Admittedly, the authors encountered in this study have stressed the importance of defining some entry points for accessing knowledge systems. In different versions, they have identified breakpoints, discontinuities, interruptions, disruptive phenomena, and controversies as the elements that allow the analyst to put together a flow of events in a sensible way. However, the issue of access to knowledge systems has never been problematized in an explicit way by the previous literature. Rather, it has been treated as a marginal, taken-for-granted question. Put another way, the purely instrumental stance towards the problem of 'looking for a way in' has impeded the development of a coherent framework for the study of knowledge as an empirical phenomenon.

The cases presented in this book show that knowledge making is based on entropy, on the presence of imbalance and discontinuity. Therefore, knowledge can only be studied as a phenomenon in motion, through displacement, surprise, controversy, and contest. The study has addressed the issue of how to study knowledge-making processes in organizations without reifying them, but taking account of the cultural specificity and context-dependency of knowledge systems. This is perceived as an important step in closing a major gap in the literature.

A salient contribution of this book has been the development and application of a three-lens framework for studying knowledge empirically. In operational terms the three lenses provide complementary tools for zooming into consolidated organizational practices which time, habit, and experience have rendered opaque and mostly taken for granted. The added value of each methodological lens has already been discussed in Chapter 3. Here it is important to reiterate that the three lenses are informed by a unifying principle: the presence of discontinuities. Discontinuities in time, action, and discourse provide not only access to background knowledge but also the narrative devices informing 'thick' description. In fact, description itself is a form of discontinuity; it unfolds by following the chains of transformations occurring within a given work setting. The technique adopted in this study has been precisely that of following organizational actors at work and describing the discontinuities informing their practices. Accordingly, the use of thick description as a narrative device has relied on the assumptions that knowledge systems are immanent to organizational practices. In this respect, description represents a mode of disentangling tacit knowledge from the variety of organizational devices in which it has been crystallized.

Although the three lenses are grounded in the specific context of this study, they can serve as a template for future research in different organizational and institutional settings. In fact, they seem to possess a generic validity which derives from their potential for deconstructing complex knowledge-related phenomena by focusing on discontinuities in the smooth functioning of organizations. A future research agenda will have to take into account the following issues. First of all, there is a problem of replicating the three lenses as a methodological framework. Here the emphasis is on the possibility of defining other kinds of knowledge problems, settings, processes that can be usually studied through the three lenses. Further work will need to consider additional organizational and institutional settings in order to corroborate the generic validity of the methodological framework and possibly fine-tune the three lenses.

A second issue concerns the possibility of developing further lenses for studying knowledge-related phenomena. The new lenses should be able to work on the cleavage between knowing and organizing; that is, look at situations where order is temporarily disrupted or recreated. Controversies, focusing on discontinuities of perspective, seem to provide a promising candidate as a fourth lens. They have been fruitfully utilized in studies on science and technology (e.g. Latour 1987) as well as in the study of social dramas underlying processes of change and continuity within a particular cultural context (Pettigrew 1979, 1985; Turner 1996). More recently, Lanzara and Patriotta (2001) have looked at the knowledge-making dynamics surrounding the controversial adoption of video recording in six Italian courtrooms. Overall, the new lenses should be able to capture the mutuality of continuity and discontinuity in dynamics of knowing and organizing. The latter point leads to a more general problem regarding the elaboration of methodological frameworks for studying co-evolutionary processes of knowing and organizing.

9.4   Implications for practice

What would a Fiat manager learn from this study? Probably things that he/she already knows but of which he/she is not aware. In this respect, the book is an attempt to unpack and enact Polany's maxim that 'we know more than we can tell'; it invites managers and practitioners to reflect about the repertoire of knowledge they possess and yet cannot articulate. In this regard, phenomenology provides a meaningful strategy of reflective inquiry. It aims at unveiling the structure and meaning of everyday experience; it stresses the importance of the details of practice; it shows how micro phenomena speak to grand realities.

Having said that, the three case studies represent a contribution in their own right. In putting together the empirical material collected on the field sites, my main purpose was to convey an image of organization in action by systematically relating abstract knowledge categories to concrete organizational activities. The choice of the shop floor as a main observational setting is emblematic of a conceptualization of knowledge as an empirical phenomenon. As discussed in Chapter 2, the existing theory of organizational knowledge displays a tendency towards deduction and abstraction which is instanced by the use of ready-made analytic concepts (e.g. tacit/explicit). The choice of a managerial focus is also indicative of the above tendency. In order to understand the inner workings of knowledge and the intricacies of knowing one needs to descend to a micro-level of analysis and observe how knowledge is empirically produced 'in action'. Our 'descent to the shop floor' was an attempt to gain hands-on experience of empirical knowledge-related phenomena associated with real actors, concrete problems, and everyday organizational practices. As a result, rather than being treated as a presence, organization was hopefully brought to life through ethnographic descriptions of the work setting. The latter was characterized as an assemblage of heterogeneous materials and situated activities: routines and standard operating procedures, tasks, technologies, products, production processes, and so on. In this respect, the shop floor stands as a metaphor of everyday life; it provides the setting for the observation of dramas in the field.

Finally, the case studies offer a distinctive perspective on a variety of themes that, although sharing a knowledge focus, could well be studied as phenomena in their own right: the evolution of the automotive industry and production systems; the role of greenfields in organizational design; the dynamics of change and innovation; the interaction between organizational routines and breakdowns; the interplay between technology and organization; the importance of time and narrative in the everyday life of organizations. A lesson to be learned from the case studies is that some classical organizational topics, such as those listed above, can possibly be revisited from a knowledge-based perspective. This should be done by systematically asking what are the knowledge implications of distinctive organizational dynamics.

9.5   Suggestions for future research

The inquiry conducted in this book calls for a new focus in research on organizational knowledge, one that emphasizes the mundane and everyday nature of knowing in organizations. In this book I have proposed a phenomenological perspective on organizational knowledge, characterized by a novel vocabulary and a compact methodological framework for studying knowledge empirically. Implementing such vocabulary and methodology will represent a major challenge for future research. In light of the considerations developed in this concluding chapter, taking up the challenge of studying knowledge empirically means:

1. Looking at what knowledge does rather than what knowledge is. This implies understanding how knowing and organizing are mutually constituted. It involves devising observational strategies for capturing the transformations and translations occurring along the knowledge chain. In operational terms this can be achieved by looking at the interplay between action and structures, flows and stocks, processes and contents, practices and assets.

2. Being able to capture the unfolding of knowledge by focusing on intermediary pathways and transient constructs rather than final outcomes. Knowledge needs to be understood as something that is always coming into being, a circulating entity that materializes through processes of temporary hooking up to organizational structures of signification.

3. Understanding the interplay between background and foreground in a given organizational setting. Knowledge making occurs in the context of pre-interpreted worlds which organizational actors perceive as obvious and natural until further notice.

4. Documenting controversies, conflicting positions, and power games by following organizational actors while they are 'busy at work'. Knowledge trajectories unfold from controversies to closures. Controversies are the engine of knowledge-creating processes. Argumentation and debate represent a natural way of formulating and resolving everyday problems in organizations. Also, controversies constitute a natural challenge to what individuals in organizations take for granted in their everyday dealings with the reality they inhabit.

5. Describing processes of opening and epistemological closure, creation and institutionalization by looking at the ways in which organizations appropriate order from disorder. Organizational inquiry needs to be performed at the boundary between continuity and discontinuity, permanence and change, organization and disorganization, being and becoming, routines and breakdowns, controversies and steady states.

6. Studying the interaction between knowing and organizing. The knowledge cycle and the taxonomy of knowledge proposed in this book hopefully constitute a preliminary effort to develop a classificatory system of knowing in the context of organizing. However, further conceptual refinement and empirical validation are needed. As for the three lens framework, future research will need to validate the theoretical model proposed in this book in a variety of organizational settings. This will involve testing (and possibly refining) the proposed conceptualization of knowledge categories as far as processes, contents, and types are concerned. Moreover, empirical indicators for observing and measuring such categories will need to be developed. The latter could provide the opportunity to conduct quantitative studies on co-evolutionary processes of knowing and organizing.

In order to achieve the above results, future theories of knowledge will need to address new questions about the modes of existence of organizations, rather than confining their inquiry solely to the relationship between knowledge factors and competitive performance. Indeed, performance cannot be even given sense or evaluated before and independently of any consideration about organizational reality, or at least what we take to be such.

Bibliography

ABERNATHY, W. J. (1978), *The Productivity Dilemma: Roadblock to Innovation.* Baltimore.

ADLER, P. (1993), 'Time and motion re-gained', *Harvard Business Review,* 1: 97–108.

——GOLDOFTAS, B., and LEVINE D. I. (1999), 'Flexibility versus efficiency? A case study of model changeovers in the Toyota production system', *Organization Science,* 10/1: 43–68.

AKRICH, M. (1993), 'The de-scription of technical objects', in W. Bijker and J. Law (eds.), *Shaping Technology/Building Society.* Cambridge, MA: MIT Press, 205–23.

ALVESSON, M. (1995), *Management of Knowledge-Intensive Companies.* Berlin: Walter de Gruyter.

AMIT, R. and SCHOEMAKER, P. (1993), 'Strategic assets and organizational rent', *Strategic Management Journal,* 14: 33–46.

APPLEYARD, M. M. (1996), 'How does knowledge flow? Interfirm patterns in the semiconductor industry', *Strategic Management Journal,* 17: 137–54.

ARGYRIS, C. (1990), *Overcoming Organizational Defenses.* Englewood Cliffs, NJ: Prentice-Hall.

——(1993), *Knowledge for Action.* San Francisco: Jossey-Bass.

——and SCHÖN, D. (1978), *Organizational Learning: A Theory of Action Perspective.* Reading, MA: Addison-Wesley.

BARLEY, S. R. and TOLBERT, P. S. (1997), 'Institutionalization and structuration: Studying the links between action and institution', *Organization Studies,* 18/1: 93–117.

BARNEY, J. (1991), 'Firm resources and sustained competitive advantage', *Journal of Management,* 17: 99–120.

BATE, S. P. (1997), 'Whatever happened to organizational anthropology? A review of the field of organizational ethnography and anthropological studies', *Human Relations,* 50/9: 1147–75.

BEAUMONT, P. and TOWNLEY, B. (1985), 'Greenfield sites, new plants and work practices', in V. Hammond (ed.), *Current Research in Management.* London: Frances Pinter.

BENYON, H. (1973), *Working for Ford.* London: Allen Lane.

BERGER, P. L. and LUCKMANN, T. (1967), *The Social Construction of Reality.* New York: Doubleday Anchor.

BERGGREN, C. (1994), 'NUMMI vs Udevalla; Rejoinder', *Sloan Management Review,* 35/2: 37–47.

BERTA, G. (1998*a*), *Mirafiori.* Bologna: Il Mulino.

BERTA, G. (1998*b*), *Conflitto Industriale e Struttura d'Impresa alla Fiat: 1919–1979.* Bologna: Il Mulino.

BEYER, J. M. and TRICE, H. M. (1987), 'How an organization's rites reveal its culture'. *Organizational Dynamics*, 15/4: 5–21.

BICKHARD, M. H. (1992), 'How Does the Environment Affect the Person?', in L. T. Winegar and J. Valsiner (eds.), *Children's Development in Social Context.* Hillsdale, NJ: Lawrence Erlbaum Assoc.

BIJKER, W. E., HUGHES, T. P., and PINCH, T. J. (1989), *The Social Construction of Technological Systems: New Directions in the Sociology and History of Technology.* Cambridge, MA: MIT Press.

BLACKLER, F. (1992), 'Formative contexts and activity systems: Postmodern approaches to the management of change', in M. Reed and M. Hughes (eds.), *Rethinking Organization: New Directions in Organization Theory and Analysis.* London: Sage, 273–94.

——— (1993), 'Knowledge and the theory of organizations: Organizations as activity systems and the reframing of management', *Journal of Management Studies*, 30/6: 863–84.

——— (1995), 'Knowledge, knowledge work and organizations: An overview and interpretation', *Organization Studies*, 16/6: 1021–46.

BLAU, P. M. (1964), *Exchange and Power in Social Life.* New York: John Wiley.

BLOCH, M. (1953), *The Historian's Craft.* New York: Knopf.

BOISOT, M. (1999), *Knowledge Assets.* Oxford: Oxford University Press.

BOLAND, R. J. and TENKASI, R. V. (1993), 'Locating meaning making in organizational learning: The narrative basis of cognition'. *Research in Organizational Change and Development*, 7: 77–103.

——— (1995), 'Perspective making and perspective taking in communities of knowing', *Organization Science*, 6/4: 350–71.

BONAZZI, G. (1993), *Il Tubo di Cristallo. Modello Giapponese e Fabbrica Integrata alla Fiat Auto.* Bologna: Il Mulino.

BOURDIEU, P. (1977), *Outline of a Theory of Practice.* Cambridge: Cambridge University Press.

——— (1990), *The Logic of Practice.* Cambridge: Polity Press.

BRAUDEL, F. (1972–74), *The Mediterranean and the Mediterranean World in the Age of Philip II.* New York: Harper and Row.

BREDO, E. (1994), Cognitivism, Situated Cognition, and Deweyian Pragmatism. *Philosophy of Education.*

BROWN, J. S. and DUGUID, P. (1991), 'Organizational learning and communities of practice: Toward a unified view of working, learning and innovation', *Organization Science*, 2/1: 40–57.

BRUNER, J. (1986), *Actual Minds, Possible Worlds.* Cambridge, MA: Harvard University Press.

BRUSS, E. (1976), *Autobiographical Acts: The Changing Situation of a Literary Genre.* Baltimore: John Hopkins University Press.

CALLON, M. (1980), 'The state and technical innovation: A case study of the electrical vehicle in France'. *Research Policy*, 9: 358–76.

CALLON, M. (1999), 'Actor-network theory—the market test', in J. Law and J. Hassard (eds.), *Actor Network Theory and After.* Oxford: Blackwell, 181–95.

CAMUFFO, A. and VOLPATO, G. (1994), 'Labor relations heritage and lean manufacturing at Fiat'. Paper presented at the conference, *International Developments in Workplace Innovation*, 15–16 June, Toronto, Ontario.

CERRUTI, G. (1994), 'La fabbrica integrata'. *Meridiana*, 21: 103–47.

CERSOSIMO, D. (1994), *Viaggio a Melfi. La Fiat oltre il Fordismo*. Roma: Donzelli.

CHAICKLIN, S. and LAVE, J. (eds.) (1993), *Understanding Practice: Perspectives on Activity and Context*. Cambridge: Cambridge University Press.

CHANDLER, A. D. (1990), *Strategy and Structure: Chapters in the History of the Industrial Enterprise*. Cambridge, MA: MIT Press.

CHOO, C. W. (1997), *The Knowing Organization: How Organizations Use Information to Construct Meaning, Create Knowledge and Make Decisions*. Oxford: Oxford University Press.

CIBORRA, C. U. (1996), 'Introduction: What does groupware mean for the organizations hosting it?', in C. U. Ciborra (ed.), *Groupware and Teamwork: Invisible Aid or Technical Hindrance?* Chichester: Wiley, 1–19.

—— and LANZARA, G. F. (1994), 'Formative contexts and information technology: understanding the dynamics of innovation in organizations', *Accounting, Management and Information Technology*, 4/2: 61–86.

CIBORRA, C. U., PATRIOTTA, G., and ERLICHER, L. (1996), 'Disassembling frames on the assembly line: The theory and practice of the new division of learning in advanced manufacturing', in W. J. Orlikowski, G. Walsham, M. R. Jones and J. I. DeGross (eds.), *Information Technology and Changes in Organizational Work*. London: Chapman and Hall, 397–418.

CLANCEY, W. J. (1991), 'A Boy Scout, Toto, and a bird: How situated cognition is different from situated robotics', in *NATO Workshop on Emergence, Situatedness, Subsumption, and Symbol Grounding*.

CLARK, J. (1995), *Managing Innovation and Change: People, Technology and Strategy*. London: Sage.

COLLIS, D. J. and MONTGOMERY, C. (1995), 'Competing on resources: Strategy in the 1990s', *Harvard Business Review*, July–August: 118–28.

COOPER, R. (1990), 'Organization/disorganization', in J. Hassard and D. Pym (eds.), *The Theory and Philosophy of Organizations*. London: Routledge.

—— (1998), 'Assemblage Notes', in R. C. H. Chia (ed.), *Organized Worlds*. London: Routledge, 108–29.

—— and LAW, J. (1995), 'Organization: Distal and proximal views'. *Research in the Sociology of Organizations*, 13: 237–74.

CZARNIAWSKA, B. (1997), *Narrating the Organization: Dramas of Institutional Identity*. Chicago: The University of Chicago Press.

—— (1998), *A Narrative Approach to Organization Studies*. London: Sage.

—— (1999), *Writing Management: Organization Theory as a Literary Genre*. Oxford: Oxford University Press.

DAFT, R. L. and WEICK, K. E. (1984), 'Toward a model of organizations as interpretation systems', *Academy of Management Review*, 9/2: 284–95.

DAVENPORT, T. H. and PRUSAK, L. (1998), *Working Knowledge: How Organizations Manage What They Know*. Cambridge, MA: Harvard Business School Press.

De Carolis, D. M. and Deed, D. L. (1999), 'The impact of stocks and flows of organizational knowledge on firm performance: An empirical investigation of the biotechnology industry', *Strategic Management Journal*, 20: 953–68.

de Certeau, M. (1984), *The Practice of Everyday Life*. Berkeley: University of California Press.

Denzin, N. K. and Lincoln, Y. S. (eds.) (1994), *Handbook of Qualitative Research*. London: Sage.

Dewey, J. (1938), *Logic: The Theory of Inquiry*. New York: Holt.

Di Maggio, P. J. and Powell, W. W. (1983), 'The iron cage revisited: Institutional isomorphism and collective rationality in organizational fields', *American Sociological Review*, 48: 147–60.

Donzelli, C. (1994), 'La fabbrica di Melfi col senno di poi. Una conversazione con Cesare Annibaldi e Maurizio Magnabosco e qualche commento', *Meridiana*, 21: 19–33.

Douglas, M. (1986), *How Institutions Think*. London: Routledge

Dreyfus, H. L. (1991), *Being-in-the-World*. Cambridge, MA: MIT Press.

Drucker, P. F. (1946), *The Concept of the Corporation*. New York: John Day.

——— (1993), *The Post-Capitalist Society*. Oxford: Butterworth-Einhemann.

Economist (1998), 'Driven by Fiat'. *The Economist*, April 25, 95–6.

Eisenhardt, K. M. and Martin, J. A. (2000), 'Dynamic capabilities: What are they?', *Strategic Management Journal*, 21: 1105–121.

Eisenhardt, K. M. and Santos, F. M. (2001), 'Knowledge-based view: A new theory of strategy?', in A. Pettigrew, H. Thomas, and R. Whittington (eds.), *Handbook of Strategy and Management*. London: Sage, 139–64.

Engestrom, Y. (1987), *Learning by Expanding: An Activity Theoretical Approach to Developmental Research*. Helsinki: Orienta-Konsultit.

Fortune (1994), 'New ideas from Europe's automakers'. *Fortune*, December 12, 159–64.

Galbraith, J. (1977), *Organizational Design*. Reading, MA: Addison Wesley.

Geertz, C. (1973), *The Interpretation of Cultures*. New York: Basic Books.

Geertz, C. (1983), *Local knowledge: Further Essays in Interpretive Anthropology*. New York: Basic Books.

Geertz, C. (1988), *Work and Lives: The Anthropologist as Author*. Stanford: Stanford University Press.

Giddens, A. (1984), *The Constitution of Society*. Cambridge: Polity Press.

Ginnet, R. C. (1990), 'Airline cockpit crew', in J. R. Hackman (ed.), *Groups that Work (and Those that Don't)*. San Francisco: Jossey-Bass, 427–48.

Ginzburg, C. (1990), *Myths, Emblems, Clues*. London: Hutchinson Radius.

Goffmann, E. (1981), *Interaction Ritual: Essays on Face-to-Face Behavior*. New York: Pantheon Books.

Goodman, N. (1978), *Ways of Worldmaking*. Hassocks: The Harvester Press.

Grant, R. M. (1991), 'The resource-based theory of competitive advantage: Implications for strategy formulation', *California Management Review*, 33: 114–35.

—— (1996), 'Toward a knowledge-based theory of the firm', *Strategic Management Journal*, 17: 109–22.

GREENWOOD, R. and HININGS, C. R. (1988), 'Organizational design types, tracks, and the dynamics of strategic change', *Organization Studies*, 9: 293–316.

GREIMAS, A. J. and COURTÉS, J. (1982), *Semiotics and Language: An Analytical Dictionary*. Bloomington, IN: Indiana Univeristy Press.

GUIMOND, S., BEGIN, G., and PALMER, D. L. (1989), 'Education and causal attributions: The development of "person-blame" and "system blame" ideology', *Social Psychology Quarterly*, 52/2: 126–40.

HAMMERSLEY, M. (1992), *What's Wrong with Ethnography? Methodological Explorations*. London: Routledge.

HATCH, M. J. (1996), 'The role of the researcher: An analysis of narrative position in organization theory', *Journal of Management Inquiry*, 5/4: 359–74.

HEDBERG, B. (1981), 'How organizations learn and unlearn', in D. Nystrom and W. Starbuck (eds.), *Handbook of Organizational Design, Vol. 1: Adapting Organizations to Their Environments*. Oxford: Oxford University Press, 3–27.

HEDLUND, G. (1994), 'A model of knowledge management and the N-form corporation', *Strategic Management Journal*, 15: 73–90.

HEIDEGGER, M. (1962), *Being and Time* (translated by John Macquarrie and Edward Robinson). New York: Harper and Row.

HILL, T. (1991), *Production/Operations Management* (2nd edn). London: Prentice Hall.

HUTCHINS, E. (1993), 'Learning to navigate', in S. Chaicklin and J. Lave (eds.), *op. cit.*, 35–63.

—— (1996), *Cognition in the Wild*. Cambridge, MA: MIT Press.

INKPEN, A. C. and DINUR, A. (1998), 'Knowledge management processes and international joint ventures', *Organization Science*, 9/4: 454–68.

JAMES, W. (1950), *The Principles of Psychology*. New York: Dover.

JAMES, W. (1977), *A Pluralistic Universe*. Cambridge, Mass: Harvard University Press.

JONES, A. M. (1994), *Creating a Learning Organization*. Unpublished PhD dissertation. University of Warwick.

JONES, A. M. and HENDRY, C. (1994), 'The learning organization: Adult learning and organizational transformation', *British Journal of Management*, 5: 153–62.

KAGHAN, W. and PHILLIPS, N. (1998), 'Building the tower of Babel: Communities of practice and paradigmatic pluralism in organization studies', *Organization*, 5/2: 191–215.

KIESER, A. (1994), 'Why organization theory needs historical analyses—And how this should be performed', *Organization Science*, 5/4: 608–20.

KNORR-CETINA, K. D. (1981), *The Manufacture of Knowledge: An Essay on the Constructivist and Contextual Nature of Science*. Oxford: Pergamon Press.

KOGUT, B., ZANDER, U. (1992), 'Knowledge of the firm, combinative capabilities, and the replication of technology', *Organization Science*, 3/3: 383–97.

KOLB, D. A. (1979), *Organizational Psychology* (3rd edn). Englewood Cliffs: Prentice Hall.

KUNDERA, M. (1997), Se Balzac ritorna all'Est. *La Repubblica*, October 22, 1997: 1.

LANZARA, G. F. (1990), 'Shifting Stories. Learning from a reflective experiment in a design process', in D. A. Schön (ed.), *The Reflective Turn: Case Studies in and on Educational Practice*, New York: Teachers College Press, 285–320.

LANZARA, G. F. and PATRIOTTA, G. (2001), 'Technology and the courtroom: An inquiry into knowledge making', *Journal of Management Studies*, 38/6: 943–71.

LATOUR, B. (1987), *Science in Action*. Cambridge, MA: Harvard University Press.

—— (1993), *We Have Never Been Modern*. Cambridge, MA: Harvard University Press.

—— (1995), 'The "pedofil" of Boavista: A photo-philosophical montage', *Common Knowledge*, 4/1: 144–87.

—— (1999a), *Pandora's Hope: Essays on the Reality of Science Studies*. Cambridge, MA: Harvard University Press.

—— (1999b), 'On recalling ANT', in J. Law and J. Hassard (eds.), *Actor Network Theory and After*. Oxford: Blackwell, 15–25.

—— and Woolgar, S. (1979), *Laboratory Life: The Social Construction of Scientific Facts*. London: Sage.

LAVE, J. and WENGER, E. (1991), *Situated Learning: Legitimate Peripheral Participation*. Cambridge: Cambridge University Press.

LAW, J. (1999), 'After ANT: complexity, naming and topology', in J. Law and J. Hassard (eds.), *Actor Network Theory and After*. Oxford: Blackwell, 1–14.

—— and Hassard, J. (1999), *Actor Network Theory and After*. Oxford: Blackwell.

LAWLER, E. E. (1982), 'Increasing worker involvement to enhance organizational effectiveness', in P. S. Goodman (ed.), *Change in Organizations*. San Francisco: Jossey-Bass.

LEONARD-BARTON, D. (1992a), 'Core capabilities and core rigidities: A paradox in managing new product development', *Strategic Management Journal*, 13: 111–25.

—— (1992b), 'The factory as a learning laboratory', *Sloan Management Review*, 34/1: 23–38.

LOUIS, M. R. and SUTTON, R. I. (1991), 'Switching cognitive gears: From habits of mind to active thinking', *Human Relations*, 44: 55–76.

MACLEAN, N. (1992), *Young Men and Fire*. Chicago: University of Chicago Press.

MARCH, J. G. and SIMON, H. A. (1958), *Organizations*. New York: John Wiley.

MEYER, J. W. and ROWAN, B. (1977), 'Institutionalized organizations: Formal structure as myth and ceremony', *American Journal of Sociology*, 83: 340–63.

MIDDLETON, D. and EDWARDS, D. (eds.) (1990), *Collective Remembering*. London: Sage.

MONDEN, Y. (1993), *Toyota Production System: An Integrated Approach to Just-in Time* (2nd edn). Norcross, Ga: Industrial Engineering and Management Press.

MORGAN, G. (1997), *Images of Organization*. London: Sage.

MOSCOVICI, S. (1982), 'The coming era of representations', in J. P. Codol, and J. -P. Leyens (eds.) *Cognitive Analyses of Social Behavior*. The Hague: Martinus Nijhoff, 115–50.

MOWERY, D. C., J. E. OXLEY, and B. S. SILVERMAN. (1996), 'Strategic alliances and interfirm knowledge transfer', *Strategic Management Journal*, 17: 77–91.

NAHAPIET, J. and GHOSHAL, S. (1998), 'Social capital, intellectual capital, and the organizational advantage', *Academy of Management Review*, 23/2: 242–66.

NELSON, R. R. and WINTER, S. G. (1982), *An Evolutionary Theory of Economic Change*. Cambridge, MA: Belknap.

NEWELL, A. and SIMON, H. A. (1972), *Human Problem-Solving*. Englewood Cliffs, NJ: Prentice Hall.

——(1991), *Field of Dreams: Evidence of New Employee Relations on Greenfield Sites*. Unpublished PhD dissertation, University of Oxford.

NONAKA, I. and TAKEUCHI, H. (1995), *The Knowledge-Creating Company*. Oxford: Oxford University Press.

NORMAN, D. A. (1993), 'Cognition in the head and in the world: An introduction to the special issue on situated action', *Cognitive Science*, 17: 1–6.

OLAFSON, F. (1979), *The Dialectics of Action*. Chicago: The University of Chicago Press.

ORGANIZATION (1998), 'Thematic issue on pluralism and incommensurability in strategic management and organization theory: Consequences for theory and practice', *Organization*, 5/2: May 1998.

ORLIKOWSKI, W. J. (1992), 'The duality of technology: Rethinking the concept of technology in organizations', *Organization Science*, 3/2: 398–427.

ORR, J. E. (1990), 'Sharing knowledge, celebrating identity: Community memory in a service culture', in D. Middleton and D. Edwards (eds.), *Collective Remembering*. London: Sage, 169–89.

——(1996), *Talking about Machines: An Ethnography of a Modern Job*. Ithaca, NY: Cornell University Press.

PARSONS, T. (1951), *The Social System*. New York: Free Press.

PATRIOTTA, G. (2003), 'Sensemaking on the shop floor: Narratives of knowledge in organizations', *Journal of Management Studies*, 40: 3.

PATRIOTTA, G. and LANZARA, G. F. (2001), 'The making of a factory: dynamics of institution building at Fiat's Melfi plant'. Paper presented at the *Annual Meeting of the Academy of Management*, Washington, 3–7 August.

PENROSE, E. (1959), *The Theory of the Growth of the Firm*. London: Basil Blackwell.

PENTLAND, B. T. (1992), 'Organizing moves in software support hot lines', *Administrative Science Quarterly*, 37: 527–48.

——and REUTER, H. (1994), 'Organizational routines as grammars of action', *Administrative Science Quarterly*, 39: 484–510.

PERROW, C. (1984), *Normal Accidents*. New York: Basic Books.

PETERAF, M. A. (1993), 'The cornerstones of competitive advantage: A resource-based view', *Strategic Management Journal*, 14: 179–91.

PETTIGREW, A. M. (1979), 'On studying organizational cultures', *Administrative Science Quarterly*, 24: 570–81.

PETTIGREW, A. M. (1985), *The Awakening Giant: Continuity and Change in Imperial Chemical Industries*. Oxford: Blackwell.

—— (1987), 'Context and action in the transformation of the firm', *Journal of Management Studies*, 24/6: 649–70.

—— (1990), 'Longitudinal field research on change: Theory and practice', *Organization Science*, 1/3: 267–91.

—— (1997), 'What is processual analysis?' *The Scandinavian Journal of Management* (Special Issue on Conducting Process Research), Autumn: 337–48.

—— (2000), 'Linking change processes to outcomes', in M. Beer and N. Nohria (eds.), *Breaking the Code of Change*. Boston: Harvard Business School Press, 243–65.

—— and WHIPP, R. (1991), *Managing Change for Competitive Success*. Oxford: Basil Blackwell.

—— BRIGNALL, S., HARVEY, J., and WEBB, D. (1999), *The Determinants of Organizational Performance*. Report to the Department of Health, Warwick Business School, Coventry.

PINCH, T. J. and BIJKER, W. E. (1989), 'The social construction of facts and artifacts: Or how science and sociology of technology might benefit each other', in W. E. Bijker, T. P. Hughes, and T. J. Pinch (eds.), *op. cit.*, 16–50.

POLANYI, M. (1966), *The Tacit Dimension*. London: Routledge.

POLLNER, M. (1987), *Mundane Reason. Reality in Everyday and Sociological Discourse*. Cambridge: Cambridge University Press.

PORTER, M. E. (1980), *Competitive Strategy*. New York: Free Press.

POWELL, W. W. and DI MAGGIO, P. J. (eds.) (1991), *New Institutionalism in Organizational Analysis*. Chicago: University of Chicago Press.

PRAHALAD, C. K. and HAMEL, G. (1990), 'The core competence of the corporation', *Harvard Business Review*, 68/3: 79–91.

PRODUCTION (1995), 'European manufacturing: The big comeback?' *Production*, August, 18–19.

PROKESCH, S. E. (1997), 'Unleashing the power of learning: An Interview with British Petroleum's John Browne', *Harvard Business Review*, 75/5: 146–62.

QUINN, J. B. (1992), *Intelligent Enterprise: A Knowledge and Service Based Paradigm for Industry*. New York: Free Press.

RICOEUR, P. (1981), 'The model of the text: meaningful action considered as text', in J. B. Thompson (ed. and trans.), *Hermeneutics and the Human Sciences*. Cambridge: Cambridge University Press.

—— (1984), *Time and Narrative, Vol. I*. Chicago: University of Chicago Press.

RIESER, V. (1992), 'La Fiat e la nuova fase di razionalizzazione'. *Quaderni di Sociologia*, 3: 35–62.

RORTY, R. (1979), *Philosophy and the Mirror of Nature*. Princeton, NJ: Princeton University Press.

RUMELT, R. P. (1984), 'Towards a strategic theory of the firm', in R. B. Lamb (ed.), *Competitive Strategic Management*. Englewood Cliffs, NJ: Prentice-Hall, 556–70.

—— (1991), 'How much does industry matter?', *Strategic Management Journal*, 12/3: 167–85.

—— (1994), Foreword, in G. Hamel and A. Heene (eds.), *Competence-based Competition*. Chichester: Wiley, XV–XX.

RYLE, G. (1949), *The Concept of Mind*. London: Hutchinson House.

SANCHEZ, R. and HEENE, A. (1997), *Strategic Learning and Knowledge Management*. Chichester: Wiley.

SANCHEZ, R. and MAHONEY, J. T. (1996), 'Modularity, flexibility, and knowledge management in product and organization design', *Strategic Management Journal*, 17: 63–76.

SCARBROUGH, H. (1998), 'Path(ological) dependency? Core competencies from an organizational perspective'. *British Journal of Management*, 9: 219–32.

—— SWAN, J., and PRESTON, J. (1999), 'Knowledge management: A literature review'. *Issues in People Management*. London: Institute of Personnel and Development.

SCHUTZ, A. (1967), *The Phenomenology of the Social World*. Evanston, IL: Northwestern University Press.

SCOTT, W. R. (1987), 'The adolescence of institutional theory', *Administrative Science Quarterly*, 32: 493–511.

SCRIBNER, S. (1987), 'Thinking in action: Some characteristics of practical thought', in R. Sternberg and R. Wagner (eds.), *Practical Intelligence. Nature and Origins of Competence in the Everyday World*. Cambridge: Cambridge University Press.

SELZNICK, P. (1957), *Leadership in Administration*. New York: Harper & Row.

SENGE, P. M. (1990), *The Fifth Discipline: The Art and Practice of The Learning Organization*. New York: Doubleday.

SHANK, R. and ABELSON, R. P. (1977), *Scripts, Goals, Plans, and Understanding: An Inquiry into Human Knowledge Structures*. Hillsdale, NJ: Erlbaum Associates.

SHINGO, S. (1989), *A Study of the Toyota Production System from an Industrial Engineering Viewpoint*. Norwalk, CN: Productivity Press.

SHRIVASTAVA, P., MITROFF, I. I., MILLER, D., and MIGLIANI, A. (1988), 'Understanding industrial crises', *Journal of Management Studies*, 25: 285–03.

SIMON, H. A. (1947), *Administrative Behavior*. New York: Macmillan.

SIMON, H. A. et al. (1992), 'Decision making and problem solving', in M. Zey (ed.), *Decision Making: Alternatives to Rational Choice Models*. Newbury Park, CA: Sage.

SIMS, H. P. and GIOIA, D. A. (eds.) (1986), *The Thinking Organization*. San Francisco: Jossey Bass.

SMIRCHICH, L. and STUBBART, C. (1985), 'Strategic management in an enacted world', *Academy of Management Review*, 10: 724–36.

SPENDER, J.-C. (1989), *Industry Recipes: The Nature and Sources of Managerial Judgement*. Oxford: Basil Blackwell.

—— (1996), 'Making knowledge the basis of a dynamic theory of the firm', *Strategic Management Journal*, 17: 45–62.

SPENDER, J.-C. (1998), 'Pluralist epistemology and the knowledge-based theory of the firm', *Organization*, 5/2: 233–56.

SPENDER, J.-C. and GRANT, R. M. (1996), 'Knowledge and the firm: Overview', *Strategic Management Journal*, 17: 5–9.

STARBUCK, W. H. and MILLIKEN, F. J. (1988), 'Executives' perceptual filters: What they notice and how they make sense', in D. C. Hambrick (ed.), *The Executive Effect: Concepts and Methods for Studying Top Managers*. Greenwich, CT: JAI, 35–65.

STINCHOMBE, A. L. (1965), 'Social structure and organizations', in J. C. March (ed.), *Handbook of Organizations*. Chicago: Rand McNally, 142–93.

SUCHMAN, L. (1987), *Plans and Situated Actions*. Cambridge: Cambridge University Press.

SZTOMPKA, P. (1991), *Society in Action: The Theory of Social Becoming*. Chicago: The University of Chicago Press.

SZULANSKI, G. (1996), 'Exploring internal stickiness: Impediments to the transfer of best practice within the firm', *Strategic Management Journal*, 17: 27–43.

TEECE, D. J., PISANO, G., and SHUEN, A. (1997), 'Dynamic capabilities and strategic management', *Strategic Management Journal*, 18/7: 509–33.

THOMAS, J. B., CLARK, S. M., and GIOIA, D. A. (1993), 'Strategic sensemaking and organizational performance: Linkages among scanning, interpretation, action, and outcomes', *Academy of Management Journal*, 36: 239–70.

TRIST, E. L. (1981), 'The sociotechnical perspective: The evolution of sociotechnical systems as a conceptual framework and as an action research program', in A. H. Van de Ven and W. F. Joyce (eds.), *Perspectives on Organization Design and Behavior*. New York: Wiley, 19–75.

TSOUKAS, H. (1996), 'The firm as a distributed knowledge system: A constructionist approach', *Strategic Management Journal*, 17: 11–25.

TURNER, S. (1994), *The Social Theory of Practices: Tradition, Tacit Knowledge and Presuppositions*. Chicago: The University of Chicago Press.

TURNER, V. (1974), *Dramas, Fields, and Metaphors: Symbolic Action in Human Society*. Ithaca; London: Cornell University Press.

——— (1996), *Schism and Continuity in an African Society: A Study of Ndembu Village Life* (2nd edn). Berg Pub. Ltd.

UNGER, R. M. (1987), *False Necessity*, Cambridge: Cambridge University Press.

VAN DE VEN, A. H. (1992), 'Suggestions for studying strategy process: A research note', *Strategic Management Journal*, 13: 169–88.

VAN MAANEN, J. (1979), 'The fact of fiction in organizational ethnography', *Administrative Science Quarterly*, 24: 539–50.

——— (1984), 'Doing new things in old ways: The chains of socialization', in J. L. Bess (ed.), *College and University Organization*. New York: New York University Press, 211–46.

——— (1988), *Tales of the Field. On Writing Ethnography*. Chicago: The University of Chicago Press.

——— (1995), 'Style as theory', *Organization Science*, 6/1: 133–43.

VERA, A. H. and SIMON, H. A. (1993), 'Situated action: A symbolic interpretation', *Cognitive Science*, 17: 7–48.

VEYNE, P. (1971), *Comment on Écrit l'Histoire*. Paris: Editions du Seuil.

VON KROGH, G., ROOS, J., and KLEIN, D. (eds.) (1998), *Knowing in Firms: Understanding, Managing and Measuring Knowledge*. Oxford: Oxford University Press.

WALSH, J. P. and UNGSON, G. R. (1991), 'Organizational memory', *Academy of Management Review*, 16: 57–91.

WEICK, K. E. (1977), 'Enactment processes in organizations', in B. M. Staw and G. Salancik (eds.), *New Directions in Organizational Behavior*. Chicago: St Clair, 267–300.

WEICK, K. E. (1979), *The Social Psychology of Organizing* (2nd edn). Reading, MA: Addison-Wesley.

—— (1988), 'Enacted sensemaking in crisis situations', *Journal of Management Studies*, 25: 305–17.

—— (1990), 'Technology as equivoque: Sense-making in new technologies', in P. Goodman, L. Sproull, et al. (eds.), *Technology and Organizations*. Oxford: Jossey-Bass, 1–44.

—— (1993), 'The collapse of sensemaking in organizations: The Mann Gulch disaster', *Administrative Science Quarterly*, 38: 628–52.

—— (1995), *Sensemaking in Organizations*. London: Sage.

WENGER, E. (1998), *Communities of Practice: Learning, Meaning, and Identity*. Cambridge: Cambridge University Press.

WERNERFELT, B. (1984), 'A resource-based view of the firm', *Strategic Management Journal*, 5: 171–80.

WHIPP, R. and CLARK, P. (1986), *Innovation and the Auto Industry: Product, Process and Work Organization*. London: Frances Pinter.

WINOGRAD, T. and FLORES, F. (1986), *Understanding Computers and Cognition: a New Foundation for Design*. Norwood, NJ: Ablex.

WOMACK, J. J. D., JONES, D. T., and ROOS, D. (1990), *The Machine that Changed the World. The Triumph of Lean Production*. New York: Macmillan.

WYNN, E. (1979), *Office Conversation as an Information Medium*. Unpublished PhD dissertation, University of California, Berkeley.

ZUBOFF, S. (1988), *In the Age of the Smart Machine*. New York: Basic Books.

ZUCKER, L. G. (1977), 'The role of institutionalization in cultural persistence', *American Sociological Review*, 42: 726–43.

—— (1983), 'Organizations as institutions', in S. B. Bachrach (ed.), *Research in the Sociology of Organizations*. Greenwhich, CN: JAI Press, 1–47.

Index